Fourth Edition

Financing College

HOW MUCH YOU'LL REALLY HAVE TO PAY —AND HOW TO GET THE MONEY

From the Editors of
Kiplinger's Personal Finance

Dearborn™
Trade Publishing
A **Kaplan Professional** Company

This publication is designed to provide accurate and authoritative information in regard to the subject matter covered. It is sold with the understanding that the publisher is not engaged in rendering legal, accounting, or other professional service. If legal advice or other expert assistance is required, the services of a competent professional person should be sought.

President, Dearborn Publishing: Roy Lipner
Vice President and Publisher: Cynthia A. Zigmund
Senior Acquisitions Editor: Mary B. Good
Cover Design: Design Solutions
Typesetting: the dotted i

Published by Dearborn Trade Publishing
A Kaplan Professional Company

Printed in the United States of America

05   06   07   10 9 8 7 6 5 4 3 2 1

Library of Congress Cataloging-in-Publication Data

Financing college : how much you'll really have to pay, and how to get the money / by the editors of Kiplinger's personal finance.
   p.   cm.
Previous ed. entered under: Davis, Kristin.
Includes index.
ISBN 1-4195-0517-3 (7.25x9 pbk.)
   1. Student aid—United States.   2. College choice—United States.   3. Parents—United States—Finance, Personal.
I. Kiplinger's personal finance.
LB2337.4.F566 2005
378.3—dc22

2005009048

Contents

INTRODUCTION ix

CHAPTER 1:
Affording the Gold-Plated Diploma 1
*Financial Aid Will Cut Your Cost • Smelling Salts for Sticker
Shock • Average College Costs • The College-Cost Spiral • Tax
Credits Will Help, Too • A College Planning Timeline • No
Need to Save It All in Advance • The Bottom Line • A
College-Cost Sampler*

CHAPTER 2:
The $64,000 Question: How Much to Save? 23
*Setting Realistic Savings Goals • Another Way to Set Your
Goal • How Much Can You Spare? • How Much You Need to
Save: The Short Range, The Long Range • Tightening Your Belt •
Smart Saving Tricks • A Budget-Cutting Worksheet •Where
Should You Save? • Saving for College or Retirement?*

CHAPTER 3:
Where to Keep Your College Money 47
*Using the Time You Have • The Safest Safe Havens •
A Small Step Up the Risk Ladder • Long-Term Investments •
Putting It All Together: A Shortcut • A Portfolio of Mutual
Funds • State-Sponsored College-Savings Plans • College
Savings and Prepaid-Tuition Plans • How to Choose an Advisor*

CHAPTER 4:
Winning the College Aid Game 99
*Cost Equals Your Contribution • What the Variables Are •
How They Decide What You Can Afford • Timing Taxes
and Aid Forms • The Financial-Aid Years • Estimate Your*

Expected Family Contribution Early • Uncle Sam's Math: The Federal Methodology • If You'll Have Two Kids in College at Once • For Divorced Parents • Calculate Your Contribution • Figuring Your Expected Family Contribution • Let Your Computer Help

CHAPTER 5:
How the Schools Build Your Aid Package   **125**
The Usual Process • How and Why Schools Adjust the Federal Formula • Preferential Packaging • Mind the Gap • No Need-Based Aid? Target a "Discount" • If You Can't Negotiate, Appeal

CHAPTER 6:
Increasing Your Eligibility for Aid   **151**
Accelerate or Defer Income • Should You Shift Assets? • How About Reducing Assets? • What About Giving Money to Your Parents? • Most Debt Doesn't Count • Can You Save Too Much? • What About a Parent in School? • Completing the FAFSA • Preparing the PROFILE • After Freshman Year • Hire a College-Aid Helper? Study First

CHAPTER 7:
The Financial Side of Choosing a College   **183**
Step One: Complete a Need Analysis • Step Two: A Financial Checkup • Weighing the Options • Public Versus Private • Honors Colleges • Good Values in Specific Fields • Go International? • Select a School with Aid in Mind • College Resources on the Internet • The Cost of Getting into College

CHAPTER 8:
The Great Scholarship Quest   **205**
The Scholarship Mirage • Who Should Seek Scholarships? • Where to Look • Tips for Scholarship Seekers • Scholarships of Broad Interest • After High School

CHAPTER 9:
Borrowing Power   **227**
College Debt Gets Cheaper • How Much Debt Is Too Much for Your Child? • How Much Debt Is Too Much for Yourself? • When You're Ready to Apply: The Loans •

Contents

Stafford Student Loans • Perkins Loans • PLUS Loans (for
Parents) • Private Loans • Are You Creditworthy? • The High
Cost of Stretching Out Your Payments • Borrowing from
Yourself • Student Loan "Relief"

CHAPTER 10:
Other Ways and Means   **263**
Cost-Conscious Ways to Get a Degree • Innovative Ways
to Pay the Bill for College • Student Jobs

CHAPTER 11:
Collegiate Cash Flow   **281**
Find a Student-Friendly Bank • Go Easy on Credit • Get
Used to "Smart" Cards • Send the Car? • A Computer's a
Must • Outfitting the Dorm Room • Don't Overlook Property
Insurance • Bargain Airfares for Students • Calling Home •
The E-Mail Alternative • "Help, I'm Broke!" • Questions for
Sophomores & Up

INDEX   **297**

Just a generation ago, college education was still a somewhat elitist experience, an optional path to success enjoyed by a small minority of Americans. Scholarship money and loans were narrowly available. Many of America's top colleges weren't even open to women, female enrollment in professional postgraduate programs was small, and racial minorities constituted a tiny fraction of enrollment in all of higher education.

Of course, a generation or two ago, millions of Americans did just fine without going to college. Young men and women with only a high school diploma—which back then typically symbolized true mastery of fundamental skills like literacy and basic math—walked into good-paying factory, clerical, and sales jobs, and they advanced just fine through diligence and on-the-job learning.

My, how times have changed. Today the high school diploma, once a badge of honor for many Americans, doesn't open many doors. Due to declining academic standards and "courtesy promotions" of failing, overaged students, the high school diploma has been debased to a point of near uselessness as an indicator of job-related academic skills. That's why academic testing of job applicants is booming, as is remedial education for college freshmen. Now there are heartening signs that public secondary education is on the mend, but it still has a long way to go.

At the same time, the job skills required by the new world economy are constantly increasing. Computer literacy is a must for all workers. Today's farmers, and factory and office workers, must be able to operate computer-controlled devices with sophisticated gauges, monitors, and printouts. That's why we're beginning to find college-educated men and women on assembly lines, behind the wheels of tractors and combines in the field, and repairing cars and trucks with all the latest computer technology.

These skills can be obtained today without going to college, as America begins to get serious about transforming secondary vocational education into high-tech programs of learning and apprenticeships for manufacturing.

But more and more, we are turning to our colleges to prepare America's youth for success in a rapidly changing global economy. And colleges are responding, by overhauling their curricula, expanding enrollment, opening adult-learning branches, offering online-degree programs, and better matching their programs to the needs of local employers. This trend is especially evident among the nation's community colleges, which have become a bridge between the less-valuable high school diploma and the stiffening skill demands of the workplace.

For most young Americans today, college is no longer a luxury, an option that might help them get a better job. It is vital path to career success. Sure, we all know a young French lit or sociology major who can't find a decent-paying job, but the lifetime earnings advantage for college graduates over high school grads is still dramatically wide and growing. A college degree is the currency of the realm in the job market, the basic credential that employers want to see. And it's fast becoming so basic a commodity that employers are now looking for postgraduate study to set one applicant apart from the others. But you probably know most of this already, which is why you're looking at this book for some help on how to afford this basic but valuable commodity called "college."

The editors of *Kiplinger's Personal Finance* magazine, led by Kristin Davis, have done a wonderful job of explaining the ins and outs of the Great College Finance Game, and I will leave the mechanics to them.

This latest edition of our best-selling guide includes all the new wrinkles in college finance, including tax-free 529 plans (state-sponsored college-savings plans), Coverdell ESAs, expanded tax deductions for college, and improved deductions for student-loan interest.

Before you get into the meat of the subject, however, I'd like to offer a few thoughts on the college-selection process. As you enter the fray, please keep in mind the following points.

Good schools, and good values, abound. Excellence in higher education is much more broadly distributed in America than many people realize. There are vastly more fine colleges than can fit on the "most-selective" lists in popular guidebooks. Arguably, how your child takes advantage of good teaching and good campus resources is more important than where he or she goes to college.

Some of the academically solid but little-known colleges, public and private, are better financial values than the expensive, high-prestige institutions. In a new trend towards chic thriftiness, it's not unusual to see an applicant turn down an acceptance from a famous college to attend a less-known one that will cost the applicant and his or her parents a lot less money.

Schools are working to attract the best. Competition among colleges to lure the very top students is creating some excellent scholarship opportunities for relatively affluent parents who would typically qualify for little or no financial aid. "Merit" scholarships, as well as low-tuition honors programs, are proliferating at colleges seeking to strengthen their student bodies academically. Even very prestigious colleges quietly vie for the best students by trying to match or top another college's financial-aid offer (a practice most colleges will deny ever doing).

Look for a college's excellence in your child's chosen field of study. Even high-prestige colleges are not outstanding in all fields. Likewise, some obscure colleges have superb departments in unusual fields of study, and if your child wants to pursue a career in one of those fields, this should matter more than the overall reputation of the college.

Majors do determine job prospects. There is a strong connection between what youths study in college and the career choices they will have when they graduate. It's fine to major in political science, anthropology, journalism, or music history, so long as students don't expect to find a lot of job opportunities in those fields when they graduate. But job offers will be plentiful and high-paying in science, engineering, and other technical fields.

Demographics play a big role in the college selection and financing game. Beginning in the early 1980s and extending into the early 1990s, America experienced a great surge in births, as the women of the enormous postwar baby boom cohort (1946–1964) finally got around to having the babies many of them had put off in their early career days. On top of that, America experienced in the 1980s a wave of immigration unparalleled since the turn of the century.

As this "baby boom echo" generation and young immigrants finished high school and applied to college in the late 1990s, colleges felt a surge of applicants. The best-known colleges saw the greatest increases in applications. And the admissions pressure hasn't abated yet. This makes it all the more important that parents help their children identify colleges that will be a good fit—in atmosphere, size, location, and especially field of study—regardless of the prestige of the institution.

The straight path isn't the only one. If your child decides not to go to college right after high school or doesn't finish a four-year program going straight through, don't despair. Many successful adults didn't follow the normal path, and millions of adults are returning to college to finish a degree or start a whole new course of study. In tomorrow's world, education will be continuous, not something one does for just four or six years of college between the ages of 18 and the mid-20s. Adult classes and online "distance learning" programs will continue to boom.

At the Kiplinger organization, we've been writing about the college-finance process since the founding of our personal-finance magazine in 1947, because it's vitally important to American families. When we surveyed the field of recent books on this subject, we found a group of books that focus on long-range planning for college expenses—basically, investment guides—and another group of books that took aim at short-run tasks, such as applying for loans, scholarships, college jobs, and so on.

This book is unusual in combining both focuses in one comprehensive guide. It's written with unusual clarity and occasional dashes of wit to lighten a very serious subject. We hope that you find it a useful ally in the daunting challenge ahead of you. Our best wishes to you and your college-bound youngsters.

Knight Kiplinger

Editor in Chief
Kiplinger's Personal Finance

Affording the Gold-Plated Diploma

What are two of the scariest words you can utter to parents of a teenager? College tuition. With the same $170,000-plus some parents will pay to put a student through one of the country's most selective private colleges, they could buy a 50-foot sailboat or a pair of Mercedes-Benzes. As one college-aid advisor quips: "Think of paying for college as buying an intellectual home for your child."

The purpose of this book isn't to scare you. It is true that by the time children reach their teen years, most parents have only a token amount saved toward the college bills. But it's also true that parents who want to finance their kids' college education—even at the country's priciest schools—usually find a way. And you can, too. Even if your kids are in high school and you don't yet have the first dollar saved, this book will show you how to marshal your resources—making the most of your own cash flow and assets, getting as much as you can in financial aid, scholarships, and low-cost loans, and taking advantage of cost-cutting tips that will hold down the amount you have to finance.

You're far better off, of course, if you're starting while your kids are in elementary school or even younger. The sacrifices you make now to put away a little each month toward college bills will pay off in more options, less debt, and less worry as the college years approach. This book will help you figure out how much to save, whose name to save it in, and where to invest it—now and as the tuition bills get closer.

Smelling Salts for Sticker Shock

First, let's get a grip on costs. The news media like to emphasize the dramatic. That's why, in stories about college costs, you'll usually read about the cost of sending a child to Harvard, Yale, Princeton, Stanford, and other elite schools where total yearly costs now top $40,000. And the average tab at a four-year private school was just over $30,000 in the 2004–2005 academic year, according to the annual survey of colleges conducted by the College Board, a nonprofit association of colleges, universities, and educational organizations. That figure includes not just tuition and fees but also room and board, books, travel costs for two or three trips home, and personal expenses—toothpaste, laundry soap, and the like, and undoubtedly some late-night pizza. (Often in discussions of college costs you'll see just the tuition—or tuition plus room and board—quoted, but it's the total bill you have to finance. Fortunately, when figuring your need for assistance, most financial-aid officers include those less-obvious costs, as we discuss in Chapter 4.)

Meanwhile, at four-year public colleges, the total cost for in-state students was about half as much—$15,000 on average. That's something over $60,000 in total for a Class of 2009 graduate, assuming the cost

---

AVERAGE COLLEGE COSTS FOR THE 2004–2005 ACADEMIC YEAR

These average costs of public and private four-year schools nationwide reflect a survey of 1,679 institutions by the College Board. The room-and-board figures assume the student lives on campus; costs for students who live at home are normally less. A student's actual expenses for books and supplies, transportation, and personal expenses will vary, of course, but these are the amounts college financial-aid officers, when compiling financial-aid packages, assume students on their campuses will spend.

Type of school	Tuition and fees	Room and board	Transpor-tation	Books and supplies	Personal expenses	Total expenses
4-year private	$20,082	$6,617	$1,031	$870	$1,524	$30,124
4-year public	5,132	6,167	1,109	853	1,943	15,204

continues to rise each year. And some of those public schools are among the nation's finest, as shown in the box below.

The College-Cost Spiral

In the mid-2000s, the costs of private colleges are rising at a slower pace (about 6% annually) than they are at public colleges (about 13% in 2004 and 10% in 2005). Through the late 1990s, costs at both public and

---

THE TOP TEN BEST VALUE COLLEGES IN 2004–2005

The schools that follow were named the top ten "best values" in America for 2005 in the 2006 edition of *America's Best Value Colleges* by Eric Owens and the staff of the *Princeton Review*. Selection was based on the 2003–2004 academic year, and costs were based on the 2004–2005 academic year. The list names schools that offer outstanding academics and enroll good students who are happy with the education they are receiving, and, additionally—and more important—do not have to mortgage their futures because their school is charging them way too much. Although some colleges on the list show high costs, they are included because of their generous financial-aid packages, especially for students from low-income families. For example, at Bates College, if your family's annual income is $16,000 per year, your contribution would be about $3,000.

Schools (in order of best value)	Cost for in-state students	Cost for out-of-state students
1. Bates College	$39,900	$39,900
2. New Mexico Institute of Mining and Technology	12,200	18,700
3. Brigham Young University	11,300*	11,300*
	12,920**	12,920**
4. Hendrix College	29,636	29,636
5. University of California—Los Angeles	21,358	37,834
6. New College of Florida	10,947	25,349
7. CUNY—Brooklyn College	9,353	13,993
8. CUNY—Queens College	4,761***	9,401***
9. William Jewell College	23,350	23,350
10. Hanover College	27,600	27,600

* Cost for members of the Church of Jesus Christ of Latter-Day Saints
** Cost for nonchurch members
*** Cost of room and board not included. No on-campus housing.

private schools rose at the lowest rates in more than a decade, although the increases still ran ahead of the inflation rate. You can credit a robust economy and stock market, which fattened state coffers and college endowments. Now, costs are again rising at higher rates, due to sharply reduced funding for public colleges and, thanks to the early 2000s stock market decline, a slowing of growth in endowments.

Parents are blanching at the $30,000-to-$40,000-a-year price tag at many private schools. Many colleges have responded with pledges to hold tuition increases to the rate of inflation, which has hovered around 3% in recent years, or to "inflation plus two" percentage points. But the cuts in state funding and decreases in endowments have made these promises difficult or impossible to keep. Still, there continue to be some suc-

HOW COSTS HAVE RISEN

This graph shows the average annual increase in tuition and fees at four-year colleges, public and private, since the 1990–1991 academic year, compared with the consumer price index rate of inflation. (Inflation rates are for the calendar year ending during the given academic year.)

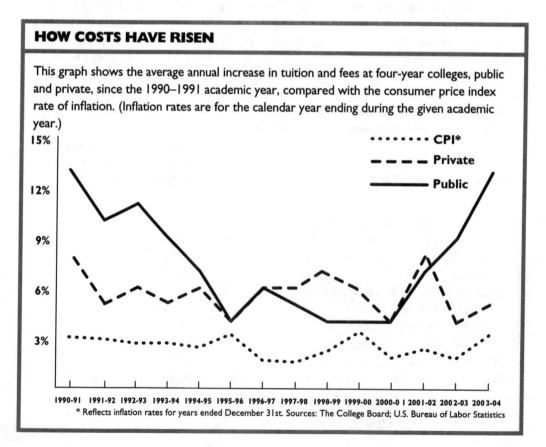

.... CPI*
– – – – Private
——— Public

1990-91 1991-92 1992-93 1993-94 1994-95 1995-96 1996-97 1997-98 1998-99 1999-00 2000-01 2001-02 2002-03 2003-04
* Reflects inflation rates for years ended December 31st. Sources: The College Board; U.S. Bureau of Labor Statistics

cessful efforts to keep costs down. Here are some examples, compiled by the National Association of Independent Colleges and Universities.

- **Wilberforce University,** in Wilberforce, Ohio, held tuition, fees, and room and board at $16,200 for 2004–2005, the third year the school maintained these costs.
- **Eureka College,** in Eureka, Illinois, reduced tuition 30% for the 2004–2005 academic year.
- **Brown University,** in Providence, Rhode Island, increased its institutional aid budget by $5 million so that all students who qualify for such aid receive larger grants and smaller loans. The initiative gives students with greatest financial need approximately $17,000 in additional grant aid over four years.
- **Salem International University,** in Salem, West Virginia, reduced tuition 35% for the 2004–2005 school year.
- **Lindenwood University,** in St. Charles, Missouri, kept tuition at $11,200 for the 2004–2005 academic year, maintaining that cost for the third year.
- **Lourdes College,** in Sylvania, Ohio, restructured its tuition for the 2004–2005 year, reducing tuition between 21% and 41% for full-time students.

So what rate of increase should you use for planning purposes? If you're facing college bills within the next six or seven years, plan on yearly increases of 7% when calculating how much your college will cost. The table on the next page shows what a year of college at today's costs will look like in the future using a 7% college-cost inflation rate.

Financial Aid Will Cut Your Cost

The numbers are unsettling. But remember that the figures cited earlier in this chapter reflect tomorrow's inflated dollars (which your income will also likely reflect), as well as the full sticker price, including living expenses, as we mentioned earlier. The welcome news is that most parents don't pay the full tab. More than half receive a financial-aid package that is, in effect, a

So what rate of increase should you use for planning purposes? If you're facing college bills within the next six or seven years, try 7%.

tuition discount based on their ability to pay. How much help might that bring? At the Massachusetts Institute of Technology, for example, the average need-based financial-aid package in 2004–2005 was $28,600, of which $20,500 was a need-based grant (that is, free money).

The amount of aid you receive will depend predominantly on your family's income. A typical family of four with one child in college and $50,000 in income would almost certainly qualify for a fat aid package to offset a $40,000-plus college tab—even with significant assets, like $150,000 in home equity and $50,000 in stocks or mutual funds. Even a family earning $125,000 in income might qualify for some aid, and almost certainly would if two or more family

WHAT COLLEGE WILL COST

This table will help you figure out the total cost of college, given projected increases of 7% annually during the college years.

If your child begins school in two years, for instance, add the annual cost of years two through five to get an estimate of the four-year cost. If she is an infant, add years 18 through 21.

Use the $40,000 starting point if you have your eye on an elite private institu-

tion, the $15,000 starting point for in-state costs at public schools, and the $30,000 starting point if you're not sure.

If you're starting early, bear in mind that the further out you go, the tougher it is to predict how quickly college costs will rise. As the years pass, you'll want to look into how much college costs are really rising and adjust your planning accordingly.

Today	1 Year	2 Years	3 Years	4 Years	5 Years	6 Years	7 Years
$40,000	$42,800	$45,796	$49,002	$52,432	$56,102	$60,029	$64,231
30,000	32,100	34,347	36,751	39,324	42,077	45,022	48,173
15,000	16,050	17,174	18,376	19,662	21,038	22,511	24,087

Today	8 Years	9 Years	10 Years	11 Years	12 Years	13 Years	14 Years
40,000	68,727	73,538	78,686	84,194	90,088	96,394	103,141
30,000	51,546	55,154	59,015	63,146	67,566	72,295	77,356
15,000	25,773	27,577	29,507	31,573	33,783	36,148	38,678

Today	15 Years	16 Years	17 Years	18 Years	19 Years	20 Years	21 Years
40,000	110,361	118,087	126,353	135,197	144,661	154,787	165,622
30,000	82,771	88,565	94,764	101,398	108,496	116,091	124,217
15,000	41,385	44,282	47,382	50,699	54,248	58,045	62,108

members attended expensive colleges at the same time. In fact, because some pricey schools have plenty of aid money to give out, families applying to them sometimes qualify for generous aid packages that bring the real cost below what they'd pay at a public university.

Chapter 4 will help you pinpoint how much schools will expect you to contribute to college costs before qualifying for any aid—your expected family contribution. That's the best indicator of how much college will really cost—no matter what the official sticker price at the school your child attends.

Tax Credits Will Help, Too

Thanks to tax legislation passed in recent years, many families will also get a boost from tax credits and tax deductions for higher-education expenses.

COLLEGE EDUCATION PAYS

Sure, some students who graduate with a six-figure diploma still wind up pouring coffee at a diner—at least for a while. But on average, a college education pays for itself in higher earnings over a lifetime. According to the Bureau of Labor Statistics, the average high school graduate earned around $28,808 in 2004, compared with about $46,800 for the average worker with a bachelor's degree. Add an advanced degree and the average is $55,328.

THE HOPE SCHOLARSHIP CREDIT. During the first two years of college, parents (or students, if they're paying the bills themselves) can qualify for a "Hope Scholarship," which is an annual tax credit equal to 100% of the first $1,000 you pay in tuition and fees and 50% of the second $1,000—for a total credit of up to $1,500 per student each calendar year. For 2005, you're fully eligible for the credit if you're a married couple filing jointly and earn up to $87,000 in adjusted gross income or if you're single and earn up to $43,000. The credit begins shrinking at higher income levels, and disappears completely at $107,000 for couples and $53,000 for singles.

Unlike a tax deduction, which reduces your taxable income, a tax credit reduces your actual tax bill dollar for dollar. So a $1,500 tax credit means you'll have an extra $1,500 you can send to your child's college rather than to Uncle Sam. Another plus: A family with two or

continued on page 10

A COLLEGE PLANNING TIMELINE

You can use this timeline to identify where you should be in the process of preparing to send your child to college. Each section identifies the appropriate steps by season and the chapters of this book that will help you take them.

If you're starting late, remember that the timeline is an ideal to shoot for. So don't be too discouraged if most of it has already passed you by. If it's the beginning of senior year, for instance, and you're just starting to look at colleges, just recognize that you have a lot of work to cram into the next few months. You may have missed the chance to arrange your finances for maximum eligibility for financial aid, but getting the aid application forms in on time (usually in January to March of the senior year) is far more important. Similarly, if you haven't managed to set aside money in a college fund, remember that every little bit helps no matter how late you start—and be aware that you will probably need to rely more heavily on your current income and loans to meet the bills.

Preschool

Start a savings plan for college. If you set aside even a small sum each month, the amounts you accumulate over the years will go a long way toward meeting the college bills. For help deciding how much to save and whether to keep the money in your own name or your child's, *see Chapter 2*. Because you have years before you need the money, you can take some risk and shoot for high returns in stocks and stock mutual funds; *see Chapter 3*.

Elementary School

Although you may need to aim for a higher monthly savings contribution than a parent who started sooner, you're still in good shape. *See Chapters 2 and 3* for guidance on how much to save and where to invest it.

Junior High

With about five years before you'll write your first tuition check, you should take less risk with money you save from now on. *See Chapter 3*.

High School
Freshman year

Complete a "need analysis" to get a rough idea of whether you're likely to qualify for financial aid. *See Chapter 4*.

If you've accumulated savings, begin shifting your money from riskier investments, like stocks and stock mutual funds, to safer investments, like bonds and money-market accounts. *See Chapter 3*.

Encourage your child to take challenging courses in high school so he or she will be a more attractive college applicant, which not only helps a student get into school but may also lead to more financial aid. *See Chapter 6*.

Likewise, encourage your child to engage in extracurricular activities, which will help with admissions and may lead to scholarships. *See Chapter 8*.

Sophomore year

Repeat the need analysis in *Chapter 4*. If your income has changed, you'll see how it's likely to affect your eligibility for financial aid.

Consider using some of the aid-boosting strategies in *Chapter 6* to increase your eligibility.

Encourage your child to begin browsing college-selection books to get an idea of what schools he or she might want to apply to. *See Chapter 7* on selecting a college.

Take a practice round of the PSAT (a shorter version of the College Board's SAT) or PLAN (a shorter version of the ACT, another national exam for college entrance).

Junior year—Fall

When colleges evaluate your income and assets to determine whether you're eligible for financial aid, the first year they examine is the one starting halfway through your child's junior year. So you have until the end of that calendar year to make adjustments to your finances that might boost your eligibility for aid. *See Chapter 6.*

Advise your child to talk with a high school guidance counselor about colleges that might be a good fit. *See Chapter 7.*

Take the PSAT or PLAN. This time it counts. Students with very high PSAT scores can qualify for National Merit Scholarships.

Strong students should consider taking advanced placement courses, which are usually offered beginning in the junior year. These help students' admissions chances at selective schools and may also earn your child credits toward his or her college degree. They might even save you money by shortening his or her time on campus. *See Chapter 10.*

Junior year—Spring

Make a preliminary list of prospective colleges by consulting guidebooks and talking to teachers and counselors. *See Chapter 7.*

Begin working campus visits into your family travel plans. You can visit in the summer, too, but a visit while a regular semester is in session will probably be more informative and revealing. *See Chapter 7.*

Begin browsing scholarship guides at the library or scholarship databases on the Internet or in the high school guidance office. *See Chapter 8.*

Make sure you have your social security card, or get a replacement.

Take the SAT or ACT.

Summer after junior year

Narrow the list of prospective colleges and request applications, catalogs, and financial-aid information. Ask about special internship or co-op programs, innovative tuition-payment plans, advanced-placement credits, and other alternatives that might influence your choice of school. *See Chapter 10.*

Senior year—Fall

Continue campus visits.

Register to receive the application materials for the PROFILE financial-aid form. *See Chapter 4.*

Apply for scholarships now and in the spring. *See Chapter 8.*

continued on page 10

A COLLEGE PLANNING TIMELINE *continued*

Begin working on college applications and essays.

Retake the SAT or ACT if you want a shot at improving your scores.

ROTC applications due by November 15.

Senior Year—Spring
College applications are typically due in January, and financial-aid forms are due in February or March (although the earlier you file them after January 1, the better). Then you'll endure the wait for acceptances and financial-aid offers.

Compare the aid packages you receive to determine how much each school will actually cost you out of pocket. If you want to appeal your aid package or try to get one school to match the offer from

another, now is the time. *See Chapter 5.*

Summer after graduation
Apply for student loans. *See Chapter 9.*

Prepare your child to handle his or her own finances. *See Chapter 11.*

And beyond
The process of planning for and paying the college bills doesn't end with the start of freshman year. You'll need to reapply each year for financial aid, and also for loans and scholarships. And chances are your child will need some friendly guidance about money management or finding a job or internship, so you'll have plenty of occasions to revisit these chapters to refresh your memory.

---

more students in the first two years of college at the same time can take advantage of multiple Hope Scholarships. So if you have twins, for instance, you could receive tax credits worth $3,000 in their freshman year and another $3,000 in their sophomore year.

THE LIFETIME LEARNING CREDIT. In the third year of college and beyond, students or their parents can take a "Lifetime Learning" tax credit that is currently worth up to $2,000 for each year of postsecondary study—which includes graduate or professional school or even "adult education" classes to brush up on job skills. Your credit equals 20% of the first $10,000 in tuition and fees paid in a calendar year. The Lifetime Learning credit is subject to the same income restrictions as the Hope Scholarship, so if you earn more than $87,000 to $107,000 as a couple or more than $43,000 to $53,000 singly, the credit will be phased out. While a family paying two or more tuition bills at once can take multiple Hope Scholarships, you're limited to one Life-time Learning credit per taxpaying household per year, no matter how many family members are in school. However, you can take a Lifetime Learning credit in the same year you claim one or more Hope Scholarships.

TAX CREDIT EXAMPLES. The total amount of tax credits a typical student can earn is more than you may think because four academic years spans five calendar years.

For example, a student who began freshman year in 2005 and who will graduate in 2009 will, over the span of his or her undergraduate career, have been eligible for up to $9,000 in tax credits from Uncle Sam, as shown here:

Freshman fall, 2005	$1,500 Hope Scholarship
Freshman spring–sophomore fall, 2006	$1,500 Hope Scholarship
Sophomore spring–junior fall, 2007	$2,000 Lifetime Learning credit
Junior spring–senior fall, 2008	$2,000 Lifetime Learning credit
Senior spring, 2009	$2,000 Lifetime Learning credit
Total	**$9,000 in tax credits**

If you'll have two students going through college simultaneously, you won't receive twice the amount of tax credits, because only one student in a taxpaying household can take the Lifetime Learning credit each year:

Freshman fall, 2005	$3,000 (2 Hope Scholarships)
Freshman spring–sophomore fall, 2006	$3,000 (2 Hope Scholarships)
Sophomore spring–junior fall, 2007	$2,000 (1 Lifetime Learning credit)
Junior spring–senior fall, 2008	$2,000 (1 Lifetime Learning credit)
Senior spring, 2009	$2,000 (1 Lifetime Learning credit)
Total	**$12,000 in tax credits**

But with two children going through college three or more years apart, a family will be able to take up to $9,000 in tax credits for each child entering college in 2005 and beyond (not that you can do much about the timing now!):

Freshman fall for student #1, 2005	$1,500 Hope Scholarship
Freshman spring–sophomore fall #1, 2006	$1,500 Hope Scholarship
Sophomore spring–junior fall #1, 2007	$2,000 Lifetime Learning credit
Junior spring–senior fall #1 and freshman fall for student #2, 2008	$3,500 (1 Lifetime credit + 1 Hope)
Senior spring #1 and freshman spring–sophomore fall #2, 2009	$3,500 (1 Lifetime credit + 1 Hope)
Sophomore spring–junior fall #2, 2010	$2,000 Lifetime Learning credit
Junior spring–senior fall #2, 2011	$2,000 Lifetime Learning credit
Senior spring #2, 2012	$2,000 Lifetime Learning credit
Total	**$18,000 in tax credits**

MORE RULES. All of the above examples assume you meet the income requirements and that you're spending enough on tuition and fees to earn the maximum credit each year.

To earn the full Hope Scholarship, you need to spend $2,000 on tuition and fees, after any grants or scholarships are taken into account. Room and board and other related expenses don't count toward the credit.

To receive the full $2,000 Lifetime Learning credit, you will have to spend $10,000 or more in tuition and fees.

The amount of the Hope Scholarship (but not the Lifetime Learning credit) is indexed for inflation, along with the income limits for eligibility for both credits, so the figures shown in the above examples may change. To be eligible for the Hope credit, a student must be enrolled at least half-time. This is true of the Lifetime Learning credit, too, unless you are taking a course to improve job skills.

TAX DEDUCTIONS FOR HIGHER EDUCATION EXPENSES. Tax legislation that passed in 2001 created an added, but temporary, tax break for college expenses that will benefit some parents. Parents can take a tax deduction for up to $4,000 of college costs, regardless of whether they itemize. Unless legislation is passed that would make this provision in the law permanent, it will be automatically repealed at the end of the 2005 tax year. To qualify for the top write-off, your adjusted gross income must be below $65,000 on a single return or $130,000 on a joint return. Taxpayers with higher incomes—but still below $80,000 on single returns and $160,000 on joint ones—can qualify for a $2,000 write-off.

You can't claim a Hope or Lifetime Learning tax credit in the same year and for the same student for whom you claim this deduction. And, in most cases, those tax credits will be more valuable than a tax deduction. But since the income limits for the credits are lower than for the deduction, some taxpayers who are locked out of the credits will get this write-off.

No Need to Save It All in Advance

What you're left to pay still won't be chicken feed—even if your true cost is less than you imagined. Unless your child wins a free ride or a generous grandparent comes to the rescue, the college bills will still be substantial. But you don't have to save the full amount in advance. Financial-aid officers like to say that a family's contribution to college costs gets paid in the past, present, and future—meaning from your savings, your income during the college years, and loans you pay off later. Just as you probably wouldn't try to save the entire cost of a home or a car before you buy it, you needn't be ready to write a check for four years of educational expenses as your child begins freshman year.

SAVINGS. Whether you're doing it or not, you probably know that the best course is to save early and often. The bigger the "down payment" you save ahead of time, the less painful the payments will be during and after the college years. But even with just a year or two to go until the first tuition bill, there's time to accumulate some cash to soften the blow. Find a way to put $200 a month into a lower-risk investment such as an

Even with just a year or two to go until the first tuition bill, there's time to accumulate some cash to soften the blow.

A good portion of a financial-aid package is likely to consist of loans, so each dollar you save now is probably one you or your child won't have to borrow—and pay interest on—later.

intermediate government bond mutual fund earning at least 5% during your child's junior and senior high school years, for instance, and you'll have made a $5,000 dent in the challenge ahead.

See Chapter 2 to get a handle on how much you need to save and in whose name to keep it, as well as how to squeeze a little more college money out of the family budget. Chapter 3 will help you choose an appropriate investment haven for your college savings.

Also remember that a good portion of a financial-aid package is likely to consist of loans rather than grants or scholarships. So each dollar that you save now is probably one you or your child won't have to borrow—and pay interest on—later.

Saving doesn't make you a chump, by the way. Some parents have the frustrating suspicion that while they're pinching pennies to save toward the equivalent of two Mercedes in the driveway, the neighbors who save nothing and actually drive a Mercedes are getting away with something—because with less savings they'll qualify for more financial aid. Don't worry. If you're saving now, you're going to be far better off than your profligate neighbors.

If the savings you put away now reduce your financial-aid package at all, it will be by a small amount. The calculations that determine how much you can afford to contribute to college costs don't even consider a portion of your savings and other assets (up to $73,700, depending on your age and marital status), and even resources above that amount are tapped at no more than 5.6% per year. So, you are hardly penalized at all for being a good saver.

And because you saved ahead of time, you'll wind up borrowing less than your neighbors to meet the portion of college costs that isn't covered by financial aid. They'll be envying you when they're still paying off college bills years and years after graduation day.

CASH FLOW. This is the painful, belt-tightening part. As a parent, you already know all about sacrifice. Maybe you will drive the old car a couple of extra years, skip a vacation, or strike shrimp and steak off the family grocery list for a while.

While your child is away at school, there will be one less mouth to feed at home, and you can probably count on fewer outlays for such expenses as sports equipment or flute lessons. Put another way, some of the board and personal costs that are rolled into the college bills are expenses you're already carrying. So it should be possible to squeeze some additional money out of the family budget to put toward college costs. In Chapter 11, you'll find tips for keeping those "incidental" costs down, from trimming the phone bill to finding a student-friendly bank account.

If you save regularly for retirement, perhaps via payroll deductions to your 401(k) plan, you might choose to put that on hold for a few years and divert cash to college bills. (Balancing the two goals, of course, can make for some tough decisions. See Chapter 2 for some guidance.)

The other alternative is to find ways to boost your income. Some parents even pick up a second job—or turn a hobby into an income-producing sideline business. A Maryland couple, for instance, turned a dog-breeding hobby into an active business to generate extra cash toward the college costs of their three children. One Minnesota family took a job cleaning their church to help put their son through business school.

Your kids are another resource. It's not unreasonable to expect them to chip in toward their own college bills. A student working full-time during the summer and semester break and/or part-time during the school year can earn perhaps $6,000 in a year. Yes, a lot of that will probably get spent on day-to-day living costs, but it's that much less sneaker and sweatshirt money you will have to come up with. (Chapter 2 discusses how your child's income will be figured into the financial-aid formula; see pages 36–39.)

LOANS. Most students also pick up some of the tab in the form of student loans, which they pay off after graduation. A typical student can borrow as much as

> **Some of the board and personal costs that are rolled into the college bills are expenses you're already carrying.**

Don't be cowed by the six-figure amounts you see in the headlines. Let them spur you to action.

$20,000 over four years, sometimes with no interest on the loan during the college years. When that's not enough, you can usually get a so-called "parent loan" to cover the balance. Federal loan programs now let you borrow up to the full cost of college, at rates that are reasonable if you don't succumb to the temptation to stretch payments out over decades. It may be even cheaper to borrow against your own assets, such as a retirement account, home equity, or cash value in a life insurance policy. (Chapter 9 will help you sort out the choices and keep a lid on interest costs.)

The Bottom Line

Yes, a college education costs a lot of money today. But don't be cowed by the six-figure amounts you see in the headlines. Let them spur you to action—using the time you have left between now and freshman orientation, whether one year or 18, to figure out how much college will really cost and map out a plan for reaching your goals for your child's college education. (Chapter 7 will help you get a handle on what those goals really are.)

A COLLEGE-COST SAMPLER, 2004–2005

This sampler isn't meant to be all-inclusive, but it will give you an idea of how college costs vary at schools in every state. For the most current information about the schools that are listed here—and those that aren't—contact the school directly or consult a guidebook such as the *College Costs & Financial Aid Handbook* ($23.95), the source for the figures below, which is published annually by the College Board.

State and school	Tuition and fees (in state/ out of state)	Room & board	Transpor- tation	Books & supplies	Personal expenses	Total costs (in state/ out of state)
Alabama						
Auburn U. (Auburn)	$4,426/12,886	$ 5,970	$ 829	$ 900	$1,689	$13,814/22,274
U. of Alabama	4,134/11,294	4,906	634	700	1,690	12,064/19,224
Alaska						
Alaska Pacific U.	$17,310	$ 6,700	$ 350	$ 840	$1,111	$26,311
U. of Alaska (Fairbanks)	3,670/9,400	5,130	324	700	2,250	12,074/17,804
Arizona						
Arizona State U.	$3,595/12,115	$ 6,453	$1,000	$ 700	$2,992	$14,740/23,260
U. of Arizona	3,603/12,373	5,610	520	714	2,212	13,859/22,629
Arkansas						
Lyon College	$13,130	$ 5,820	$ 900	$ 700	$ 900	$21,450
U. of Arkansas (Fayetteville)	4,768/11,518	5,087	1,100	800	1,100	12,855/19,605
California						
Stanford U.	$28,923	$ 9,049	NA	$1,155	NA	$39,127
U. of California (Berkeley)	5,250/19,460	11,212	604	1,108	1,156	19,330/33,540
Colorado						
Colorado College	$28,644	$ 7,216	$ 720	$ 844	$ 900	$38,324
U. of Colorado (Boulder)	4,020/20,366	6,754	567	1,163	2,673	15,177/31,493
Connecticut						
U. of Connecticut	$7,308/19,036	$ 7,300	$ 900	$ 725	$1,800	$18,033/29,761
Yale U.	29,820	9,030	NA	2,520	NA	41,370
Delaware						
Delaware State U.	$4,726/10,383	$ 7,411	$1,576	$1,050	$ 777	$15,540/21,197
U. of Delaware	6,498/16,028	6,118	NA	800	1,500	14,916/24,446

continued on page 18

A COLLEGE-COST SAMPLER, 2004–2005 *continued*

State and school	Tuition and fees (in state/ out of state)	Room & board	Transpor- tation	Books & supplies	Personal expenses	Total costs (in state/ out of state)
District of Columbia						
Georgetown U.	$28,209	$10,033	$ 410	$ 940	$1,105	$40,697
U. of the District of Columbia	2,520/4,710	NA	1,260	800	1,600	6,180/8,370
Florida						
Stetson U.	$22,640	$ 6,855	NA	$ 800	$1,620	$31,915
U. of Florida	2,780/13,283	5,800	310	700	2,280	11,870/22,373
Georgia						
Emory U.	$29,322	$ 9,650	$ 600	$1,000	$ 700	$41,272
U. of Georgia	4,078/14,854	5,756	NA	610	1,682	12,126/22,902
Hawaii						
Hawaii Pacific U.	$11,002	$ 9,020	$1,000	$1,200	$ 600	$22,822
U. of Hawaii (Manoa)	3,465/9,945	6,043	243	1,017	1,166	11,934/18,414
Idaho						
Boise State U.	$3,251/9,971	$ 4,513	$1,000	$1,000	$2,258	$12,022/18,742
U. of Idaho	3,348/10,740	4,868	998	1,130	1,996	12,340/19,732
Illinois						
Northwestern U.	$30,085	$ 9,393	$ 426	$1,353	$1,611	$42,868
U. of Illinois (Urbana-Champaign)	7,010/18,046	7,018	440	740	1,610	16,818/27,854
Indiana						
Indiana U. (Bloomington)	$6,517/17,552	$ 5,892	$ 750	$ 740	$2,200	$16,099/27,114
U. of Notre Dame	27,612	6,930	500	850	900	36,792
Iowa						
Grinnell College	$25,820	$ 6,870	$ 500	$ 400	$ 400	$33,990
Iowa State U.	5,028/14,370	5,740	424	754	2,320	14,266/23,608
Kansas						
Kansas State U.	$4,060/11,950	$ 5,080	302	$ 684	$2,520	$12,646/20,536
U. of Kansas (Lawrence)	4,101/11,577	4,822	1,222	750	1,904	12,799/20,275

State and school	Tuition and fees (in state/ out of state)	Room & board	Transpor- tation	Books & supplies	Personal expenses	Total costs (in state/ out of state)
Kentucky						
U. of Kentucky	$4,546/11,226	$4,286	$ 560	$ 600	$1,148	$11,140/17,820
U. of Louisville	4,450/12,166	3,872	1,176	700	2,004	12,202/19,918
Louisiana						
Louisiana State U. and A&M	$3,964/9,264	$5,216	$ 822	$1,000	$1,427	$12,429/17,729
Tulane U.	31,210	7,925	800	800	800	41,535
Maine						
Bowdoin College	$30,120	$7,670	NA	$ 800	$1,160	$39,750
U. of Maine (Machias)	4,115/10,055	5,150	900	650	1,600	12,415/18,355
Maryland						
Johns Hopkins U.	$30,640	$5,456	$ 700	$ 850	$ 800	$38,446
U. of Maryland (College Park)	6,759/17,433	7,468	604	785	1,940	17,556/28,230
Massachusetts						
Harvard and Radcliffe Colleges	$30,620	$9,260	NA	$ 873	$2,638	$43,391
U. of Massachusetts (Amherst)	8,232/17,085	5,811	400	500	1,000	115,943/24,796
Michigan						
Michigan State U.	$6,703/16,663	$5,230	NA	$ 778	$1,314	$14,025/23,988
U. of Michigan (Ann Arbor)	7,975/24,777	6,704	NA	756	2,060	17,495/34,297
Minnesota						
Carleton College	$30,666	$6,309	$ 500	$ 620	$ 100	$38,195
U. of Minnesota (Twin Cities)	7,116/18,746	6,044	NA	730	2,392	16,282/27,912
Mississippi						
U. of Mississippi	$3,916/8,826	$4,358	$ 600	$ 750	$2,000	$11,624/16,534
U. of Southern Mississippi	3,874/8,752	4,297	380	700	1,840	11,091/15,969
Missouri						
U. of Missouri (Columbia)	$6,558/16,005	$5,380	NA	$ 835	$2,436	$15,209/24,656
Washington U.	30,546	9,640	NA	1,000	1,600	42,786

continued on page 20

A COLLEGE-COST SAMPLER, 2004–2005 *continued*

State and school	Tuition and fees (in state/ out of state)	Room & board	Transpor- tation	Books & supplies	Personal expenses	Total costs (in state/ out of state)
Montana						
Montana State U.	$4,180/11,540	$2,300 (room)	$ 900	$ 800	$2,200	$10,460/17,820
U. of Montana (Missoula)	4,104/11,475	5,292	NA	750	2,030	12,176/19,547
Nebraska						
Creighton U.	$21,118	$7,200	$ 600	$1,000	$1,400	$31,318
U. of Nebraska (Lincoln)	4,711/12,293	5,204	NA	720	2,356	12,991/20,573
Nevada						
Sierra Nevada College	$19,650	$7,450	$ 500	$ 750	$2,035	$30,385
U. of Nevada (Las Vegas)	2,670/8,607	7,364	530	850	1,900	13,314/19,251
New Hampshire						
Dartmouth College	$29,256	$8,740	NA	NA	NA	$37,996
U. of New Hampshire	8,664/19,024	6,234	300	1,100	1,800	18,098/28,458
New Jersey						
Princeton U.	$29,910	$8,387	$ 450	$ 790	$1,719	$41,256
Rutgers at New Brunswick	7,927/14,441	8,027	544	733	1,453	18,684/25,198
New Mexico						
New Mexico State	$3,372/11,250	$4,560	$1,228	$ 664	$2,686	$12,510/20,388
U. of New Mexico	3,738/12,500	5,576	1,396	792	1,562	13,064/21,826
New York						
Columbia U.	$29,788	$8,802	NA	$1,000	$1,060	$40,650
State U. of New York (Binghamton)	5,687/11,637	7,100	250	800	NA	13,837/19,787
North Carolina						
Duke U.	$30,720	$8,520	$ 475	$ 940	$1,640	$42,295
U. of North Carolina (Chapel Hill)	3,993/15,841	6,216	NA	800	1,850	12,859/24,707
North Dakota						
No. Dakota State	$3,965/9,600	$4,471	$ 270	$ 650	$2,230	$11,586/17,221
U. of North Dakota	4,156/9,902	4,234	750	600	2,038	11,778/17,524

State and school	Tuition and fees (in state/ out of state)	Room & board	Transpor- tation	Books & supplies	Personal expenses	Total costs (in state/ out of state)
Ohio						
Oberlin College	$29,688	$7,250	NA	$ 761	$ 978	$38,677
Ohio State U. (Columbus)	6,651/16,638	6,429	192	936	2,346	16,554/26,541
Oklahoma						
U. of Oklahoma	$3,983/10,112	$5,485	$ 917	$ 899	$2,821	$14,105/20,234
U. of Tulsa	16,830	5,896	1,119	1,200	2,238	27,283
Oregon						
Linfield College	$22,022	$6,370	$ 200	$ 600	$1,100	$30,292
U. of Oregon (Eugene)	4,959/16,698	6,981	NA	675	1,975	14,590/26,329
Pennsylvania						
Penn State (University Park)	$9,706/19,328	$6,430	$ 378	$ 816	$2,016	$19,346/28,968
U. of Pennsylvania	29,318	8,642	300	760	1,576	40,596
Rhode Island						
Brown U.	$31,573	$8,474	NA	$1,000	$1,306	$42,353
U. of Rhode Island	6,202/16,334	7,518	NA	600	1,576	15,896/26,028
South Carolina						
Clemson U.	$7,144/14,742	$5,038	$2,194	$ 768	$1,640	$16,784/24,382
U. of South Carolina (Columbia)	5,778/15,116	5,327	1,104	720	2,420	15,349/24,687
South Dakota						
Augustana College	$17,980	$5,423	$ 200	$ 700	$ 800	$25,103
South Dakota State U.	4,254/8,966	3,854	900	700	1,568	11,276/15,988
Tennessee						
U. of Tennessee (Knoxville)	$4,450/13,282	$4,710	$2,494	$ 998	$2,002	$14,654/23,486
Vanderbilt U.	28,440	9,457	NA	NA	NA	37,897
Texas						
Rice U.	$21,206	$8,380	NA	$ 800	$1,500	$31,946
Texas A&M (College Station)	5,051/12,131	6,030	532	802	1,522	13,937/21,017

continued on page 22

A COLLEGE-COST SAMPLER, 2004–2005 *continued*

State and school	Tuition and fees (in state/ out of state)	Room & board	Transpor- tation	Books & supplies	Personal expenses	Total costs (in state/ out of state)
Utah						
Brigham Young U.	$3,150	$5,354	$1,370	$1,110	$1,550	$12,534
U. of Utah	3,646/11,292	5,586	NA	1,086	NA	10,318/17,964
Vermont						
Middlebury College	$40,400	NA	NA	$ 750	$1,000	$42,150
U. of Vermont	9,636/22,688	6,680	NA	696	1,039	18,051/31,103
Virginia						
U. of Virginia	$5,964/21,934	$5,591	NA	$ 900	$1,610	$14,065/30,035
Washington & Lee U.	23,295	6,368	NA	1,000	1,395	32,058
Washington						
U. of Puget Sound	$25,360	$6,400	$ 500	$ 750	$1,300	$34,310
Washington State U.	5,210/13,312	6,054	1,212	710	1,962	15,148/23,250
West Virginia						
West Virginia U. (Morgantown)	$3,548/10,768	$5,822	$1,035	$ 720	$1,208	$12,333/19,553
West Virginia Wesleyan College	20,450	5,200	750	600	1,500	28,500
Wisconsin						
Lawrence U.	$26,343	$5,559	$ 300	$ 600	$1,005	$33,807
U. of Wisconsin (Madison)	5,136/19,136	4,299	340	660	1,550	11,985/25,985
Wyoming						
U. of Wyoming	$3,243/9,273	$5,953	$ 679	$1,000	$2,000	$12,875/18,905

The $64,000 Question: How Much to Save?

How much money do you need to shovel into the college fund? A lot, but not as much as some mutual fund companies and brokerages would have you believe. The worksheets they give customers to help them compute how much to invest tend to employ the big scare, which goes like this: Take today's sticker price at one of the country's costliest universities, inflate it at 7% per year, and conclude that parents of a newborn must save more than $600,000—or about $1,100 a month—over 18 years to pay four years' college costs out of their own pockets the day the child sets foot on campus. For parents of junior-high students the prognosis is even worse—on the order of almost $2,800 a month to come up with a cash-on-the-barrelhead payment to the bursar at Ivy League U.

Very disturbing. But as we explained in Chapter 1, most parents won't pay the full sticker price, and you don't need to save in advance every penny of what you will spend. In this chapter, we'll help you get a handle on how much you really need to be saving toward college costs. We'll also provide some guidance on how to squeeze more cash out of your budget to put into savings and how to decide whether to keep those savings in your own name or in your child's name.

Setting Realistic Savings Goals

There's no right answer to the how much to save question. It's a personal goal that you need to set—and no one is going to hold you to it. Still,

Changing your assumptions can transform the ridiculous into a manageable goal.

it can be a useful exercise to crunch some numbers. Working backward, we'll start with assumptions that produce impossibly huge numbers and then show you how changing the assumptions can transform the ridiculous into a manageable goal.

BAD ASSUMPTION #1: YOU NEED TO SAVE IT ALL UP FRONT. Imagine your sixth grader will attend one of the most expensive schools and you'll foot the whole bill. The goal would be $285,000 (about what four years at an Ivy League school will cost for the class of 2016, assuming 7% annual inflation). If you start from scratch and earn a 7% return on your investments, you'd need to put away a gasp-inducing $2,624 per month.

But as you know, you wouldn't need to hand over the whole $285,000 the day your scholar reports for freshman orientation. By assuming you'll keep up the contributions during your child's undergraduate years, you'd cut the tab to $1,637 per month. If you already have a $10,000 head start, the savings goal would be reduced to $1,522 a month.

BAD ASSUMPTION #2: YOU'LL PAY 100% OF THE SCHOOL'S STICKER PRICE. That's still an impossibility for most family budgets. But remember, you're probably not going to have to pay the entire tab yourself. After all, financial aid, student loans, a summer job, a scholarship or grant, and/or a grandparent's largesse will probably trim the final bill.

- **Aiming to amass 75% of the total expense** from scratch requires a $1,228 monthly savings contribution, or $1,112 if you already have $10,000 put away.
- **Aiming to foot half the bill** brings those numbers down to $819 and $703, respectively.
- **Saving even a quarter of the total** could be enough if it seems likely that you'll get significant financial aid. That's $409 a month from scratch, or $294 with $10,000 already in the bank.

QUESTIONABLE ASSUMPTION #3: YOU'RE AIMING FOR AN IVY LEAGUE SCHOOL. Let's assume instead that your goal is an average-priced private college, which will probably cost closer to $214,000 than $285,000 by the time your sixth grader is ready to go.

- **Shooting for 75% of that cost** means you would need to save $922 a month from scratch, or $806 with a $10,000 head start.
- **To save 50% of the cost,** your monthly savings goal would be $615, or $499 with $10,000 already saved.
- **And to save 25%,** your goal is $307 a month, or $192 a month with $10,000 in the kitty.

REASONABLE POSSIBILITY: YOU'RE SAVING FOR A PUBLIC COLLEGE. How about saving for a public college, where the total bill will probably be about $107,000 over four years?

- **If you aim to save the whole amount,** your goal is $615 from scratch, or $499 with $10,000 already saved.
- **Aim for 75%,** and you'd want to save $461 a month from scratch, or $346 a month with $10,000 saved.
- **Shoot for 50%,** and the numbers are $307 and $192, respectively.

The point is that you can juggle the numbers and rescale your goal until you reach a number that doesn't make you want to quit before you start. Also remember that these numbers are much higher than they'd be if you were saving for a newborn or a toddler. Using a 10% return (because you can aim for higher returns when you have a longer time horizon, as discussed in Chapter 3), saving ahead for the full four years at an Ivy League would require $991 per month for today's newborn—rather than the $2,624 cited above for a sixth grader—and saving to cover 50% of public-college costs would require just $88 a month.

Another Way to Set Your Goal

An even more precise approach is to start the number crunching with your "expected family contribution" (Chapter 4 will show you how) rather than with any school's sticker price. Your expected

You need to decide how much you can afford or are willing to save toward college, versus competing goals such as saving for retirement.

contribution is the amount of money colleges will expect you to come up with out of pocket before qualifying for any financial aid, so using that number as a starting savings goal is more realistic than looking at the full sticker price. If you determine from the worksheet in Chapter 4 that you would be expected to contribute $10,000 a year to college costs today, for example, then use that figure as your starting point and multiply it by four to represent the cost of four years of school. Even if you can't quite match the savings goal that emerges from the calculations in this chapter, you'll have a handle on the amount that you'll probably be expected to pay and just how far your efforts will take you toward it.

The worksheets on the following pages will help you determine what you should save monthly. Use the "short-form" version if college is five or fewer years away, and the "long-form" version if college is more than five years off.

How Much Can You Spare?

No matter how much you estimate your contribution to college costs should be, you need to decide how much you can afford or are willing to save toward college, versus competing goals such as saving for retirement. And you probably already have a feel for how much you can squeeze out of your paycheck each month or each week to funnel into a college fund. One computer programmer who lives in New Jersey says his savings plan for his son's college education started with, "Okay, I think we can do $100 a month, and if that's too much we'll knock it back." Then it became just another bill to pay, "and we just did it." Later, he bumped up his monthly mutual fund contribution by $50 when he got a raise. That's the quickest way (and for many people, the best way) to take the plunge.

But if you really want to feed the college fund as much as possible in years ahead—or you want to come as close as possible to the goal you've set—it will

continued on page 30

HOW MUCH YOU NEED TO SAVE: THE SHORT RANGE

This worksheet is for families with a child in the eighth grade or older. The first two columns show the monthly savings necessary over nine years to pay full price at an average private or public college; the third column shows the amount needed to come up with an expected family contribution of $10,000, an example of the minimum out of pocket a school might expect. The last column lets you figure out what you should save monthly in the years left until your child graduates from college. (The payments in the last four years represent a contribution from cash flow toward college costs, rather than actual savings.)

This worksheet assumes that the return you earn on your investments will just about match the rate of increase in college costs. In other words, the 7% or so that college costs will go up each year will about match the 7% or so you can earn in a lower-risk mutual fund. That's a reasonable assumption for parents with five years or fewer until the first tuition bill.

	Example: Private College	Example: Public College	Example: Expected Contribution	Your Family's Numbers
A. Cost of college OR Expected Family Contribution The average annual cost for tuition, room and board, and other costs at public schools in 2004–2005 is about $15,000; at private schools, it's $30,000.	$30,000 x 4	$15,000 x 4	$10,000 x 4	$_____ x_____
B. Total cost Multiply the result in Step A by 4.	120,000	60,000	40,000	_____
C. Savings goal Multiply the result in Step B by the percentage of the cost you wish to save (for example, 60%).	x 60% 72,000	x 60% 36,000	x 60% 24,000	x_____% _____
D. Existing savings Subtract the amount of your existing savings for college from the result in Step C.	– 5,000 67,000	– 5,000 31,000	–5,000 19,000	–_____ _____
E. What you should save annually Divide the result in Step D by the number of years until *college* graduation.	÷ 9 7,444	÷ 9 3,444	÷ 9 2,111	÷_____ _____
F. What you should save monthly Divide the result in Step E by 12.	÷ 12 $620	÷ 12 $287	÷ 12 $176	÷_____ $_____

HOW MUCH YOU NEED TO SAVE: THE LONG RANGE

When you have more than five years to go until college (and more than nine years until graduation), you have time on your side in two ways. You can stretch your savings out over a longer period of time, and you can afford to put your money in investments that earn a rate of return likely to outpace college-cost inflation. That means you can make a smaller contribution each month than the parent who starts later, or perhaps aim to save a higher percentage of the total bill up front. This worksheet allows you to take higher returns into account as you figure what you should save monthly.

A. Projected cost of college

Estimate college costs for all four years, using the table on page 6 in Chapter 1. This far out, don't aim for precision, but rather a rough idea of what your costs will be. (You may also want to complete the financial-aid worksheet in Chapter 4 to get an idea of what your expected family contribution would be today. If you would qualify for a lot of aid, you may want to lower your cost estimates. But remember that your financial position could change a lot over the years—and so could the financial-aid rules.) $ _____

B. Savings goal

Multiply the result in Step A by the percentage of the cost you wish to save—say, 80%.

x _____

$ _____

C. Estimate the return on your investments

Estimate how much you can earn on your money—10% is a fair before-tax estimate if you invest in stocks or stock mutual funds (which you'll read more about in Chapter 3). If you'll pay income taxes directly from your investment earnings, then use an after-tax return. If you're earning 10% and you're in the 25% federal bracket, your return after federal taxes is 7.5%. (It's actually a bit less after taking state taxes into account.) To figure your after-tax return, subtract your federal tax bracket from 1 and multiply the result by your estimated before-tax return. For example,

$$1 - 0.25 = 0.75$$
$$0.75 \times 10\% = 7.5\%$$

Those figures represent your after-tax return, no matter where you get the money to pay tax on your earnings. But if you can handle the tax bill from current income, your funds set aside for college keep growing at the before-tax rate, which can be a relatively painless savings trick. The tax bill in the early years will be small; and in the later years your income may have risen enough to easily handle the tax bill on larger gains. If you plan to pay the taxes out of current income (or if you're saving in a tax-free account), use your expected before-tax return (for example, 10%) in the table below.

D. Figure your monthly contribution

Say you have a 3-year-old, who will finish college 19 years from now. In the table below, find where 19 years intersects with the estimated after-tax rate of return on your savings, say, 7%. The result, $21, is the approximate amount you need to save monthly to accumulate $10,000 by your deadline. If your savings goal is $100,000, you need to save ten times this amount, or $210, each month.

Your goal (the result in Step B) divided by $10,000

Multiplied by monthly contribution per $10,000 (from table) _____

Equals monthly contribution to meet your goal _____

$ _____

What you need to save per month for each $10,000 of college expenses

Years	3%	4%	5%	6%	7%	8%	9%	10%	11%	12%
1	$820	$815	$811	$807	$802	$798	$794	$789	$785	$781
2	404	400	395	391	387	383	379	375	371	367
3	265	261	257	253	249	245	241	237	234	230
4	196	192	188	184	180	176	173	169	165	162
5	154	150	146	143	139	135	132	128	125	121
6	127	123	119	115	112	108	104	101	98	95
7	107	103	99	96	92	89	85	82	79	76
8	92	88	85	81	78	74	71	68	65	62
9	81	77	73	70	66	63	60	57	54	51
10	71	68	64	61	57	54	51	48	46	43
11	64	60	57	53	50	47	44	42	39	36
12	58	54	51	47	44	41	39	36	33	31
13	52	49	45	42	39	36	34	31	29	27
14	48	44	41	38	35	32	30	27	25	23
15	44	41	37	34	31	29	26	24	22	20
16	41	37	34	31	28	26	23	21	19	17
17	38	34	31	28	25	23	21	19	17	15
18	35	32	29	26	23	21	19	17	15	13
19	33	29	26	24	21	19	17	15	13	11
20	30	27	24	22	19	17	15	13	12	10
21	29	25	22	20	17	15	13	12	10	8

Every $25 a week you can trim from your spending means a potential $15,000 you could accumulate by the time today's eighth grader finishes college.

undoubtedly pay off to get a handle on how much flab there is in your everyday spending. That requires a candid look at your income and outgo.

If you already keep track via a checking and budgeting software program, such as *Quicken* or *Microsoft Money,* the data-gathering job is easy—just print out an income-and-expense statement for the past few months. Otherwise, you can start by gathering your checkbook, ATM receipts, and credit card statements and filling out the budget worksheet on pages 32–33. You'll sharpen the picture if you spend a month or two also tracking where your cash goes, using a notebook to write down each day's expenses. Lots of potential college money can slip through your fingers for coffee on the way to work, lunch at the deli, drinks after work, DVD rentals, and other incidentals.

Tightening Your Belt

Once you have an accurate picture of what's coming in and how you're spending it, the next step is to look for the least painful places to cut back. Big overspending, perhaps on clothes or gifts or dinners out, will probably leap out at you once you see the numbers on paper. But seemingly small economies add up, too. Every $25 a week you can trim from your spending—by brown-bagging lunch, mowing your own lawn, eating dinner out less often, or whatever strikes you as dispensable—means a potential $15,000 you could accumulate by the time today's eighth grader finishes college in nine years (assuming you invested the savings and earned a 7% return on your money). Here are other possibilities:

- **Dropping a $140-a-month membership at the gym** you use only sporadically contributes nearly $21,000 over the nine years.
- **How about the $50 monthly cable TV bill?** Another $6,000.
- **Keeping your car long enough** to have two years free of $300-a-month loan payments can put $7,750 into the college fund after two years.

- **Taking one $2,000 vacation a year** instead of two frees up a potential $25,600.
- **Trimming the Christmas-gift budget** by $300 each year nets another $3,845.

Of course, you don't want a budget so rigid that there's no room for fun or an occasional indulgence. The idea isn't to live like monks. If a gym membership has helped you stick to your workout schedule, the fee is a defensible investment in your health. If having someone else clean the house or take care of the lawn is the expense that keeps your life sane or your marriage harmonious, maybe you shouldn't give it up. The point is to take an honest look at your spending, pinpoint expenditures that aren't essential, and put that money to better use.

Smart Saving Tricks

The next chapter will help you find the best places to stash your monthly savings, but more important than where you put it is making sure it gets put away somewhere. That probably won't happen if you wait until the end of the month, after all the bills are paid and pocket money spent, to find that extra $100 or $200 or $300. Instead, make it a top-priority fixed expense.

Call It Your "College Payment"
Think of it like your mortgage or car payment. If you think it will help, make yourself a coupon book and keep it with your bills.

Make It Automatic
Better still, eliminate the need for willpower by setting up an automatic transfer from your bank account to a mutual fund each month (the fund company will be happy to send you forms) or an automatic payroll deduction into a savings account or U.S. savings bond (talk to your company's personnel department). Most large no-load mutual fund families, such as American

continued on page 34

More important than where you put your money is making sure it gets put away somewhere.

A BUDGET-CUTTING WORKSHEET

Use the first column to record your actual expenses. In the second column, set a spending goal in areas where you feel you can cut back. Add up your monthly savings in the third column.

Month_____

Your monthly income

Take-home pay $ _____

Other (specify)   _____

                  _____

         Total $ _____

Your monthly expenses	Actual	Spending goal	Savings
(For irregular expenses you pay out of current income, such as insurance premiums, divide the annual cost by 12.)			
Mortgage or rent	$_____	$_____	$_____
Taxes not withheld from pay	_____	_____	_____
Installment loans/	_____	_____	_____
Credit card payments	_____	_____	_____
	_____	_____	_____
Insurance premiums			
Life	_____	_____	_____
Auto	_____	_____	_____
Home	_____	_____	_____
Health	_____	_____	_____
Disability	_____	_____	_____
Food and beverages			
Groceries	_____	_____	_____
Meals out	_____	_____	_____
Fuel and utilities			
Gas or oil	_____	_____	_____
Electricity	_____	_____	_____
Telephone	_____	_____	_____
Water and sewer	_____	_____	_____
Subtotal	$_____	$_____	$_____

Your monthly expenses	Actual	Spending goal	Savings
Household maintenance	$_____	$_____	$_____
Home furnishings	_____	_____	_____
Automobile			
Gas and oil	_____	_____	_____
Repairs	_____	_____	_____
Other transportation	_____	_____	_____
Public transportation	_____	_____	_____
Clothing			
Mom	_____	_____	_____
Dad	_____	_____	_____
Kids	_____	_____	_____
Pocket money			
Mom	_____	_____	_____
Dad	_____	_____	_____
Kids	_____	_____	_____
Personal care			
(haircuts, cosmetics, and so on)	_____	_____	_____
Recreation and entertainment	_____	_____	_____
Medical and dental	_____	_____	_____
Charity	_____	_____	_____
Vacations	_____	_____	_____
Special expenses			
(tuition, alimony, and so on)	_____	_____	_____
Miscellaneous other	_____	_____	_____
Savings	_____	_____	_____
Emergency fund	_____	_____	_____
Retirement or 401(k)	_____	_____	_____
Subtotal, previous page	$_____	$_____	$_____
Total	$_____	$_____	$_____

Century, Dreyfus, Fidelity, Janus, T. Rowe Price, and Vanguard, can even arrange automatic contributions straight from your paycheck.

Stash Your Raise

An increase in salary is one of the best opportunities you have to "find" money to save. Tell yourself that you got no raise at all and shuttle the monthly increase in your paycheck straight to a savings or mutual fund account. Or treat yourself to a reward with the first month's extra take-home pay, and then start squirreling the extra away.

TEN WAYS TO KEEP MORE CASH

It was Benjamin Franklin who said, "Beware of little expenses; a small leak will sink a great ship." In the spirit of Ben, here are some Franklin-like ways to plug holes in your budget and enrich your college fund.

1. Reduce the cost of your debt.
One way is to switch to a credit card that charges less interest. Transferring a $2,000 balance from an 18% card to an 8.25% card will save you $730 if you pay off your balance at the rate of $50 per month.

Another good choice is a no-fee, no-points home-equity line of credit, which you'd use to pay off higher-cost debt. An average balance of $3,000 on a 20% credit card costs $600 per year in interest; with a 9.5% home-equity loan, the carrying cost is $285. That's tax-deductible, so Uncle Sam pays $71 of it if you're in the 25% tax bracket.

Better still, get your credit card and loan balances down to zero to avoid interest charges entirely. Then divert your debt payments to college savings.

2. Will your electric utility pay to make your home energy-efficient?
Caulking and insulating your house can cut your electric bills by 25%. Many utility companies will perform a free or low-cost "energy audit" of your home, and some will help foot the bill for energy-saving fix-ups.

3. Shop term life insurance rates.
The easiest way is to let a shopping service, such as SelectQuote (800-343-1985; www.selectquote.com), MasterQuote (800-337-5433; www.masterquote.com), or IntelliQuote (888-622-0925; www .intelliquote.com), scout prices for you.

4. Shop around for car and home-owners insurance, too. Premium rates can vary by more than 25%. Once you get the best deal, knock another 10% or so off the premium by raising your collision-and-comprehensive deductible to $500.

That may sound Spartan, but it's far easier than cutting back on expenses you've grown used to. Financial planners often tell of clients who readily agree they can cut back on vacations or lawn-care expenses in order to boost college savings. But the next year's client review often reveals the Visa and Master-Card balances out of whack, whereas they had been paid off in the past. It takes some people a few tries. Saving seems much less like self-deprivation when you've never had your hands on the extra money.

5. Cancel your private mortgage insurance. If you have at least 20% equity in your home, ask your lender to cancel your private mortgage insurance. That will trim your mortgage payment each month.

6. Exploit a set-aside plan. The idea is to set aside part of your salary to pay medical expenses with pretax dollars. Money channeled through a set-aside plan escapes federal income and social security taxes and, in almost all states, state income taxes, too. Using the program to pay $1,000 worth of bills can save $400 or more.

7. Stop smoking. Aside from being bad for your health, the habit costs about $1,460 a year for a pack-a-day smoker. A year after you quit, you can apply for cheaper life insurance rates. Quitting would knock the premium from $984 to $492 a year for a 40-year-old male with a $250,000 policy from Prudential Financial/

Pruco Life Insurance Company. That's a typical reduction.

8. Don't buy a brand-new car. Buy nearly new. You can save big on the cost of the car and financing, and keep payments low. Let someone else take the big hit on depreciation; cars lose their value the fastest in the first couple of years on the road. You'll also save on the cost of car insurance.

9. Reconsider the value of your tax preparer. If your taxes are complicated, a tax pro is probably well worth the fee. But, if not, doing it yourself can save a pretty penny. For most returns, tax-preparation software does the job for less than $40.

10. Visit your public library. If you haven't been to the library in a while, you might be surprised at the opportunities to save on books, compact discs, Internet access, videotapes, investment research, and other services.

Now that 529 plans and the education IRA allow you to enjoy tax-free earnings, there's little reason to use a custodial account, once a college-savings staple.

Save Bonuses and Gifts

If saving the entire raise is impractical—perhaps this is the year you need to replace the nine-year-old clunker in the garage—at least try to squirrel away some of it. Bonuses and other windfalls, like tax refunds and holiday gifts, are other golden opportunities to save money you're unlikely to miss.

Divert the Cost of Day Care

If you have young children and have made room in your budget to pay for the cost of day care, one of those golden opportunities comes when day care expenses end and your child heads off for elementary school (assuming you opt for a public school). A Haddam, Connecticut, couple spend $250 a week on day care for their two young children. When day care expenses end, they plan to redirect that money into a college fund. If each child's share—$125 per week—grows at a modest 8% between ages 5 and 18, each will have roughly $150,000 to put toward college bills.

Where Should You Save?

Once you've begun saving for your child's college education, you'll have to decide what kind of savings vehicle in which to put the money. Your primary choices: A custodial account, a Coverdell Education Savings Account (ESA), formerly known as the education IRA, or a state-sponsored college savings plan, commonly know as a 529 plan. (There's also an "Independent 529 plan," which is discussed in Chapter 3.) The best choice depends on your circumstances. The last two options allow you to enjoy tax-free earnings. But custodial accounts can still be a good choice for many people.

Why Custodial Accounts Are Just About Obsolete

The big draw to saving for college in a child's name, using a custodial account—also called an UTMA (Uniform Transfers to Minors Act) or UGMA (Uniform Gifts to Minors Act) account—has been to reduce the family tax bill. In 2005, the first $800 of annual investment income earned in the child's name is tax-free, and the next $800 is taxed at the child's rate, presumably 10%. So, for example, the tax bill on the first $1,600 of interest or dividends would be $80, compared with $400 if that income were yours and taxed at the 25% rate. Also, the tax rate on dividends and capital gains is now as little as 5% for those in the lowest tax bracket. Custodial accounts also offer a wide range of investment choices.

That's certainly a benefit, but consider a potential tax bill of $0, available with a Coverdell ESA or a 529 plan. Plus, custodial accounts have other disadvantages. Money you put in your kid's name (even in an account where you're the custodian) is an irrevocable gift. It belongs to the child, and you generally can't take it back. That means you lose the ability to use the money for other purposes should the need arise. As the account's custodian, you can use the money for the child's benefit, such as for private high school or braces, but not for a "family" emergency, such as a parent's medical bills or for household bills in the event that a parent becomes unemployed. Practically speaking, your state won't send the "custodial account police" after you for using your child's college fund to pay the mortgage or take a vacation, but a child would have the legal right to fight your decision, if so inclined. (Granted that seldom happens, but it is the law.)

Your children are entitled to spend the money however they wish once they reach the age at which the custodial arrangement ends in your state—typically either age 18 or 21. If you live in a state where custodial accounts end at age 18, you'll have to trust your child to use the money to pay for college tuition and books, not a red Porsche or a year bumming around Europe. You have less to worry about if custodial accounts in your state end at age 21, because normally at least three-quarters of the college bills are paid before a student's 21st birthday. (In a few states, such as California, the age is 18 by default, but it can be higher—in some cases, up to age 25—if you choose

> **Money you put in your kid's name in a custodial account is an irrevocable gift. It belongs to the child, and you can't take it back.**

to specify an age in the account documents. See the box below for state-by-state rules.)

The other disadvantage to saving in your child's name is that the financial-aid formulas consider 25% to 35% of a student's savings to be available for paying college bills each year, while parents are expected to contribute only 5.6% of theirs, at most. That makes

---

WHEN CAN YOUR CHILD HAVE THE MONEY?

If you save for college in your child's name using a custodial account under the Uniform Transfers to Minors Act or Uniform Gifts to Minors Act, state law dictates when you must turn the money over to your child. In most states it's age 18 or 21, but in a handful of states you choose an age between 18 and 21 or between 18 and 25.

Note that the ages listed below are current as of 2005. Many states have changed their laws in recent years, and if you opened a custodial account before a change

in the law, the old law applies to that account. The financial institution where you opened the account can verify the age at which you no longer control the money. (The following information is adapted with permission from *Plan Your Estate* by attorneys Denis Clifford and Cora Jordan. Copyright 2004. Published by Nolo Press, Berkeley, California. Available in bookstores, online at www.nolo.com, or by calling 800-728-3555.)

State	Age	State	Age	State	Age
Alabama	21	Kentucky	18	North Dakota	21
Alaska	18 to 25	Louisiana	18	Ohio	18 to 21
Arizona	21	Maine	18 to 21	Oklahoma	18
Arkansas	18 to 21	Maryland	21	Oregon	21 to 25
California	18 to 25	Massachusetts	21	Pennsylvania	21 to 25
Colorado	21	Michigan	18 to 21	Rhode Island	21
Connecticut	21	Minnesota	21	South Carolina	18*
Delaware	21	Mississippi	21	South Dakota	18
Dist. of Columbia	18 to 21	Missouri	21	Tennessee	21
Florida	21	Montana	21	Texas	21
Georgia	21	Nebraska	21	Utah	21
Hawaii	21	Nevada	18 to 25	Vermont	18**
Idaho	21	New Hampshire	21	Virginia	18 to 21
Illinois	21	New Jersey	18 to 21	Washington	21
Indiana	21	New Mexico	21	West Virginia	21
Iowa	21	New York	21	Wisconsin	21
Kansas	21	North Carolina	18 to 21	Wyoming	21

*Had not adopted UTMA when this book went to press.
**UTMA legislation was pending when this book went to press.

sense because parents have numerous other financial responsibilities. But if you look at all the funds—yours and your child's—as "family" money, putting college money in your child's name could cost you financial aid. (For more about how schools determine your aid, see Chapter 5.)

Custodial accounts may still be useful for some parents and grandparents who are seeking a tax-advantaged way to save money for children and like the idea of choosing their own investments. But for college savings, Coverdell ESAs and 529 plans offer superior tax benefits, better financial-aid results, and more control for the parent or other owner of the account.

The Benefits of 529 Plans

State-sponsored college savings plans are among the top choices for college savings. Withdrawals from the accounts are tax-free. You can use a 529 plan to save for your child's college education regardless of your family income, and anyone can open and fund the account— a parent, grandparent, aunt, uncle, or friend. (You could even use a 529 plan to save for your own higher-education expenses.) The owner of a 529 plan account (usually the person who opens it) is the person who controls the money until it's actually used for college expenses—regardless of the age of the beneficiary—so you don't have to worry about the Porsche scenario.

In fact, you can change the beneficiary of the account at any time, so if the child for whom it was originally intended doesn't go to college, you could transfer the money to a sibling or other family member (even a cousin). The money does, however, need to be used for higher education expenses when it's withdrawn. If it's used for some other purpose, the earnings are taxable to the account owner, who also pays a penalty tax equal to 10% of the earnings. The money can be used at any accredited college in the U.S. (and at some foreign schools) regardless of the state sponsoring the plan.

Unlike Coverdell ESAs (described in the following section), which limit your contributions to $2,000 a

> **You can use a 529 plan to save for your child's college education regardless of your family income, and anyone can open and fund the account.**

The states' 529 plans also fare better than custodial accounts under federal and private financial-aid formulas.

year per beneficiary, 529 plans allow you to make large contributions all at once and to accumulate significant sums toward college expenses. The actual maximum depends on the state that sponsors the plan, but $100,000 or more is typical, and some states have maximums that exceed $200,000.

The states' 529 plans fare better than custodial accounts under federal and private financial-aid formulas. Generally, money in a 529 plan is considered a parental asset, which means the family is expected to use no more than 5.6% per year toward college costs before qualifying for financial aid. (The exception is the "prepaid tuition plan" version of the 529 plan. Prepaid plans—which are described in greater detail in Chapter 3—are considered a "resource" under current aid formulas, which means they can reduce your aid eligibility dollar for dollar.)

There are some drawbacks to 529 plans, however:

LIMITED INVESTMENT CHOICES. While a custodial account or a Coverdell ESA allows you to invest your money in just about anything you like, in a 529 plan you're restricted to the investment choices offered by the state plan you use. You may have just one choice, or you may have four or five. Once you've chosen an investment, you can't switch to another selection in that state's plan later on, but you can roll your money to another state's plan and change your investment choices that way. Generally, the investment plans the states offer are good ones, tailored specifically to college savings. However, keep in mind that it is possible to lose money if the investments do not perform well, as happened to people who started their 529 plans just before the last down stock market. (Chapter 3 provides more detail on the investment aspects of 529 plans.) But if having unlimited investment control is important to you, then a Coverdell ESA may be a better choice for at least some of your college savings.

POSSIBLE REVERSAL OF TAX-FREE STATUS. The second drawback is the prospect (remote, in our opinion) that the plans could cease to be tax-free after 2010. In the legislation that granted 529 plans tax-free status, Congress chose to "sunset" all provisions of the new law in 2011. That means, unless the tax-free provisions are extended or made permanent, 529 plans would then go back to the way they were before the legislation was passed: Earnings in the plans would return to being tax-deferred, and then taxable to the student in his or her tax bracket when withdrawn. (That's not a bad deal, either, but it isn't as generous as the current rules.) We think that tax-free 529 plans will be popular and that Congress will respond to the inevitable call to retain a tax break aimed at families saving for college. But parents who are saving for younger children should be aware of the possibility for reversal.

SHIFTING SANDS. Owners of 529 plans are at the mercy of state government, federal government, and plan sponsors, all of whom can make changes. In 2003, for example, New York's contract with TIAA-CREF expired, and the state switched to a Vanguard-run 529 plan. Participants' money was moved into entirely new investments. The new plan lacks the TIAA-CREF option that paid a guaranteed 3%.

Oregon dropped Strong Capital Management as its plan administrator in November 2003 after the CEO was charged with illegal market-timing activity. Parents now have to choose from a different slate of options under a new plan that uses Oppenheimer and Vanguard funds.

FEES ARE HIGH. Even among plans that aren't sold by brokers (and thus don't have high up-front loads or annual sales fees), expenses are higher in most 529 plans than in equivalent mutual funds. Fund-rating service Morningstar calls a 529 plan "reasonably priced" if the annual expense ratio is less than 1% for a portfolio that's half in stocks and half in bonds. Below 0.70% is considered cheap. The reinvested expense savings can add five digits to the outcome of college savings for a preschooler.

The main reason to use a Coverdell ESA rather than a 529 plan is to retain complete control over the investments in the account.

THE THREAT OF PENALTY. You'll pay a penalty (10% of earnings) plus taxes if the money isn't used for education by the original beneficiary or by a family member.

Who Should Use Coverdell ESAs?

In the same legislation that made 529 plans tax-free, Congress vastly improved the Coverdell ESA, making it a viable choice for college savers. The most important change was raising the annual contribution limit from $500 per year per beneficiary to $2,000 per year—perhaps not enough to cover college costs entirely, but enough to make a dent. If you made a $2,000 contribution each year for 18 years and it earned 10% per year, your savings would grow to just over $100,000. Plus, you'd owe no taxes on withdrawal because Coverdell ESA earnings are tax-free when used for educational expenses. Coverdell ESAs get the same favorable financial-aid treatment as 529 savings plans; the money is considered a parental asset.

The main reason to use a Coverdell ESA rather than a 529 plan is to retain complete control over the investments in the account. If you would want to purchase individual stocks or bonds for your child's college account, or would want to select your own mix of mutual funds, the Coverdell is for you. Another advantage is that, under the law, you can withdraw Coverdell ESA money tax-free to pay for private elementary school or secondary school expenses. If you anticipate sending your child to private school, you might want to take advantage of that flexibility—perhaps using the Coverdell for primary school or high school expenses and a 529 plan for college expenses. The law formerly prevented you from contributing to both kinds of plans in the same year, but that restriction has been lifted.

There are other restrictions, however:

■ **You can contribute to a Coverdell ESA** only if your income falls beneath certain limits. Eligibility phases out between $95,000 and $110,000 for single taxpayers and between $190,000 and $220,000 for married taxpayers filing jointly. So high earners will need to look elsewhere, or give your child $2,000 and let him or her contribute to the account. Or the child's grandparents can make the contribution if their income is below the threshold.

- **You must use the money for educational expenses** in order for the earnings to be tax-free. Withdrawals for any other purpose are subject to tax and to a penalty of 10% of the earnings.
- **Also, you must use funds in a Coverdell ESA** by the time the beneficiary is 30 years of age (except for individuals with special needs) or transfer the funds to another family member who is under the age of 30.
- **Finally, the accounts are not practical** for those who can set aside a large lump sum for college all at once (from an inheritance, for instance), because of the annual limit of $2,000 on contributions.

How Grandparents Can Help

Are you a grandparent? State-sponsored 529 plans also shine as a way for you to help save for your grandchildren's college expenses. As the owner of a 529 plan account—with your grandchild as beneficiary—you retain complete control over the money until it's used for college expenses. That means you could transfer the money to other grandchildren if the intended beneficiary decided not to go to college, or you could even take the money back, subject to taxes and a 10%-of-earnings penalty.

A Coverdell ESA offers similar flexibility, and more control over choosing the investments within the account, but you're subject to the income restrictions and contribution limits discussed above.

If it's likely that your grandchild will qualify for financial aid, the biggest no-no is to put savings in your grandchild's name via a custodial, or UTMA, account. Students are expected to pony up pretty much all their own savings over the course of an undergraduate career; thus savings in a student's name can significantly reduce his or her eligibility for aid. Again, 529 plans or Coverdell ESAs are a better choice if aid is a concern because the savings in those accounts will be

Coverdell ESAs aren't practical for those who can set aside a large lump sum for college, because of the annual limit of $2,000 on contributions.

An even better strategy for grandparents: Hang on to the savings a little longer and help pay off student loans after your grandchild graduates.

considered a parental asset, with much less impact on aid eligibility.

When college bills are imminent, you may be thinking of giving your children money to pay your grandchildren's tuition bills, or paying the bills directly. If your children's household income is modest, and thus financial aid is a concern, it may be better for you to hold the savings in your own name and time your gift to coincide with college bills. (Don't give a large gift at Christmastime, as it will inflate your children's bank account at precisely the time they must report such things on college financial-aid forms.) Even better: Hang on to the savings a little longer and help pay off student loans after your grandchild graduates. By then, a new grad trying to make ends meet on an entry-level salary is likely to really appreciate the help.

If your net worth is high enough to cause estate-tax headaches (in 2005 the tax kicks in when a taxable estate exceeds $1,500,000), there are two good ways to boost the amount of money you can give away and thus reduce estate taxes at your death:

■ **For college-age grandkids,** you can pay tuition directly to the school, and that gift will not count against the $11,000 per year that you can give an individual before having to worry about federal gift taxes.
■ **For younger children,** 529 plans shine once again: You can contribute $11,000 per year without gift-tax implications, even though the beneficiary can't use the money right away. You can even make up to five years' worth of gifts—$55,000—at once.

Saving for College or Retirement?

College and retirement are the twin financial towers for many families. Ideally you'd try to build both at the same time, but usually families find themselves forced to concentrate on just one or the other. Which one should take priority?

Your own convictions may lead to a natural choice, but if you're torn, your age is probably the most important variable to consider. The older you are, the more sense it makes to weight your savings toward retirement accounts because you'll have less time to build your retirement savings after your kids are through with college. If you'll be 59½ or older while your child is in college, you may want to put the bulk of your savings into retirement accounts, such as IRAs or Keogh plans. That will let you take advantage of the tax-deferred growth in those accounts, but because you'll be old enough to make penalty-free withdrawals by that time, you'll have the flexibility to tap the money for college costs if you choose to.

Maximizing contributions to a 401(k) plan with your employer also makes sense, but unless you leave your employer, you'll have to tap the money through a loan rather than an outright withdrawal.

- **If you leave your employer after age 55,** you can then withdraw the money without penalty.
- **If you leave before age 55,** you can roll the money over into an IRA, then withdraw it penalty-free after age 59½ (or earlier if it is part of a series of roughly equal payments, determined by your life expectancy, that lasts for at least five consecutive years and until you're 59½).

Another plus for retirement accounts is that, at most schools, they're not taken into consideration when determining your financial-aid eligibility.

If you're relatively young, you might choose to save more heavily toward college first, then concentrate on retirement after your kids graduate from college. But don't ignore retirement savings entirely. If you have a 401(k) plan at work, for instance, contribute at least enough to take full advantage of any employer match. That free money is too good an offer to pass up. You may even want to contribute up to the maximum, to take advantage of the tax break that lets your account grow tax-deferred, bearing in mind that you can borrow the money later for college expenses.

> **Your age is probably the most important variable to consider when deciding whether to focus on saving for retirement or college.**

Consider this option: Open a Roth IRA and use your contributions to help pay college costs. You can withdraw them tax- and penalty-free.

In Keoghs, SEP–IRAs, and some IRAs, your contribution is tax-deductible, but you can't borrow from these plans, and there's a 10% penalty for withdrawing money before you reach age $59\frac{1}{2}$ (with the one exception described above). So contribute to these only after you've met your college savings goals.

Or consider this option. Open a Roth IRA, which allows you to take out your contributions (since you've already paid tax on the contribution) tax- and penalty-free. You can tap your contributions for college expenses if you need to or let the money ride for retirement if you don't.

Here's how it works: A husband and wife can each contribute up to $4,000 annually ($5,000 annually starting in 2008) and withdraw their contributions without taxes or penalty. If the couple starts their contributions when their child is a newborn, they'll have contributed $174,000 in the two accounts over 18 years. That sum could be tapped for college bills or left to continue growing for retirement. The earnings on their contributions, another $208,000 at an 8% annual growth rate, could be withdrawn penalty-free (but tax would be due); or the money could continue to grow inside the accounts and be withdrawn tax-free by the couple in retirement.

Where to Keep Your College Money

O nce you have started putting money aside for college, your next decision is where to save or invest it. CDs? Savings bonds? Mutual funds? A state-sponsored college-savings plan? The answer depends primarily on the amount of time you have left before you'll start writing tuition checks. In this chapter, we'll describe the best choices for your long-term investments—funds you don't need to touch for five years or more—and short-term savings. But, because it's fairly common for parents to get a late start at saving, we'll work backward, starting with the safest choices for short-term money, including money-market mutual funds, certificates of deposit, and government bonds, and progressing to investments that provide better returns but involve a little more risk, such as growth-and-income, long-term-growth, and aggressive-growth mutual funds. All of those investments are among your choices for college savings that you keep in a Coverdell ESA, Roth IRA, custodial account, or ordinary taxable account in your own name.

If you're willing to give up some investment discretion, turn to page 79, where you'll find the beginning of a thorough discussion of, in our opinion, the best college-savings vehicle: state-sponsored college-savings plans, which give you many of the same investment choices in a convenient—and tax-free—package. And if you really don't want to formulate a saving and investing plan yourself, you'll learn how to find a financial planner who can help you.

Before we begin discussing specific types of investments, let's consider why and how your strategy

Short-term or long-term, there's a way to invest your college savings for growth balanced with safety.

should change with the time you have left before college. In this instance, it makes most sense to begin with a look at the long-term.

Using the Time You Have

If the first tuition payment will be due more than five years in the future, you can put the pedal to the metal—that is, go for the highest possible returns by investing most of your college savings (or as much as your tolerance for risk will allow) in stocks or stock mutual funds. The stock market invariably rises in some years and falls in others, but when you average out the ups and downs, stocks historically have earned more than any other investment. This data from Ibbotson Associates, for investment returns from 1925 through 2004, makes that clear. One dollar in 1926, compounded at the rate of inflation, equaled $10.03 at the end of 2004.

■ **Invested in Treasury bills it would be worth $17.01;**
■ **In long-term government bonds, $65.12;**
■ **In large-company stocks, $2,247; and**
■ **In small-company stocks, $11,617!**

You won't be saving for college over 78 years, of course, but the point is that over the long haul, nothing else will keep you as far ahead of inflation as stocks. A longtime horizon mitigates the risk of the market's going down in any given year—you can simply wait for a better time to cash out. (It's interesting to note that the results above include the impact of the 1929 market crash.)

How does the last decade compare? According to data compiled by Ibbotson Associates, one dollar at the beginning of 1995 was worth $1.27 at the end of 2004, after inflation.

■ **Invested in Treasury bills it would be worth $1.47;**
■ **In long-term government bonds, $2.54;**
■ **In large-company stocks, $3.13; and**
■ **In small-company stocks, $4.56.**

With fewer than five years until your child heads off to college, you don't need to avoid stocks entirely, but you want to reduce your risk by keeping some of your money in less-volatile investments, such as bonds, certificates of deposit, or money-market accounts. By pulling your chips off the stock-market table gradually (or if you're starting late, by putting only a modest stake into the market in the first place), you avoid the potential for disaster—say, having to tap a stock mutual fund to pay tuition just after a 1,000-point drop in the market. By the time you're writing tuition checks, in fact, you probably want your college fund to be entirely or almost entirely out of the stock market.

Here's a rough guideline to follow for allocating your savings among stocks or stock mutual funds (equities) and bonds, money-market accounts, or CDs (fixed-income investments).

- **Elementary school years:** up to 100% equities
- **Junior high school years:** 75% equities, 25% fixed-income investments
- **Freshman and sophomore high school years:** 50% fixed income, 50% equities
- **Junior and senior high school years:** 75% fixed income, 25% equities
- **College freshman year:** 100% fixed income.

This isn't a rigid schedule. The point is to give yourself roughly five years to get out of equities so that you won't be forced to sell in a lousy market when you need the money. You don't need to bring your investment mix down to 50% stocks and 50% bonds the very day your son starts his freshman year of high school—and you shouldn't if the market has just suffered a big drop. But that's the right time to begin looking for a good opportunity to sell some stocks and buy bonds or CDs.

The Safest Safe Havens

If you have a short time horizon, you want to concentrate primarily on safety, which means keeping the bulk of your money in interest-bearing accounts or

By the time you're writing tuition checks, in fact, you probably want your college fund to be entirely or almost entirely out of the stock market.

Because these investments are designed for safety, there's no need to avoid putting your eggs in one basket.

investments, including CDs, bonds, and bond funds. Among the short-term selections, your best choice often boils down to the instrument that's paying the best yield when you're ready to buy, for the length of time you can lock up your money. Since interest rates change rapidly, the discussions below include information on how to check rates for yourself.

Because these investments are designed for safety, there's no need to avoid putting your eggs in one basket. You will want to choose your investments so that you can get your money when you need it for tuition, perhaps using a money-market fund for money needed in the next year and CDs or bond funds for money needed a little further out. You could reach for a little extra yield by putting some money in an intermediate-term bond fund and the rest in a short-term fund or money-market fund. But using more than two places is probably overdoing it.

Certificates of Deposit

SUMMARY: *Government-insured up to $100,000 for maximum safety. Modest returns, but can sometimes beat Treasury bills or notes when interest rates are falling. Penalty for early withdrawal. Shop nationwide for the best rates.*

A saver's staple, certificates of deposit pay a higher-than-passbook rate of interest in return for your commitment to leave the money on deposit with a bank, savings and loan, or credit union for a fixed length of time, usually from one month to five years. The longer you commit your money, and in some cases the more money you deposit, the higher the interest rate you earn. Minimum denominations are normally $500 to $1,000.

The only catch to CDs is that if you need the money before the CD matures, you'll pay a penalty that could be as much as six months' interest. On a two-year, $5,000 CD paying 3.7%, for instance, you might forfeit $93 in interest to cash in early. So you need to time the maturities of your CDs to correspond with tuition-bill due dates. One strategy for shifting gradually out of more-aggressive investments is to buy a two-year CD with one-fourth of your savings as your child begins his or her junior year of high school (so it will mature just before the college tuition bill for freshman year), buy another two-year CD with the next fourth before senior year (to be redeemed for sophomore-year tuition), and so on.

SHOPPING FOR THE BEST RATE. If you're buying CDs in large denominations, consider an out-of-town bank. While there's little point in chasing an extra tenth of a percentage point on $1,000, you can often beat what's available from local banks in your area by a full percentage point or more by choosing from the top-yielding certificates of deposit that are listed in newspapers, such as the *Wall Street Journal* and *Barron's,* and magazines, including the "Managing" section each month in *Kiplinger's Personal Finance* magazine. Web sites such as Bank Rate Monitor (www.bankrate.com) also list top-yielding CDs nationwide. In early 2005, a top-yielding, one-year CD paid just under 3.5%. Banks tend to adjust CD rates more slowly than interest rates change in the general economy. That means CDs will often be a good bet when interest rates are falling (because you lock in a higher-than-market rate) but will often lag other choices, such as money-market mutual funds or Treasury bills, when interest rates are rising (because then you lock in a below-market rate).

RISK. The banks that issue the highest-yielding CDs may not be in your home state. But there's no reason to avoid keeping your money in a faraway institution. At home or out of state, the Federal Deposit Insurance Corporation (FDIC) covers your losses if the bank goes out of business—as long as your deposits in any one bank, including accrued interest, don't exceed $100,000.

The College CD

SUMMARY: *A good idea in principle, but less attractive because of low returns.*

The College Savings Bank, in Princeton, New Jersey, sells certificates of deposit specifically geared to

If you're buying CDs in large denominations, consider an out-of-town bank.

college savers, with a variable return that's based on the rate of college-cost inflation at 500 schools in the U.S. Deposits in the bank's CollegeSure CD are FDIC-insured, as explained above, and are guaranteed to earn no less than 2%. The CollegeSure CD is more flexible than ordinary bank CDs: After a $500 minimum initial deposit, you can make regular automatic contributions of $250 or more through a draft from your bank account or $50 a month or more via payroll deduction. But as with bank CDs, there's a substantial penalty if you withdraw your money early—10% of the withdrawal if you tap the money within the first three years and less in later years.

Unfortunately, returns on the CD haven't been great in the past. You earn a rate of return equal to the rate of increase in the College Board's Independent College 500 Index, an index of 500 widely attended private schools. Between 1996 and 2004, returns have ranged from 4.24% to 5.35%.

Money-Market Mutual Funds

SUMMARY: *Best place to keep money you'll need to pay tuition bills within a year. Shop for the highest-yielding fund with good check-writing privileges.*

A money-market fund is a mutual fund that invests in short-term corporate and government bonds and passes the interest payments on to shareholders. Unlike other mutual funds, a money-market fund's share price stays the same ($1 a share), so your principal doesn't gain or lose value. (See "Risk" below.) Most money-market funds allow you to write checks from your account at any time, so your money can earn interest up to the day it's needed for college bills.

If you strive for maximum simplicity, the easiest move is to keep all your short-term savings in a money-market mutual fund that offers check-writing privileges. Then you can simply write checks from the account as needed. Be sure to find out, however, whether the fund restricts the number of checks you can write per month, imposes a minimum for each check (such as $500), or charges any fees for checks.

If the check-writing fee is significant or the policies are too restrictive, look for another fund.

If you want to reach for a bit more yield, put money you'll need for the coming year in a money-market fund and keep the rest in CDs or bonds that mature before each succeeding year's annual tuition bill.

SHOPPING FOR THE BEST YIELD. As long as the check-writing features meet your needs, you can shop for a fund by looking for the best current yield. The return on money-market funds fluctuates with market interest rates, and you'll find the top-yielding funds listed in the same financial publications that list CD rates (see page 51). *Kiplinger's Personal Finance* magazine lists top-yielding money-market funds monthly in its "Managing" section. In 2005, a top-yielding money-market fund paid around 2.04%, compared with a national average of 1.81%, according to the iMoneyNet publication *Money Fund Report*, another source for yields (check iMoneyNet's Web site at www.ibcdata.com).

RISK. Unlike bank deposits, money-market mutual funds are not FDIC-insured, making them a hair less safe than a CD or bank money-market account. Still, because they buy bonds with very short maturities (see the discussion of maturities and safety on page 59), they're among the safest uninsured investments around. In a few rare instances, money-market funds have lost money, but in all but one instance the investment companies sponsoring the funds have voluntarily kicked in extra cash to maintain the price at the standard $1 per share (the exception was a fund open only to institutional investors).

U.S. Savings Bonds

SUMMARY: *A good buy if you'll qualify for tax-free earnings, available to some parents when the bonds are used to pay college tuition. Also good to hold if you have older bonds earning at least 6%.*

Most people don't think of savings bonds as short-term savings vehicles. In fact, they're a popular gift for

> **Money-market mutual funds are not FDIC-insured, making them a hair less safe than a CD or bank money-market account.**

newborns and young children, and most parents have at least a few tucked away somewhere. If you anticipate qualifying for the tax break available to parents who use savings-bond proceeds to pay for their children's college tuition (see the following page), the bonds are an attractive short-term haven for your college kitty. But if your income will be too high to qualify for the tax break, you'll probably find better returns elsewhere.

RULES, RULES, RULES. Savings bonds would be fairly simple savings vehicles—if only the federal government would stop changing the rules for them every couple of years. Currently, rates are set using a formula that is 90% of the average yield on five-year Treasury securities for the preceding six months. (The bonds yielded 3.25% in early 2005.) Earlier bonds (purchased between May 1993 and May 1995) earned a flat 4% during their first five years and are guaranteed to earn no less than 4% overall. Before that, many bonds were guaranteed to earn 6%. So what your bonds pay depends on when you purchased them.

The latest rules revive an old rule of thumb that you should hold U.S. savings bonds for at least five years. If you cash in a bond earlier, you'll pay a penalty equal to three months of interest. That's not as stiff a penalty as previously, so if you're eligible for the tax break, you may still come out ahead using savings bonds for a short-term time horizon. On a $1,000 bond that pays 4.5%, three months' worth of interest comes to about $11.25.

Because your earnings from savings bonds are free from state and local taxes, the 4.5% short-term return is equal to a higher after-tax return—about 4.8% if your combined state and local tax rate is 7%. And your

---

YIELDS: TAXABLE, TAX-EXEMPT

To figure out how a tax-exempt yield compares with a taxable yield, taking only federal taxes into account, use the following formula:

tax-free rate ÷ (1 − federal tax bracket) = taxable-equivalent rate

For savings bonds paying 4.5%, here's the taxable-equivalent yield for someone in the 25% federal tax bracket:

4.5% ÷ 0.75 = 6.0%

If the investment is free of state taxes, too, your taxable-equivalent yield will be even higher.

return is tax-deferred (unless you choose to pay yearly; few people do), which means you can wait until you cash the bonds to pay taxes on your earnings.

WHEN SAVINGS BONDS ARE TAX-FREE. Savings bonds really begin looking attractive when the returns are completely tax-free:

- **A break from federal tax in the 25% bracket** would boost the taxable-equivalent return to 6.0%. (Add the effect of avoiding state taxes at a rate of 7%, and your return is a not-so-shabby 6.6%.)
- **If you're in the 15% bracket,** the equivalent return is 5.3% (or 5.8% if the returns are also exempt from state taxes of 7%).
- **If you're in the 33% bracket or higher,** you won't qualify for the tax break.

Here's how you qualify for the full tax break (available only on bonds issued after 1989):

The bonds must be held in a parent's name. And the parent must be at least 24 years old on the first day of the month in which the bond is issued. This requirement can be a bit awkward if family members like to give your child savings bonds as a birthday or holiday gift. If you think you'll be eligible for the tax break, you'll have to convince your relatives (and your child) of the benefits of having the bonds in your name—or forgo the break on those bonds.

The proceeds must be used to pay college tuition and fees only. You can't use them to pay for room and board, textbooks, or other expenses. As a practical matter, that means the value of the bonds you redeem tax-free can't exceed the amount of tuition you pay in a given year. If your tuition bill is $5,000 in the freshman year, for instance, you can avoid the tax by cashing in no more than $5,000 in bonds that year.

Your adjusted gross income must not exceed certain thresholds. Your adjusted gross income when the bonds are redeemed must not exceed $91,850 on a joint tax return or $61,200 on a single return. (Those figures are for 2005 and will increase annually to keep pace with inflation.) The thresholds are for the full tax break, which disappears gradually as income increases. You get a partial break if your income is between $91,850 and $121,850 on a joint return and between $61,200 and $76,200 on a single return. The take-back is in direct proportion to the amount your income exceeds the end of the low range. (See the table below.) A couple making, say, $106,850 is about halfway between the low and high ends and thus could escape taxes on about half the interest.

If your income is close to the thresholds, you'll have to make an educated guess as to where it will be in the future. Using a 3% rate of inflation as your benchmark, do you think your income will lag, keep up with, or outpace inflation? If you would qualify for only a partial break now and expect your income to grow faster than inflation, for instance, the tax break probably isn't an attraction for you.

Bear in mind, also, that your income in the year you redeem the bonds will include the savings-bond earnings you've built up over the years you've held the bonds. So if you initially bought the bonds for $5,000 and they're worth $10,000 when you redeem them (at 5%, a doubling in value would take about 14 years), the $5,000 in earnings would be considered income in the year you redeem the bonds.

If you don't expect to qualify for all or part of the savings-bond tax break, you're probably better off

IS YOUR SAVINGS BOND INTEREST TAX-FREE?

Adjusted gross income		
Single	Joint	Tax status
Less than $61,200	Less than $91,850	Fully tax-free
$61,200 to $76,200	$91,850 to $121,850	Partially tax-free
More than $76,200	More than $121,850	Not tax-free

shopping among U.S. Treasuries, certificates of deposit, and money-market mutual funds for the best supersafe yields.

WHERE TO BUY. You can buy (and redeem) U.S. series EE savings bonds at most banks, and you may also be able to buy them via payroll deduction through your employer. For current rates, which change every May 1 and November 1, call 800-722-2678 (or visit www.savingsbonds.gov).

U.S. Treasury Bills and Notes
SUMMARY: *A good way to get supersafe returns—free from state and local taxes—if you are confident you'll hold the bill or note until maturity.*

Treasury bills and notes are another bedrock storage vault for money you'll need soon. You lend Uncle Sam $1,000 or more for a specified period of time; he pays you interest and returns your principal when the bill or note matures. The yield will nearly always outpace that of savings bonds. At press time, six-month Treasury bills (T-bills have maturities of less than one year) were yielding about 2.7% and five-year Treasury

---

WHEN IT'S TIME TO CASH IN

Which bonds should you redeem first, and which should you keep or redeem last, if you own a stack of bonds dating back a number of years?

On most bonds purchased before May 1997, interest is credited to you only every six months. So you must take care to redeem your bonds shortly after a six-month anniversary of the issue date to avoid losing as much as six months' worth of interest. The issue date, printed on the face of the bond, is always the first day of the month during which you bought the bond. So, for example, a bond you bought on July 15 will have an issue date of July 1 and will have interest credited each January 1 and July 1. You squeeze out the maximum interest if you buy a bond at the end of the month and redeem it the day after the six-month anniversary. If the interest-crediting date falls in July but tuition bills don't come due until September 1, switch the money into a money-market mutual fund to capture that last two months' interest.

Try to hold bonds for at least five years to avoid the penalty (three months' interest) for early redemption.

**If you're
18 months
from the
first tuition
bill, a bank
or broker
should be
able to find
a Treasury
that matures
right at
the wire.**

notes (T-notes have maturities of two to ten years) about 3.7%. (Note: Treasury bonds, which have maturities longer than ten years, aren't really appropriate for college savers. If you have that long, you should be in an investment earning more than Treasuries.)

Because your earnings are free from state and local taxes, your real return is somewhat better than the stated yield. A 3.7% yield, for instance, is worth about 4.0% to someone paying 7% income tax to his or her state.

WHERE TO BUY. You can buy T-bills and T-notes from a bank or a broker for a modest fee, usually about $50, and there's one good reason to consider doing so. Banks and brokers are selling already-issued notes and bills from their own inventory, which is likely to contain a variety of maturities. New bills mature in three or six months, and new notes in two, three, five, or ten years. But if you're 18 months from the first tuition bill, a bank or broker should be able to find a Treasury that matures right at the wire.

The minimum investment is $1,000, whether you're buying T-bills or Treasury notes, which mature in two to ten years.

Treasury Direct, a service of the Bureau of the Public Debt, makes it easier than in the past to purchase new bonds directly. It has also simplified the paperwork involved in purchasing bonds. You can establish a Pay Direct account that allows you to request an automatic withdrawal from your bank account when you submit your tender form. Your assets will remain in your account earning interest until the day the security is issued. Treasury Direct also allows you to order tender forms (on which you specify what bonds you'd like to buy), check your account balance over the phone, or reinvest bond assets that have matured. Information regarding the Treasury Direct program is available online at www.publicdebt.treas.gov or by phone at 800-722-2678.

WHERE TO CHECK RATES. Most newspapers list current Treasury yields in the business section. The *Wall Street*

Journal publishes an extensive list of Treasury bonds, notes, and bills of varying maturities, with their current yields, in section C each weekday.

RISK. Treasury bills and notes (and bonds, too) are backed by the full faith and credit of the U.S. government. As long as you don't sell your T-bill or T-note before maturity, you're guaranteed the return of your principal. Sell early and your bond may be worth less—or more—than you paid for it. (See the box below for an explanation of why bond prices change in relation to maturity.)

A BOND PRIMER

Before you purchase a bond or bond fund, make sure you understand how bonds work and how they react to changes in interest rates.

When you buy a bond, you're basically lending money to a company or government entity, which pays you interest—usually every six months—at a set rate. When the term of the "loan" ends (that is, the bond matures), you get your principal back. Say you bought a ten-year, $1,000 bond that pays you 8% interest. Hold it to maturity and you'll get $80 of interest each year, plus you'll get the $1,000 face value back at the end of ten years.

Between the time a bond is issued and the time it matures, the value of the bond itself can rise or fall. As interest rates rise, bond prices fall; as interest rates fall, bond prices rise. So if you sell the bond before maturity, you'll probably get back more or less than the $1,000 face value. Here's an example:

■ **If interest rates rise to 9%,** an 8% bond becomes less valuable because investors won't pay as much for it as they will for a bond paying 9% interest. (The price would fall to around $889, the amount on which a 9% interest rate produces the same $80 a year in income.)

■ **If interest rates fall to 7%,** an 8% bond becomes more valuable to investors. (It would be worth around $1,143, the amount at which a 7% interest rate produces $80 a year.)

A bond's price and yield are also affected by the length of time left until the bond matures. The further away a bond's maturity, the more volatile its price tends to be (the more likely it is to go up or down) and the higher your yield is likely to be. That's because there's less risk that a bond will default or will lose value because of huge swings in interest rates when there are only three months until maturity rather than ten years. Investors in longer-term bonds are compensated for the extra risk with a higher yield.

In exchange for taking a smidgen of risk, you'll achieve a better return, more convenience, or some combination of the two.

THE DOWNSIDE. The drawback to Treasuries is that the government pays you your interest semiannually, automatically depositing it in a bank account you designate. There's no easy way to automatically reinvest the earnings—you have to have the discipline to stash them away (or, preferably, the foresight to have them deposited in a money-market account) rather than allowing them to be dumped into your checking account and spent.

A Small Step Up the Risk Ladder

The investment options in this section are nearly as safe—and under some specific circumstances we'll describe, just as safe—as the choices above. But in exchange for taking a smidgen of risk, you'll achieve a better return, more convenience, or some combination of the two. All are appropriate for money you'll need to use in the next few years.

Treasury Funds

SUMMARY: *Buying Treasury bills and notes directly is your best bet if you can hold them to maturity. Otherwise, consider funds, which allow you to regularly invest smaller amounts and automatically reinvest your dividends. You can lose some principal if interest rates rise.*

Instead of investing directly in Treasury bills and notes, you can put your money into a mutual fund that buys Treasuries (and, often, other government securities). One advantage is that you can automatically reinvest the dividends in more shares of the fund, so you don't have to find someplace else to put your earnings every six months, as you do with Treasuries you hold yourself. In addition, you can withdraw your money at any time. Minimum investments are as low as $1,000.

THE DOWNSIDE. But there are a couple of disadvantages to bond funds, too.

Management fees. First, assuming you were able to buy a portfolio of Treasury bonds that matched the holdings of a Treasury bond fund, you'd earn a bit less in the fund because, as with all mutual funds, the fund company automatically deducts a management fee each year. The T. Rowe Price U.S. Treasury Long-Term Fund, for instance, has a 0.67% expense ratio, which means that for every $1,000 you have invested in the fund, you pay $6.70 each year in management fees. The Vanguard Long-Term Treasury fund's expense ratio is just 0.26%. (When you buy the bonds themselves, there's no commission if you buy them directly from the U.S. Treasury and only a small one-time commission if you buy them from a broker.)

The possibility of taxes. Second, while income from U.S. Treasuries held in a mutual fund is generally free from state and local income taxes, just as if you held the bonds directly, your returns may not be 100% free from those taxes if the fund also holds other government securities, such as Ginnie Maes (government-backed mortgage issues).

RETURNS. The returns on Treasury bond funds will be similar to the returns on Treasury bonds and will fluctuate with market interest rates. Over the past decade the average government-securities fund has earned about 6.6% per year. (The yield on a bond fund is the average rate of interest the bonds in the portfolio pay, independent of any fluctuations in value of the bonds.

U.S. GOVERNMENT BOND FUNDS

All the funds listed here are no-load funds, which means they charge no up-front sales fees.

Fund	Minimum purchase	800 #	Web site
T. Rowe Price Long-Term Treasury Fund	$2,500	638-5660	www.troweprice.com
Vanguard Long-Term U.S. Treasury Fund	$3,000	635-1511	www.vanguard.com

Zero-coupon bonds are ideal if you know exactly when you're going to need your money.

A bond fund's total return will include the impact of changes in the price of bonds themselves.)

RISK. By holding a Treasury bill or note to maturity, you're assured of getting all your principal back. But bond funds never "mature," so there's always a small risk that if interest rates rise dramatically, your investment will lose money (see the box on page 59). Treasury-fund managers try to keep this risk to a minimum by buying a diversified mix of bonds and, in some cases, by sticking with bonds that have relatively short maturities.

Zero-Coupon Bonds

SUMMARY: *Just as safe as ordinary Treasuries if you hold the bonds to maturity. Interest is paid at maturity, so you needn't worry about reinvesting earnings. But you may have to pay taxes on "phantom" earnings each year instead of waiting until you redeem the bond.*

Zero-coupon bonds are an ideal investment if you know exactly when you're going to need your money—as you ordinarily do when you're counting down to the day your first tuition bill is due. While ordinary bonds usually pay interest every three or six months, zero-coupon bonds don't pay any interest at all until they mature, at which time you get all the accumulated interest at once. You can think of it as a bond that automatically reinvests your interest payments at a set interest rate, so you don't have to worry about putting the income to work elsewhere.

Zero-coupon bonds come in denominations as low as $1,000 and are sold at discounts from face value, depending on how long you have to wait until maturity. The longer to maturity, the less you pay. A $1,000 Treasury zero yielding 5% and maturing in five years, for example, would cost around $784. A $1,000 Treasury zero yielding 5.5% and maturing in ten years would cost around $585.

You'll need to use a broker to buy zeros. You may want to check with more than one, in fact, to compare yields and find bonds that fit your time frame.

If your child will be a freshman in 2010 and you have $15,000 already saved toward college expenses, you could buy four zero-coupon bonds, each with a face value of $5,000, one maturing in 2010, the second in 2011, the third in 2012, and the last in 2013. In mid-2005, Treasury zeros with those maturities would have cost about $3,935, $3,670, $3,485, and $3,290 (for a total of $14,380, not including commissions). Each bond would be worth $5,000 when redeemed, reflecting yields to maturity of 4.7% to 5.2%.

The most popular zeros are Treasury zeros, or Treasury strips, so called because brokerages "strip" the interest coupons from the bond and sell you just the discounted bond. They almost always pay more than savings bonds. The brokerage redeems the coupons to collect the bond's interest income (or it might sell the coupons separately to an investor who will redeem them). If you buy the "stripped" bonds, you don't get any interest from the bond. But you pay a discounted price for the bond, as illustrated above, and get the full face value at maturity.

Treasury strips are popular—and are a good choice for short-term savers—because there's no risk that the government will default on its obligations. You can also buy municipal zeros and corporate zeros, described beginning on page 67, which pay you a higher rate of interest to compensate for the additional risk that a company or municipality may fail to repay its bondholders.

THE TAX CATCH. The catch to zeros is that while you might be willing to postpone receiving interest until your zeros mature, the IRS isn't so patient. Taxes on the interest are due year by year as it accrues, just as though you had received it. You'll get a notice each year from the issuer or your broker showing how much interest to report to the IRS. Treasury zeros are free from state and local tax, but you'll still pay federal tax on the "phantom" income.

The prospect of reporting and paying tax on phantom interest is one reason taxable zeros are often

You might be willing to postpone receiving interest until your zeros mature, but the IRS isn't so patient. Taxes on the interest are due year by year.

When shopping for zeros, ask your broker for the yield to maturity. That's the return you're guaranteed to earn if you hold the bond until it matures.

found in tax-deferred vehicles, like IRAs. But an IRA isn't practical for college savings unless the parent holding the account will be at least 59½ when the account needs to be tapped for college bills.

But don't let the tax consequences scare you away from zeros. You can get around paying a lot of the phantom income tax if you put the bonds in your child's name so that the income will be taxable to the child. (The first $800 of investment income a child reports each year is tax-free, and the next $800 is taxed in the child's tax bracket. After the child turns 14, all the income over the first $800 is taxed in the child's bracket.) Or you can avoid the phantom tax entirely by accumulating money in a Coverdell ESA and eventually buying the bonds in that account, where the earnings will be tax-free.

RETURN. When shopping for zeros, ask your broker for the yield to maturity. That's the return you're guaranteed to earn if you hold the bond until it matures.

Treasury strips are not callable, but some other zero-coupon bonds can be "called" early, meaning that the corporation or municipality can pay off the principal ahead of time. Usually this is done when interest rates have fallen, which prompts companies to pay off their existing debts (bonds) and refinance them by issuing lower-rate bonds. If your zero is callable, also ask your broker for the yield to call. That's the rate of return you'd earn if the bond was called at the earliest possible date.

RISK. Zero-coupon Treasuries, or Treasury strips, are just as safe as ordinary Treasury notes or bills if you hold them to maturity. Like any Treasury, the value of a zero fluctuates with interest rates in the meantime. But because investors wait until the bond matures to get their money and get no interest in the meantime, zeros are more volatile. If interest rates rise, for instance, a five-year zero-coupon bond will fall further in value than an ordinary five-year Treasury. That's because the "yield" you're getting doesn't include any interest payments; it's all built into the discounted price of the bond. So the discount shrinks or swells with greater magnitude in response to interest-rate changes than it does on a bond with the buffer—so to speak—of a steady income stream. Treasury strips are a bit riskier than Treasuries in the sense that if you must cash out early, the penalty for doing so may be higher.

Zero-Coupon Bond Funds

SUMMARY: *Here's a good way to buy zeros with small monthly contributions.*

Individual zero-coupon bonds primarily make sense for money you've already accumulated toward college bills. They generally aren't practical for ongoing contributions of, say, $100 a month. The smallest zero you're likely to find is $1,000, and $5,000 is more typical. In early 2005, to buy a $1,000 bond that matures in five years you would have needed to invest about $818. You could save $100 a month and buy one $1,000 bond every eight months or so, but a more practical solution is to invest in a zero-coupon bond mutual fund, such as American Century's Target Maturities Trust (800-345-2021), part of the largest family of such funds. American Century's no-load zero-coupon bond funds hold Treasury strips, and each fund is scheduled to "mature" when the bonds in the fund mature. So the fund called American Century Target Maturities 2010 holds Treasury strips that mature in (or very close to) 2010, and American Century Target Maturities 2015 holds Treasury strips that mature around 2015. There are also funds that mature in 2020, 2025, and 2030.

You can hang on to the fund until maturity, at which time you're paid 100% of your principal plus interest, or you can cash in your shares at any time prior to maturity. There's no up-front sales fee to buy shares. The minimum initial investment is $2,500, and you can add to the fund with as little as $50 if you contribute via monthly bank draft.

If your child will begin college in 2017, you'd probably want to buy the fund that matures in 2020. That way you could withdraw some money in 2017, some in

2018, some in 2019, and the last of it to pay for your child's senior year when the fund matures in 2020. A more conservative approach would be to buy the fund that matures in 2015, take your principal and interest all at once, then move the money to a money-market fund. The discussion of risk, below, explains why.

TAXES. The tax treatment of phantom income is the same as for Treasury strips themselves—you must pay tax on the interest as it accrues, instead of when you redeem your shares.

RETURN. In 2005, you could expect to earn an annual return of about 4.1% if you bought American Century Target Maturities 2010 and held your shares to maturity. In American Century Target 2015, you could expect to earn a return of about 5.0%.

RISK. There's little risk in buying a zero-coupon bond fund if you plan to hold it to maturity. But the value of the bonds can rise and fall dramatically in the meantime, so you could lose money if you had to sell shares early. As we've explained previously, the further away the fund's final maturity, the greater your risk of a loss should interest rates rise. As the fund gets within a few years of maturity, the bonds (at that point, short-term bonds) are less volatile, meaning that interest-rate swings will have less impact on your return. So, if you're not going to wait until the fund matures, the next best thing is to wait to cash out within those last few years when the fund is close to maturity.

MORE RISK, BETTER RETURNS. Some parents with five years or less until the college bills come due will want to stick entirely with the low-risk choices we've discussed so far, even if it means they'll have to settle for a return on their money that may just keep pace with college-cost inflation. If you have low tolerance for risk—in other words, you would lose sleep if your investments dropped in value even temporarily—that's probably the best course for you.

But if you're willing to tolerate a modest amount of risk in order to reach for better returns on your money, consider putting some of your college savings in higher-yielding bond funds or in conservative stock mutual funds. These choices, particularly the conservative stock funds, are also appropriate for parents who have a longer time to save but who don't care for the ups and downs that more-aggressive funds (discussed later) are susceptible to.

Corporate-Bond Mutual Funds

SUMMARY: *You can reach for a bit more return than you'll get with Treasuries by buying shares in a short-term or intermediate-term high-quality corporate-bond fund. In exchange for the higher income, you risk that your shares may lose some value if interest rates rise or if some bonds in the portfolio default.*

Although not as secure as Treasuries, corporate bonds and municipal bonds are another option for short-term savings. Usually, those bonds pay a higher rate of interest to compensate for the extra risk. But since you need $50,000 or more to build a well-diversified portfolio of individual bonds, most investors are better off using bond mutual funds. Bond funds invest in a pool of bonds with varying interest rates and maturities and pass the interest payments on to you. Apart from the income, the shares you buy may fluctuate in price due to interest-rate changes in the economy. High-quality funds invest in bonds issued by top-rated companies with the best prospects for paying interest and principal on time. You can invest in a corporate-bond fund with only $1,000 and add contributions, usually of $100 or more, at any time. You can also automatically reinvest the income from the fund in additional shares, and you can redeem your shares at any time.

RETURN. Corporate bonds—and corporate-bond funds—typically earn a bit more than Treasury bonds or funds to compensate for the additional risk. Over the past decade, the average high-quality corporate bond fund earned 6.7% per year.

Since you need $50,000 or more to build a well-diversified portfolio of individual bonds, most investors are better off using bond mutual funds.

RISK. As mentioned above, the shares in a bond fund can fluctuate in price—they go down when interest rates rise and go up when interest rates fall. Usually those swings are modest, especially when the fund buys short-term and intermediate-term bonds—that is, bonds with maturities of less than about seven years. Funds that restrict themselves to short-term bonds, with maturities of three years or less, are even less volatile, but they pay correspondingly lower returns. A short-term bond fund, in fact, is only a small step up in risk from a money-market mutual fund.

The other risk in bonds is that the company issuing a bond will default (fail to pay interest or principal on time). Owning a fund minimizes that risk because even if one bond defaults, there are many others in the port-folio. You can also minimize your risk by buying high-quality bond funds (those that invest in top-rated companies) rather than high-yield, or junk, bond funds (which reach for extra yield by investing in lower-rated companies). A fund's prospectus should tell you what kind of bonds it's investing in, but its name may tip you off first; junk-bond fund names often include the words "high-yield."

HIGH-QUALITY CORPORATE-BOND FUNDS

All the funds listed here are no-load funds, which means they charge no up-front sales fees.

Fund	Minimum purchase	Toll-free #	Web site
Harbor Bond	$1,000	800-422-1050	www.harborfund.com
Loomis Sayles Bond	$5,000	800-633-3330	www.loomissayles.com

Municipal-Bond Funds

SUMMARY: *A good choice among bond funds for investors in the highest federal tax brackets.*

If you're in the 28% bracket or higher, you may want to take a look at municipal-bond funds, which pay lower yields but are free from federal (and some-times state and local) taxes. A municipal-bond fund that's yielding 5% is the equivalent of a taxable fund yielding 6.94%, if you're in the 28% tax bracket. (In the 33% bracket, the taxable-equivalent yield jumps to 7.5%, and in the 35% bracket it's 7.7%.) These funds buy pools of tax-free bonds issued by state and local governments and their agencies. The funds listed below buy a broad range of issues from around the country. But if you live in a state with a high income tax (such as California, Maryland, or New York), you can do even better buying single-state municipal-bond funds, with income that is free from both federal and state taxes, and perhaps even local taxes, too.

RETURN. Over the past ten years, the annualized total return on high-quality municipal-bond funds (including yield and appreciation in the price of the shares) was 5.0% tax-free.

RISK. Your shares could lose some value if interest rates rise. As with corporate-bond funds, investors with short time horizons should stick with funds that invest in high-quality bonds. In an ideal world, you would also stick with funds that buy bonds with short-term or intermediate-term maturities, which also reduces risk. But good short-term muni-bond funds are relatively rare. (One short-term fund is Vanguard Municipal Bond Limited Term, which earned about 4.67% annually over the past ten years.) So you may have to accept a bit more interest-rate risk in a muni-bond fund than you would in a corporate-bond fund bought for the same purpose.

MUNICIPAL-BOND FUNDS

All the funds listed here are no-load funds, which means they charge no up-front sales fees.

Fund	Minimum purchase	Toll-free #	Web site
Vanguard High Yield Tax Exempt	$3,000	800-635-1511	www.vanguard.com
Vanguard Intermediate Term Tax Exempt	$3,000		
Vanguard Limited Term Tax Exempt	$3,000		

Conservative Stock Mutual Funds

SUMMARY: *Growth-and-income funds are a good bet for investors seeking steady returns. These funds won't soar in the best markets, but won't crash in the worst, either.*

Stock mutual funds, which buy a pool of stocks and then issue shares in the pool to investors, come in every stripe, though they fall between these two extremes:

- **Low-risk growth-and-income funds** concentrate their portfolios on steadily growing blue-chip stocks that pay good dividends.
- **High-flying aggressive-growth funds** look for promising small companies that could soar in value—but could also take a nosedive.

Investors with a short time horizon—or a low tolerance for risk—want to stick with the growth-and-income variety, which aim to provide long-term growth without much fluctuation in share price, even in declining markets. They may not have the potential for sizzling returns, but they also won't fall as hard when the market is down. (If you have a longer time horizon, see the next section, which discusses the more aggressive possibilities.)

RETURNS. Over the past ten years, the average growth-and-income fund returned 11.5% per year. That's above the historical average for the stock market—about 10.4% per year going back to 1926.

RISK. As in any stock fund, you can lose money in any given year. But because they invest in large, well-

---

GROWTH-AND-INCOME FUNDS

All the funds listed here are no-load funds, which means they charge no up-front sales fees.

Fund	Minimum purchase	Toll-free #	Web site
Selected American Shares	$1,000	800-243-1575	www.selectedfunds.com
T. Rowe Price Equity Income	$2,500	800-638-5660	www.troweprice.com
Vanguard 500 Index	$3,000	800-662-2739	www.vanguard.com

established companies that pay good dividends, growth-and-income funds, with the exception of the 2000–2002 down market, have had few losing years in the past decade.

Long-Term Investments

If you're reading this book while your kids are still in diapers, bravo. A long time horizon allows you to pursue the higher returns you can earn by investing in growth stocks or growth-stock mutual funds. In any given year, stocks can lose money—the S&P 500 index tends to fall in one year out of every four. But historically the index has returned an average of 10.4% per year, compounded. A long-term investment horizon lets you ride out the fluctuations of the market so you can take advantage of those double-digit returns.

> ## MUTUAL FUND RESOURCES
>
> Want to update the mutual funds recommended in this chapter? Each year, *Kiplinger's Personal Finance* magazine updates its recommended mutual fund portfolios for investors with short-term, medium-term, and long-term investment goals. You'll find our latest suggested portfolios on our Web site (www.kiplinger.com) under "Investing."

How much of a difference does a couple of percentage points make?

- **A hundred dollars invested every month at 8% produces $48,329 at the end of 18 years.**
- **At 10%, the same contributions grow to $60,557.**
- **At 12%, they reach $76,544.**

Such above-average returns are possible with a long time horizon and growth-oriented mutual funds.

Long-Term-Growth Funds

SUMMARY: *These funds are appropriate as core choices for a long-term stock portfolio. Returns will be similar to the stock market as a whole.*

Growth mutual funds seek long-range capital gains (gains in the value of the shares themselves) by investing mostly in medium-size and large, well-established companies, regardless of whether they pay big dividends. They'll produce returns that should keep pace with or exceed the large-company stock indexes, such as the Dow Jones industrial average. They're good choices primarily for long-term savers, but even parents of high schoolers may want to keep up to half of their money in growth funds to give their savings a chance to beat college-cost inflation.

RETURN. The average long-term-growth fund has earned 8.6% annually over the past ten years.

RISK. Growth funds are considered a bit more risky than growth-and-income funds because they don't seek the extra cushion of high dividends (which companies don't guarantee but usually pay regardless of whether the market goes up or down). When the stock market drops, you can expect a growth fund to drop by at least a similar percentage.

LONG-TERM-GROWTH MUTUAL FUNDS

All the funds listed here are no-load funds, which means they charge no up-front sales fees.

Fund	Minimum purchase	Toll-free #	Web site
Harbor Capital Appreciation	$1,000	800-422-1050	www.harborfunds.com
Legg Mason Opportunity	$1,000	800-368-2558	www.leggmason.com
Marsico Growth	$2,500	888-860-8686	www.marsicofunds.com
Oakmark Fund	$1,000	800-625-6275	www.oakmark.com

Aggressive-Growth Funds

SUMMARY: *These funds will soar in good markets and sink in bad ones. But average out the ups and downs and they outperform other funds over the long haul. Appropriate for a portion of a long-term investor's portfolio.*

Aggressive-growth funds typically specialize in stocks of small to medium-size, fast-growing companies and will usually outperform the averages during boom markets and get flattened during poor ones. You don't want to build your entire investment plan around such funds, but having one-fourth to one-third of a long-term portfolio in aggressive funds gives your investments the chance to outperform the averages. Over the long haul, stocks of small companies have returned about two percentage points more a year than stocks of larger companies, albeit with greater volatility.

RETURN. The average aggressive stock fund returned 8.6% per year over the past ten years.

RISK. In down years, double-digit losses are not unusual in aggressive-growth funds.

AGGRESSIVE-GROWTH FUNDS

All the funds listed here are no-load funds, which means they charge no up-front sales fees.

Fund	Minimum purchase	Toll-free #	Web site
Bridgeway Aggressive Investors 2	$2,000	800-661-3550	www.bridgewayfunds.com
Masters' Select Value	$5,000	800-656-8864	www.mastersfunds.com
Meridian Growth	$1,000	800-446-6662	www.meridianfund.com

International Funds

SUMMARY: *Risk-averse investors might want to limit international-stock funds to 10% or less of a long-term, college-saving portfolio. But if you have lots of time and are aiming for maximum returns, consider putting as much as 20% of your money in international funds.*

The theory goes that in today's global economy, a well-diversified stock portfolio includes some exposure to international stocks. But over the past decade, international funds have disappointed investors with consistently low returns. Some pros feel that investing in large U.S. corporations with overseas operations (the kinds of companies you'd find in a growth-and-income or long-term-growth fund) provides enough international exposure. Others believe that after a decade of weak performance for international funds, the pendulum is sure to swing the other way.

Investors who want the extra diversification of international stocks should stick with broad-based international funds—that is, funds that spread their money in markets around the world. Funds that invest in just one country or region, such as Latin American funds or Pacific Rim funds, may top the charts with eye-popping returns one year but suffer dismal losses the next because of a single political or economic event.

RETURN. The average international-stock fund returned an annualized 5.3% over the past ten years. Over the past five years, returns have been a disappointing 2.7% per year.

INTERNATIONAL FUNDS

The funds listed here are no-load funds, which means they charge no up-front sales fees.

Fund	Minimum purchase	Toll-free #	Web site
Dodge & Cox International Stock Fund	$2,500	800-621-3979	www.dodgeandcox.com
Julius Baer International Equity A	$2,500	800-387-6977	www.juliusbaer.com

---

RISK. International funds that specialize in a given region tend to have the same kind of up-one-year, down-the-next volatility as domestic aggressive-growth funds. But broadly diversified funds that spread their investments into Europe, Asia, and developing markets tend to be more stable. Nonetheless, the average international-stock fund lost about 48% in 2000–2002.

Putting It All Together: A Shortcut

We'll give you an easy way out first. The prospect of choosing from among thousands of mutual funds (or even the few dozen listed here) can be overwhelming, even paralyzing, to new investors. If your instinct is to flee for the safety and simplicity of CDs or money-market funds, consider instead buying shares in an index fund that replicates the S&P 500 stock index. By simply buying the 500 widely held stocks in the index, these funds aim to match rather than beat the market. That may sound uninspiring, but since most stock funds don't outperform the S&P 500, an index fund should put your returns well above average—which isn't bad at all for any investor.

Because the S&P 500 index funds all buy the same stocks, there isn't much difference between them except in the annual expenses that you pay for fund management.

- **Selected American Shares** lets you open an account with just $1,000, making it a good get-your-feet-wet choice for parents just getting started. Expenses are 0.94%, meaning that your total return is shaved by only $9.40 annually for each $1,000 invested.
- **Vanguard Index 500** holds expenses to about 0.18% but requires $3,000 to open an account.

The track records of these two funds are almost indistinguishable over the past ten years. Both are listed in the table of growth-and-income funds on page 70.

A Portfolio of Mutual Funds

The downside to investing in a single fund is that the market is fickle. Some years the pendulum swings toward stocks of large companies (like those in an S&P 500 index fund). Other times small companies are in favor. Growth stocks are "in" some years and "out" others. You'll be "in" all the time if you own a diversified portfolio of mutual funds that owns stocks of different-size companies and that reflects different investing styles. We've presented three suggested fund portfolios on the following pages that illustrate how to put together a broadly diversified mix of funds appropriate to the amount of time you have left until your child enters college. The sample portfolios reflect recommendations that come from *Kiplinger's Personal Finance* magazine in 2005; in future years you can find updated recommendations

Since most stock funds don't outperform the S&P 500, an index fund should put your returns well above average.

Want something that's well rounded, but a little easier to manage? By combining two or three index funds, you can diversify your portfolio.

at www.kiplinger.com under "Investing." All stock and bond funds selected for these sample portfolios are listed in the tables on the preceding pages, which provide the funds' minimum investments, telephone numbers, and Web site addresses.

A Middle Path

Want to consider something that's well rounded, but that's also a little easier to manage? By combining two or three index funds, you can diversify your portfolio to include bonds, large and small domestic stocks, and international stocks. And by keeping the funds all in the same fund family, you'll receive a single statement each month, instead of having to hassle with many. For each time horizon, we show two or three index funds that, in combination, are a good, no-fuss alternative to an ideally diversified portfolio of actively managed funds. We've chosen Vanguard funds because the Vanguard Group has by far the largest number of index funds, as well as the lowest expense ratios. The only downside is that Vanguard is not particularly friendly to very small investors. Each fund has a $3,000 minimum purchase, and there's a $10 annual fee for each fund account with less than $2,500. For prospectuses, call 800-871-3879 or visit the company's Web site at www.vanguard.com.

With Five Years to Go

Parents of junior high school students can afford to keep roughly half of their money invested in stocks. The portfolio on the following page is invested 40% in bond funds, with the other 60% spread among four stock funds—two growth-and-income funds, one long-term-growth fund, and one international fund—and one fund that invests in realty.

Because minimum initial investments range from $1,000 to $5,000, you'd need $17,000 to replicate this portfolio all at once. If you're starting with less, buy one of the domestic-stock funds first, then add the others later. As college gets closer, you would look for a good opportunity to redeem your shares in the long-term-growth fund first, shifting that money to bonds or CDs.

Fund	% of portfolio	Investment category
American Century Equity Income	20%	growth-and-income
T. Rowe Price Growth Stock	10%	growth-and-income
Dodge & Cox International Stock Fund	10%	international
Masters' Select Smaller Companies	10%	long-term-growth
Third Avenue Real Estate Value	10%	realty
Fidelity Floating Rate High Income	10%	high-yield corporate bond
Harbor Bond Fund	30%	intermediate-term corporate bond

THE SIMPLE PORTFOLIO

Fund	% of portfolio	Invests in
Vanguard Total Stock Market Index	50%	large and small domestic stocks
Vanguard Total Bond Market Index	50%	short- and intermediate-term bonds

With Six to Ten Years to Go

Parents of elementary schoolers who want to go for maximum growth can afford to be fully invested in stock mutual funds, including international funds. But this portfolio includes a small investment in bonds, to reduce volatility and to give you a convenient place to begin shifting your money to as the college bills get closer. You'd need $15,500 to buy this mix of funds outright, but if you're starting with less, buy shares first in the U.S. stock funds, then add some international exposure and bonds.

Fund	% of portfolio	Investment category
T. Rowe Price Growth Stock	20%	growth-and-income
Oakmark Select	15%	aggressive-growth
Dodge & Cox International Stock Fund	20%	international
Masters' Select Smaller Companies	15%	long-term-growth
Third Avenue Real Estate	10%	realty
Loomis Sayles Bond	10%	international corporate bond
Harbor Bond Fund	10%	intermediate-term corporate bond

THE SIMPLE PORTFOLIO

Fund	% of portfolio	Invests in
Vanguard Total Stock Market Index	60%	large and small domestic stocks
Vanguard Total Bond Market Index	20%	short- and intermediate-term bonds
Vanguard Total International Stock Index	20%	European, Asian, and emerging-market stocks

With 11 or More Years to Go

Parents of newborns and toddlers can afford to go for maximum growth, so this portfolio includes an aggressive-growth fund, two long-term-growth funds, an international fund, and a growth-and-income fund. You'd need $12,000 to buy these funds all at once. If you're starting with less, buy any of the U.S. funds first, then add the others as you're able.

Fund	% of portfolio	Investment category
T. Rowe Price Growth Stock	25%	growth-and-income
Oakmark Select	20%	aggressive-growth
Legg Mason Opportunity	10%	long-term-growth
Dodge & Cox International Stock Fund	25%	international
Masters' Select Smaller Companies	20%	long-term-growth

THE SIMPLE PORTFOLIO

Fund	% of portfolio	Invests in
Vanguard Total Stock Market Index	80%	large and small domestic stocks
Vanguard Total International Stock Index	20%	European, Asian, and emerging-market stocks

State-Sponsored College-Savings Plans

State-sponsored college-savings plans—also known as 529 plans after the section of the tax code that governs them—have had their ups and downs in recent years, but are the savings vehicle of choice for many parents—thanks to improved plans from the states, along with changes in the tax law that took effect in 2002 that make earnings in the plans tax-free. In mid-2005, all 50 states and the District of Columbia had some kind of 529 plan to offer.

Tax-free earnings give your college savings a potent kick. To appreciate the power of the new federal tax break, consider what could happen to a single $1,000 investment over 18 years, assuming a 10% annual return. In a taxable account, with the IRS claiming 25% of the earnings each year, the account would grow to

Using a state-sponsored plan does not restrict you to using the money at a college in the sponsoring state.

$3,676. In a tax-free college-savings plan, it would grow to $5,560. That gives you 51% more money to pay college bills. Even better, some states allow residents to deduct their contributions on their state-tax returns. (See the state-by-state details on pages 87–94.)

There are two types of 529 plans to choose from: a savings plan, which invests your money in mutual funds or similar accounts, or a prepaid-tuition plan, which promises that your payments today will cover tuition tomorrow no matter how much costs rise.

If you're saving over the long haul, savings plans let you reach for stock market returns, which are likely to outpace tuition inflation. There's a risk, of course, that you'll lose money in a prolonged bear market, the same risk you'd take investing in stocks and bonds outside a savings plan. But most plans offer investment options that tilt toward stocks when your children are younger and gradually ease you into bonds as they get older, which matches our overall prescription for long-term college savings.

Prepaid plans are more conservative. You're not likely to lose money in a prepaid plan (although only about half the states that offer them back their "guarantee" to provide for tomorrow's tuition with the full faith and credit of the state). But in exchange for less risk, you can expect lower returns.

You can participate in either kind of 529 plan no matter what your household income and can take advantage of low minimum contributions. And because the account owner—usually a parent—controls the money until it is used for college, there's no way Junior could empty the account at the nearest car dealership. Using a state-sponsored plan does not restrict you to using the money at a college in the sponsoring state—you may use the proceeds at any accredited college in the U.S. and at some foreign institutions. The main catch is that you'll pay a penalty (usually 10% of earnings, although often higher in prepaid plans) if you don't use your 529 plan account for college. If the beneficiary never goes to college, you can dodge that hazard by transferring the account to a sibling or other family member.

Savings-Style Plans

The majority of state-sponsored 529 plans are savings-style plans—the best choice for most parents. Maximum investments (whether defined as total contributions or total balance, including earnings) are high—usually exceeding $200,000. Typically, you can choose from three or more investment "tracks," and one of them is usually an "age-based" portfolio that may be 80% or more in stocks when a child is in his or her preschool years and shifts gradually into bonds as the child ages. The good news is that such a choice puts your college savings on autopilot, so you don't have to bother with rebalancing your investments (or worry about forgetting to adjust them) over time. The bad news is that once you've chosen your investment track, you must stick with it—you can't later shift from the age-based portfolio to another track your state offers or to an investment mix of your choice.

Under the current tax law, you can, however, roll your 529 plan from one state to another as frequently as once a year, giving you a roundabout way to make new investment choices if you're unhappy with the performance of your plan or if your investment philosophy changes. Still, because each state has only a few choices, a savings plan does not give you as much investment discretion as you would have in a taxable account, an IRA or a Coverdell ESA, where you have complete control. This is the chief disadvantage of 529 savings plans—but we think the overall merits of the plans outweigh the investment limitations.

In 2005, most states offered savings plans that are open to any U.S. resident (although some plans are open only to nonresidents through brokers and financial advisors or with higher fees), so you're not restricted to the plan offered by your home state. However, if your state offers a generous tax deduction for contributions (as 24 states and the District of Columbia do, for example), you have an added incentive to use your state's plan. (Taxation of 529 plan earnings also varies from state to state, so check your state's plan.)

> In a savings-style plan, you can typically choose from three or more investment "tracks," and one of them is usually an "age-based" portfolio.

Prepaid-tuition plans let you buy up to four years' worth of tuition at current prices, either in installments or as a lump sum.

Aside from any tax benefits, consider whether the investment choices reflect your own philosophy, and take a look at fees, which eat into your return. If you don't like your own state's offerings, consider the plans we designate as "recommended" in the listing on pages 87–94. Those are the plans whose investment choices come closest to the strategies we lay out in this chapter, and whose underlying expenses and program restrictions we consider reasonable.

Prepaid-Tuition Plans

The older sibling of 529 savings plans, prepaid-tuition plans are based on the idea of paying for tomorrow's college education at today's prices. Prepaid-tuition plans let you buy up to four years' worth of tuition at current prices, either in installments or as a lump sum. The appeal is the guarantee that when your child is ready for freshman year, your account will cover tuition, no matter how much it has risen. By paying costs in full now or in installments over several years, you lock in current prices and guarantee that your investment will appreciate at the same rate that college costs rise.

There are two kinds of prepaid plans:

"Contract" type plans. In "contract" type plans, you commit in advance to buying a certain amount of future tuition—such as a year's worth, or a full four years' worth. In Florida's plan, for instance, the parents of an eighth grader could put up a lump sum of $10,646 to prepay four years of tuition at any public university in the state. Or they could pay in 55 monthly installments of $211, for a total of $11,605. Tuition at Florida's ten, four-year universities is about $2,940 a year, so if costs rose 6% annually, today's eighth grader would expect to pay about $17,200 in the future in tuition for a four-year education.

One major disadvantage to contract-type plans is that you commit to a long-term schedule of payments—not unlike a car loan. The only way to stop paying is to discontinue the plan, withdraw your principal, and incur a penalty. Because they're pegged to the cost of lower-priced public colleges, a prepaid contract plan will also make only a minor dent in the tab if it's transferred to an expensive private school. Many of them also cover only tuition and fees, not room, board, books, and personal expenses. Savings plans, on the other hand, can be used to cover all those costs.

Tuition units. Prepaid unit plans sell units that represent a fixed percentage of tuition, with one unit typically corresponding to 1% of a year's tuition. Everybody pays the same price for the units and the price of a unit increases each year. The parents can buy as many units as they want each year. In prepaid plans that offer "tuition units," you can be more flexible with your investment. In Tennessee, for instance, tuition units sold for $50.80 apiece in 2004–2005; you can buy as many or as few as you like, as regularly or erratically as you want. If your goal is to cover four years of tuition at an average-priced institution in Tennessee, you would aim to amass 400 units. That would leave you with a small refund if your child attended Tennessee Tech University (which costs 92

THE INDEPENDENT 529 PLAN ALTERNATIVE

The Independent 529 plan lets you pay tomorrow's tuition (or part of it) at today's prices for more than 240 private colleges. (See www.independent529plan.com for the list of participating colleges.) Basically, the money you invest represents a percentage (possibly 100%) of a school's current tuition. For example, say you prepay $10,000 today to cover one year of tuition and current tuition at the school your child ultimately attends is $20,000. Your $10,000 investment is 50% of that current tuition, so you'll be covered for 50% of the future tuition once your child starts college. If current tuition is $30,000, your $10,000 investment represents one-third of the total tuition, and you'll be responsible for coming up with the remaining two-thirds tuition in the future.

If your child doesn't go to a participating school, you get your money back, but the annual return is capped at just 2%. If you worry that your child won't attend one of the schools on the list, you might be better off investing in a traditional 529 state college savings plan.

PROS AND CONS OF SAVING VIA LIFE INSURANCE

Should you use cash-value life insurance (whole life, universal life, or variable universal life) to save for college? There are generous tax advantages, to be sure. Money you "invest" in a cash-value policy grows tax-deferred, and you may be able to avoid tax on your earnings entirely by withdrawing your original investment after a long period of time and then borrowing against the policy. But for most middle-income families, the answer is no, since you have to be able to commit a substantial amount of money to a policy—and stick with it for at least ten years—to make life insurance worthwhile as an investment.

Don't consider buying life insurance as a savings vehicle unless the following are true:

- **You have a long-term need for life insurance**—at least ten years and preferably longer. Because up-front commissions are high, it seldom makes sense to buy a cash-value policy unless you plan to keep it at least a decade, during which the benefit of tax-deferred earnings can overtake the drag of up-front costs.
- **You have maxed out on other forms of tax-deferred saving,** such as IRAs, Keoghs, or 401(k) plans. There's no point in paying the extra expenses of

an insurance policy if you can get similar tax benefits elsewhere.

- **You can afford to "fully fund" the policy,** which means you can afford to pay the "target" or "recommended" premium—even though the policy will probably permit you to put in less. Fully funding the policy lets you take maximum advantage of tax-deferred growth, and ensures that your policy won't lapse once you begin withdrawing money to cover college costs. (Since you wouldn't want a life insurance policy to be your only form of savings, you should really have enough cash flow to pay the premium and invest elsewhere.)

If you do buy life insurance as a long-term savings vehicle, your best bet is probably variable universal life. VUL policies, as they're known, allow you to invest the "savings" portion of your premium in a variety of mutual fund accounts, including stock funds. With a long-term time horizon, that's where you want your money. Other forms of cash-value insurance—whole life and universal life—essentially invest your money in bonds and similar investments, so there's not the same potential for high returns.

---

units a year) or leave you a bit short at the University of Tennessee in Knoxville (110 units a year). You could aim to save even more than 400 units if your goal is to save for a private college.

RETURN. In either kind of prepaid plan, your return is roughly equivalent to the rate of tuition inflation at public colleges and universities in your state—which made the plans extremely attractive when tuitions were rising at 10% and more a year. Even today, with the average rate of tuition inflation closer to 7%, prepaid plans remain a good deal, but many plans have run into trouble because of the continuing rise in tuitions and weak investment returns. And the plans are no match for investing in the stock market when you have many years before you'll need the money. But prepaid plans are a good alternative to low-paying savings bonds or CDs for short-term college savings. With five years or so to build a college kitty, parents should invest most of it for safety, as described earlier, perhaps in zero-coupon bonds, bond funds, certificates of deposit—or prepaid-tuition plans. Compared with those of fixed-income investments, returns of prepaid plans have been competitive, particularly considering their now-improved tax advantages.

TRANSFER. As with 529 savings plans, you can transfer the value of a prepaid plan to any accredited private or out-of-state public school in the U.S. In most cases, using the funds at a school outside the plan won't affect your return because the state will transfer the full value of your account to any school. But a few states limit your return if the beneficiary doesn't attend an in-state public college. Florida, for instance, caps your return at 5% if the account is used out of state, and Massachusetts pays just the rate of inflation if the account isn't used at one of 80-plus participating schools (among them, prestigious private institutions such as Smith and Amherst—but not Harvard or MIT).

AFFECT ON FINANCIAL AID. Prepaid plans are a bad idea for families that expect to be eligible for substantial need-based financial aid because prepaid tuition is considered a resource that reduces your financial need dollar for dollar. College-savings plans reduce your financial need, too, but to a lesser degree. They're included among the parents' assets, which reduces your financial need by up to 5.6% of the balance in the account each year. There's a chance that Congress will

> **As with 529 savings plans, you can transfer the value of a prepaid plan to any accredited private or out-of-state public school in the U.S.**

eventually grant prepaid-tuition plans more favorable treatment in financial-aid formulas, but for now savings plans have the edge.

THE APPEAL OF A SURE THING. Financial advisors have been lukewarm to prepaid plans because of their restrictions and below-market returns. But many parents have enthusiastically signed up for them anyway because prepaid plans deliver what savings plans and the stock market don't—a sure thing. Whether college costs rise by 2% or 10% annually, prepaid-plan participants know that their contributions will cover all or a predetermined portion of the tuition bill at a public college—or even a private one in a few states. If that reassurance is a sufficient return for you, then a prepaid plan may be your preference. But you may need to save separately for room and board (only a few plans include it) or for the cost of a private college over a public one. Savings plans, on the other hand, seldom guarantee returns and can even lose money, depending on how the plan invests. The prospectus or annual report should specify what kinds of investments the plan may make and whether you can expect a minimum return. (Kentucky, for instance, guarantees at least 3%.)

PENALTIES AND ALTERNATIVES. If you have doubts that your child will attend college at all, a prepaid plan is not for you. In many cases you pay a significant penalty (higher than the 10% of earnings that's standard on 529 savings plans) if you withdraw entirely, either because your child doesn't attend college or because you can't keep up the payments in a state where monthly payments are required. Alabama extracts the stiffest penalty: You get your principal back with no interest, minus a cancellation fee of up to $150. However, in most states the beneficiary can wait up to ten years after graduating from high school to use the account. Or you can avoid the penalty by transferring the account to another family member, such as a sibling. In addition, penalties are usually waived if the beneficiary

continued on page 95

COLLEGE SAVINGS AND PREPAID-TUITION PLANS

This listing provides details on a sampling of the savings and prepaid plans offered by all 50 states and the District of Columbia. States frequently tinker with their plans, so request further information directly, using the phone numbers or Internet addresses listed, or check www.savingforcollege.com.

Some notes on the listings:

■ **Most savings plans** allow you to enroll at any time, while many prepaid plans limit enrollment to just a few months during the year.

■ **529 plans are federal-tax-free,** but taxation of 529-plan earnings varies from state to state, so check your state's plan.

■ **All savings and prepaid plans** are transferable to out-of-state and private institutions (although a few prepaid plans may make lower payouts to those schools).

■ **Our "recommended" choices** (marked with an asterisk) are open to nonresidents (in some cases open only if the account owner or beneficiary is a resident) and have multiple investment choices, at least one of which approximates the graduated investment allocations suggested in this chapter. Consider your home state's offerings first—especially if your contributions would be state-tax-deductible. If they're not suitable, look for alternatives among our recommendations, which include plans offered by Colorado, Illinois, Iowa, Michigan, Minnesota, Nevada, New York, Utah, and Virginia.

Alabama Prepaid Affordable College Tuition (PACT) Program
Type: Prepaid (contract)
Phone: 800-252-7228
Web link: www.treasury.state.al.us
State-tax deduction for residents: No deduction
Open to nonresidents: Yes

University of Alaska College Savings Plan
Type: Savings
Phone: 800-369-3641 or 866-277-1005 in Alaska
Web link: www.uacollegesavings.com
State-tax deduction for residents: Alaska does not have an income tax
Open to nonresidents: Yes

Arizona Family College Savings Program
Type: Savings
Phone: 800-888-2723 (College Savings Bank); 888-667-3239 (Securities Management and Research)
Web link: www.acpe.asu.edu
State-tax deduction for residents: No deduction
Open to nonresidents: Yes

Arkansas Tax-Deferred Tuition Savings Program (GIFT College Investing Plan)
Type: Savings
Phone: 877-615-4116
Web link: www.thegiftplan.com
State-tax deduction for residents: No deduction
Open to nonresidents: Yes

continued on page 88

COLLEGE SAVINGS AND PREPAID-TUITION PLANS *continued*

California Golden State ScholarShare College Savings Trust
Type: Savings
Phone: 887-728-4338
Web link: www.scholarshare.com
State-tax deduction for residents: No deduction
Open to nonresidents: Yes

* Colorado Stable Value Plus College Savings Program
Type: Savings
Phone: 800-448-2424
Web link: www.collegeinvest.org
State-tax deduction for residents: Full contribution is deductible
Open to nonresidents: Yes

Connecticut Higher Education Trust (CHET)
Type: Savings
Phone: 888-799-2438
Web link: www.aboutchet.com
State-tax deduction for residents: No deduction
Open to nonresidents: Yes

Delaware College Investment Plan
Type: Savings
Phone: 800-544-1655
Web link: www.fidelity.com/delaware
State-tax deduction for residents: No deduction
Open to nonresidents: Yes

District of Columbia 529 College Savings Plan
Type: Savings
Phone: 800-987-4859 (D.C. residents); 800-368-2745 (nonresidents)
Web link: www.DCCollegeSavings.com
State-tax deduction for residents: Deductions for contributions up to $3,000 ($6,000 for married couples filing jointly if both own accounts)
Open to nonresidents: Yes. However, D.C. nonresidents may have to pay an up-front sales load.

Florida Prepaid College Program
Type: Prepaid (contract)
Phone: 800-552-4723
Web link: www.floridaprepaidcollege.com
State-tax deduction for residents: Florida does not have an income tax
Open to nonresidents: No

Georgia Higher Education Savings Plan
Type: Savings
Phone: 877-424-4377
Web link: www.gacollegesavings.com
State-tax deduction for residents: Deductions for contributions up to $2,000 per dependent beneficiary per year by parent/guardian who itemizes federal tax return and has an adjusted gross income under $50,000 for single filer ($100,000 for joint)
Open to nonresidents: Yes

Hawaii Tuition EDGE
Type: Savings
Phone: 866-529-3343
Web link: www.tuitionedge.com
State-tax deduction for residents: No
Open to nonresidents: Yes. Account owner or beneficiary must be Hawaiian resident at time of enrollment.

Idaho College Savings Program (IDeal)
Type: Savings
Phone: 866-433-2533
Web link: www.idsaves.org
State-tax deduction for residents: Contributions deductible up to $4,000 per year per contributor ($8,000 for joint filers)
Open to nonresidents: Yes

College Illinois
Type: Prepaid (contract)
Phone: 877-877-3724
Web link: www.collegeillinois.com
State-tax deduction for residents: Deductions for contributions up to $10,000 per contributor
Open to nonresidents: Yes. Account owner or beneficiary must be an Illinois resident for 12 months before enrollment

* Bright Start College Savings Program (Illinois)
Type: Savings
Phone: 877-432-7444
Web link: www.brightstartsavings.com
State-tax deduction for residents: Deductions for contributions up to $10,000 each year
Open to nonresidents: Yes

Indiana CollegeChoice 529 Investment Plan
Type: Savings
Phone: 866-400-7526
Web link: www.collegechoiceplan.com
State-tax deduction for residents: No deduction
Open to nonresidents: No

* College Savings Iowa
Type: Savings
Phone: 888-672-9116
Web link: www.collegesavingsiowa.com
State-tax deduction for residents: Deduction for contributions up to $2,375 per beneficiary each year
Open to nonresidents: Yes

Kansas Learning Quest 529 Education Savings Program
Type: Savings
Phone: 800-579-2203
Web link: www.learningquestsavings.com
State-tax deduction for residents: Deduction for contributions up to $3,000 per beneficiary per year ($6,000 if married filing jointly)
Open to nonresidents: Yes

Kentucky Education Savings Plan Trust
Type: Savings
Phone: 877-598-7878
Web link: www.kentuckytrust.org
State-tax deduction for residents: No deduction
Open to nonresidents: Yes

continued on page 90

COLLEGE SAVINGS AND PREPAID-TUITION PLANS *continued*

Louisiana Student Tuition Assistance and Revenue Trust Program (START)
Type: Savings
Phone: 800-259-5625
Web link: www.osfa.state.la.us/START.htm
State-tax deduction for residents: Deduction for contributions up to $2,400 per beneficiary each year
Open to nonresidents: Yes. Account owner or beneficiary must be a Louisiana resident at time of enrollment

Maine NextGen College Investing Plan
Type: Savings
Phone: 877-463-9843
Web link: www.nextgenplan.com
State-tax deduction for residents: No deduction
Open to nonresidents: Yes

Maryland Prepaid College Trust
Type: Prepaid (contract)
Phone: 888-463-4723
Web link: www.collegesavingsmd.org
State-tax deduction for residents: Deduction for up to $2,500 per year per contract
Open to nonresidents: No. Must be Maryland or D.C. resident

Massachusetts U. Plan
Type: Prepaid
Phone: 800-449-6332
Web link: www.mefa.org/savings
State-tax deduction for residents: No deduction
Open to nonresidents: Yes

Massachusetts U. Fund College Investing Plan
Type: Savings
Phone: 800-544-2776
Web link: www.fidelity.com/ufund
State-tax deduction for residents: No deduction
Open to nonresidents: Yes

Michigan Education Trust
Type: Prepaid (contract)
Phone: 800-638-4543
Web link: www.met4kid.com
State-tax deduction for residents: Contributions are fully deductible
Open to nonresidents: No

* Michigan Education Savings Program
Type: Savings
Phone: 877-861-6377
Web link: www.misaves.com
State-tax deduction for residents: Deduction for contributions up to $5,000 per single tax return per year ($10,000 for married couples filing jointly)
Open to nonresidents: Yes

* Minnesota College Savings Plan
Type: Savings
Phone: 877-338-4646
Web link: www.mnsaves.com
State-tax deduction for residents: No deductions
Open to nonresidents: Yes

Mississippi Affordable College Savings
Type: Savings
Phone: 800-486-3670
Web link: www.collegesavingsms.com
State-tax deduction for residents:
Deductions for contributions up to $10,000
per year ($20,000 for joint filers)
Open to nonresidents: Yes

Mississippi Prepaid Affordable College Tuition Program (MPACT)
Type: Prepaid (contract)
Phone: 800-987-4450
Web link: www.treasury.state.ms.us
State-tax deduction for residents:
Unlimited deduction
Open to nonresidents: No

Missouri Saving for Tuition (MO$T) Program
Type: Savings
Phone: 888-414-6678
Web link: www.missourimost.org
State-tax deduction for residents:
Deduction for contributions up to $8,000
per year per contributor
Open to nonresidents: Yes

Montana Family Education Savings Program
Type: Savings
Phone: 800-888-2723
Web link: montana.collegesavings.com
State-tax deduction for residents:
Deductions for contributions up to $3,000
per year ($6,000 for couples) for Montana
residents
Open to nonresidents: Yes

*College Savings Plan of Nebraska
Type: Savings
Phone: 888-993-3746
Web link: www.PlanForCollegeNow.com
State-tax deduction for residents:
Deduction for contributions up to $1,000
per year ($500 if couple filing separately)
Open to nonresidents: Yes

* Nevada Prepaid Tuition Program
Type: Prepaid (contract)
Phone: 888-477-2667
Web link: www.prepaid-tuition.state.nv.us
State-tax deduction for residents:
Nevada has no state income tax
Open to nonresidents: Yes. Account
owner or beneficiary must be Nevada resi-
dent or account holder must be an alumnus
of a Nevada college

New Hampshire UNIQUE College Investing Plan
Type: Savings
Phone: 800-544-1722
Web link: www.fidelity.com/unique
State-tax deduction for residents: New
Hampshire does not have state income tax
Open to nonresidents: Yes

New Jersey Better Education Savings Trust (NJBEST)
Type: Savings
Phone: 877-465-2378
Web link: http://www.hesaa.org/njbest/
index.asp
State-tax deduction for residents:
No deduction
Open to nonresidents: No

continued on page 92

COLLEGE SAVINGS AND PREPAID-TUITION PLANS *continued*

New Mexico Education Plan's College Savings Program
Type: Savings
Phone: 877-337-5268
Web link: www.theeducationplan.com
State-tax deduction for residents:
Deduction for all contributions
Open to nonresidents: Yes

* New York's 529 College Savings Program
Type: Savings
Phone: 877-697-2837
Web link: www.nysaves.com
State-tax deduction for residents:
Deduction for contributions up to $5,000 for single return per year ($10,000 for couples)
Open to nonresidents: Yes

North Carolina's National College Savings Program
Type: Savings
Phone: 800-600-3453
Web link: www.cfnc.org/savings
State-tax deduction for residents:
No deduction
Open to nonresidents: Yes

North Dakota College SAVE
Type: Savings
Phone: 866-728-3529
Web link: www.collegesave4u.com
State-tax deduction for residents:
No deduction
Open to nonresidents: Yes

Ohio CollegeAdvantage 529 Savings Plan
Type: Savings
Phone: 800-233-6734; 800-225-1581 (out of state)
Web link: www.collegeadvantage.com
State-tax deduction for residents:
Deductions for contributions up to $2,000 per year, per contributor, per beneficiary
Open to nonresidents: Yes. Benefciary or the account holder must be a resident

Oklahoma College Savings Plan
Type: Savings
Phone: 877-654-7284
Web link: www.ok4saving.org
State-tax deduction for residents:
Deductions for contributions up to $2,500 per account per year
Open to nonresidents: Yes

Oregon College Savings Plan
Type: Savings
Phone: 866-772-8464
Web link: www.oregoncollegesavings.com
State-tax deduction for residents:
$2,000-per-year deduction and $1,000 for married filing separately
Open to nonresidents: Yes

Pennsylvania Tuition Account Program (TAP 529)
Type: Prepaid (tuition units)
Phone: 800-440-4000
Web link: www.tap529.org
State-tax deduction for residents:
No deduction
Open to nonresidents: Yes. Account owner or beneficiary must be Pennsylvania resident

Rhode Island CollegeBound Fund
Type: Savings
Phone: 888-324-5057
Web link: www.collegeboundfund.com
State-tax deduction for residents:
Deductions for contributions up to
$500 per single tax return ($1,000 joint
return)
Open to nonresidents: Yes. Account
owner or beneficiary must be Rhode Island
resident

**South Carolina Tuition Prepayment
Program**
Type: Prepaid (contract)
Phone: 888-772-4723
Web link: www.scgrad.org
State-tax deduction for residents: Yes
Open to nonresidents: No. Beneficiary
must be resident of South Carolina for 12
months

South Dakota CollegeAccess 529
Type: Savings
Phone: 866-529-7462
Web link: www.collegeaccess529.com
State-tax deduction for residents: South
Dakota does not have an income tax
Open to nonresidents: Yes

Tennessee's BEST Prepaid Tuition Plan
Type: Prepaid unit/guaranteed savings
Phone: 888-486-2378
Web link: www.treasury.state.tn.us/best.htm
State-tax deduction for residents:
No deduction
Open to nonresidents: No

Tennessee's BEST Savings Plan
Type: Savings
Phone: 888-486-2378
Web link: www.tnbest.com
State-tax deduction for residents:
No deduction
Open to nonresidents: Yes

Texas Guaranteed Tuition Plan
Type: Prepaid (contract)
Phone: 800-445-4723
Web link: www.texastomorrowfund.org
State-tax deduction for residents:
Texas does not have an income tax
Open to nonresidents: Yes. Beneficiary
(except newborn) must be Texas resident
for 12 months or account owner must be
Texas resident

* Utah Educational Savings Plan Trust
Type: Savings
Phone: 800-418-2551
Web link: www.uesp.org
State-tax deduction for residents: De-
duction of up to $1,510 per year ($3,020 for
married couple)
Open to nonresidents: Yes

Vermont Higher Education Savings Plan
Type: Savings
Phone: 800-637-5860
Web link: www.vsac.org
State-tax deduction for residents: 5%
Vermont income tax credit up to $2,000 in
annual contributions per beneficiary
Open to nonresidents: Yes

continued on page 94

COLLEGE SAVINGS AND PREPAID-TUITION PLANS *continued*

Virginia Prepaid Education Program
Type: Prepaid (contract)
Phone: 888-567-0540
Web link: www.virginia529.com
State-tax deduction for residents: Deduction of up to $2,000 per contract per year (no cap for donors over age 70)
Open to nonresidents: No

* Virginia College Savings Trust
Type: Savings
Phone: 888-567-0540
Web link: www.virginia529.com
State-tax deduction for residents: Deduction of up to $2,000 per contract per year (no cap for donors over age 70)
Open to nonresidents: Yes

Washington Guaranteed Education Tuition (GET)
Type: Prepaid units/guaranteed savings
Phone: 877-438-8848
Web link: www.get.wa.gov
State-tax deduction for residents: Washington does not have personal income tax
Open to nonresidents: No

West Virginia SMART 529 Prepaid Tuition Plan
Type: Prepaid (contract)
Phone: 866-574-3542
Web link: www.smart529.com
State-tax deduction for residents: Deduction for full amount of contribution
Open to nonresidents: Yes. Account owner or beneficiary must be West Virginia resident

Wisconsin Edvest College Savings Program
Type: Savings
Phone: 888-338-3789
Web link: www.edvest.com
State-tax deduction for residents: State-tax deduction up to $3,000 per contributor per child per year
Open to nonresidents: Yes

Wyoming College Achievement Plan
Type: Savings
Phone: 877-529-2655
Web link: www.collegeachievementplan .com
State-tax deduction: Wyoming has no state income tax
Open to nonresidents: Yes

dies, becomes disabled, or earns a scholarship that makes the state savings account unnecessary.

How to Choose an Advisor

Would you rather have help setting up a savings plan, choosing investments, and keeping track of when it's time to shift from stocks to bonds? Helping parents build a college fund is bread-and-butter work for financial planners. Some charge $150 or so an hour for advice on an ad hoc basis, some will manage your investments for an annual fee of 0.5% to 1.5% of your portfolio, and still others charge no up-front fee but earn a commission on the investment products you buy. Whichever approach you prefer, it's essential to do some legwork to choose a competent planner who suits your investment style and tolerance for risk.

Consider Credentials

Anyone can hang out a "financial planning" shingle, but certain credentials show that the planner has formal training in the mechanics of investing, insurance, and financial planning. The Certified Financial Planner (CFP) designation is awarded by the Certified Financial Planner Board of Standards, Inc. (CFP Board). To earn it, planners must pass a ten-hour comprehensive exam, usually after completing roughly two years' worth of home-study courses from board-approved educational institutions or classroom courses offered at many colleges and universities, fulfill experience requirements, and participate in continuing education. Designations that reflect similar training are the Chartered Financial Consultant (ChFC) from the American College in Bryn Mawr, Pennsylvania, and the Personal Financial Specialist (PFS) awarded to certified public accountants by the American Institute of CPAs.

Start the Search

The best way to find a planner is to ask for recommendations from people whose business acumen you

If you're going to use an advisor, it's essential to do some legwork to choose a competent planner who suits your investment style and tolerance for risk.

You're relying on this person to advise you on decisions that can make the difference between meeting your goals and falling short.

trust—perhaps your tax preparer or lawyer, a business associate, or a friend. But absent a personal recommendation, you can get lists of credentialed planners in your area by contacting the following professional associations:

- **The Financial Planning Association** (800-322-4237; www.fpanet.org)
- **The American Institute of CPAs** (888-777-7077; www.cpapfs.org)
- **The National Association of Personal Financial Advisors** (fee-only planners; 800-366-2732; www.napfa.org)

Don't simply take your business to the most convenient planner. Take the time necessary to choose carefully, because you're not only paying a lot for a planner's services—either via a direct fee or a commission deducted from your investment—but you're also relying on this person to advise you on decisions that can make the difference between meeting your goals and falling short.

Start by interviewing at least three planners. Use the initial interview (for which there is usually no charge) to get a feel for whether the planner listens to you, answers your questions, addresses your concerns, and is willing to explain financial strategy in terms that make sense to you. Above all, make sure the planner is someone you're comfortable with and can communicate with. Also use the initial interview to get answers to these questions:

HOW ARE YOU COMPENSATED? Knowing up front how much you'll pay and how fees are calculated will help you evaluate the advice you're getting.

- **Fee-only planners** may charge by the hour or charge an annual fee, but their compensation doesn't depend on what products you buy. When they help you select a mutual fund, they'll ordinarily suggest no-load funds. Using a fee-only planner eliminates the worry that you'll be sold a product you don't need or one that has a high commission when one with a lower commission is just as good.

- **Commission-based planners** appear to cost less because they don't charge an up-front fee, but when they recommend mutual funds, they'll choose funds with a load (around 5%), which is deducted from your investment.
- **Planners who switch-hit,** taking a commission when one is available and charging a fee when one is not, are sometimes called fee-based planners.

HOW LONG HAVE YOU BEEN DOING THIS? Every financial planner has first-year clients, but you don't have to be one of them. And someone who's spent most of his or her career selling insurance or preparing tax returns may not be so sharp on the twists and turns of the financial-aid process. So look for someone who has at least a few years of experience in financial planning and, even better, who is a specialist in college planning.

WHO IMPLEMENTS YOUR ADVICE—YOU OR ME? You may want to turn all the details over to a planner, or you may simply want a once-a-year review of a savings plan you manage yourself. Either way, make sure you clarify your expectations up front, and ensure that the planner is willing to carry out your wishes. Some planners insist on implementing as well as creating a financial plan, having observed that a carefully crafted road map is useless if it isn't used correctly—or used at all. Others are happy to draw the map and let you do the driving.

WILL YOU PROVIDE REFERENCES? Specifically request names of clients whose financial position is similar to yours—if you're a business owner, for instance, you don't want a planner who's never dealt with how business assets affect financial-aid formulas. And check the references. You can gain a lot of insight by asking current clients what they like and don't like about the planner, whether they've ever considered switching, how their investments have done, and how you might work with the planner most effectively.

> Look for someone who has at least a few years of experience in financial planning and, even better, who is a specialist in college planning.

Winning the College Aid Game

Halfway through high school is the two-minute warning for parents with college-bound kids who hope to receive financial aid. The forms you fill out to apply for aid—the "Free Application for Federal Student Aid" and others discussed later—ask about your finances for the calendar year starting in January of a typical student's junior year in high school. Some strategic planning at that point (and earlier if you want to exercise certain strategies discussed in Chapter 6) can help you get all the aid for which you're eligible.

Even if your income is above average, don't assume you won't qualify for financial aid. Families with household income of $75,000 or more can qualify for substantial aid, especially when a student attends an expensive college or when two or more students are in college at the same time.

Financial advisors and financial-aid officers almost unanimously stress the same point. It's a myth that families earning more than $50,000 won't qualify for aid. Even families with incomes into the six figures can qualify for aid at expensive schools.

Many parents think they're not eligible because their neighbor didn't get any aid. It might look like they make the same thing, but after the needs analysis it could be very different.

To help you get started on this often critical component of financing college, this chapter will lay out the aid process, step by step. It will help you project the amount almost any school will expect your family

Subtract your expected family contribution from the sticker price, and the balance is the amount of financial aid you're eligible for.

to contribute toward your child's education—that's the real cost of college—and how much aid you will qualify for. And if the aid picture doesn't look promising, you'll at least have time to put together a plan for making the most of what you've saved and figuring out the best way to finance any gaps (topics covered in Chapters 7 and 9).

Of course, you never know for sure what you'll get until you receive a college's financial-aid offer, which typically arrives shortly after the congratulatory letter of admission. At that point, the more you know about the process, the better the odds you can negotiate a better package—using the tips for negotiation outlined in the next chapter.

Cost Equals Your Contribution

If you take away a single message from this chapter, it should be this: Don't rule out any college—even Harvard or Yale, where tuition, room, board, and expenses topped $40,000 for the 2004–2005 academic year—because of the expense. The sticker price is the maximum price, and parents who can afford that amount are expected to cough it up. But otherwise, your cost is *not* the sticker price. Your cost is the "expected family contribution." That's the amount the federal government and the schools themselves deem you can afford to pay out of pocket, based on federal and private "need analysis" formulas. Subtract your family contribution from the sticker price, and the balance is the amount of financial aid you're eligible for. In theory, at least, it's a simple equation:

total cost of college – expected family contribution (EFC)
= financial-aid eligibility

Here's how this formula would apply to a family whose expected contribution is $15,000 as they consider various colleges. At a public school where the bill is $15,000 or less, the family would receive no aid. But the family would be eligible for $5,000 of aid at a school where the cost is $20,000, $10,000 in aid where the total cost is $25,000, and a whopping $25,000 in aid at a school with a total cost of $40,000.

Many parents don't fully appreciate the message in that equation: Assuming you qualify for financial aid, sending your child to an expensive private school, generally speaking, should cost no more than sending him or her to a less-expensive public school. In fact, some families wind up paying less at expensive private schools than at less-expensive public institutions because the financial-aid package at the private school was more generous.

What the Variables Are

As you'll see in more detail later in this chapter, the financial-aid equation can become somewhat more complicated—because there's a lot of play in all three parts of the equation.

Total cost may mean different things at different schools. For instance, some schools include travel expenses in that figure and others don't.

Expected family contribution can vary depending on how you fill out the financial-aid forms, as you'll find out in this chapter. In addition, the expected contribution may be different at a private school than it is at a public school because while all colleges must stick with the federal formulas when giving out federal money (and state money, in many cases), they can adjust the expected family contribution using their own criteria when deciding how much of their own financial-aid money you'll be awarded.

Financial aid isn't always "free money." Some colleges will make up the difference between their cost and your expected family contribution with an aid package mostly filled with loans that you or your child will

You could pay less at an expensive private school than at a less-expensive public institution if the private school's aid package is more generous.

Don't skip applying to a desirable school you think is out of reach financially. Wait until you see what comes in the financial-aid package.

have to pay back with interest, while others may award you a package rich with grants or scholarships that cost you nothing.

All the same, the lesson here still applies: Don't skip applying to a desirable school you think is out of reach financially. Wait until the financial-aid package arrives before you decide whether you can manage the amount you're expected to pay.

How They Decide What You Can Afford

Around January of your son's or daughter's senior year in high school, you'll be subjected to the rigors of filling out at least one, and perhaps several, financial-aid forms, which ask for information about income and assets—yours and your child's. Using the numbers you report on these forms, the federal government and the schools your child applies to will determine your expected family contribution.

The Free Application for Federal Student Aid (FAFSA)

Every school will ask you to complete this form, which determines your eligibility for federal aid at all schools and your eligibility for other aid at most public schools and some private schools. It's available from high school guidance counselors and college financial-aid offices. FAFSA forms are now also available on the Web (at www.fafsa.ed.gov; see the box on page 107) or over the phone (800-433-3243 or 319-337-5665).

Regional processors, which handle financial-aid forms for the federal government, crunch the numbers you enter on the FAFSA through a formula called the federal methodology. Several weeks after mailing the form (or 10 to 14 days after submitting it electronically), you'll receive a document called a Student Aid Report (SAR), which shows your expected family contribu-

---

SPEED COUNTS

It's critical not to miss a school's deadline for completing financial-aid forms. Many schools are able to fully meet your financial need only if you file on time—and February 1 or February 15 deadlines are typical.

The first day you can mail the FAFSA form for the 2006–2007 academic year is January 1, 2006. And the sooner after January 1 you file, the better, since some schools give out aid on a first-come, first-served basis.

Also be sure to review your forms carefully before dropping them in the mail because a mistake can put you at the end of the line for financial aid. Form processors say they return forms that are photocopied, illegible, or missing a signature. Other errors, such as supplying a range of numbers instead of the specific dollar amount requested, won't cause your form to bounce, but they may delay the process at your school's financial-aid office.

---

tion. The all-important number appears in the upper right of the report, under the date, and looks something like this: EFC:8500. That means your expected family contribution is $8,500. This EFC determines your eligibility for federal financial aid.

Copies of the report are also sent to the schools you designate. Until you receive the school's financial-aid offer in the mail, you won't know what it has decided you can afford, and that amount may differ from the EFC.

The PROFILE Aid Form

When giving out their own aid (as opposed to federal or most state-funded aid), colleges are free to calculate your EFC using formulas that differ from—and may be less generous than—the federal methodology. The schools use this supplementary form to ask for data that the FAFSA excludes—such as how much equity you have in your home and whether your child has received any scholarships or assistance from relatives (for more on why those items are excluded or included in a need analysis, see page 127.

If a school your child is applying to requires the PROFILE, you'll need to get a registration form, send it to the College Scholarship Service—which administers the forms—and complete the packet of forms you receive from the CSS. You can obtain a registration form from your child's high school guidance office, college financial-aid office, or from the CSS directly by calling 800-915-9990. Even easier, you can visit the CSS's Web site at www.collegeboard.com to register and complete the PROFILE form online. You'll pay a flat $5 registration fee, plus $18 to have the information forwarded to each school that requires it.

> ## DRAFT REGISTRATION
>
> Men ages 18 to 25 must register with the Selective Service to qualify for federal financial aid. If they're not registered and can't explain why they're exempt, Uncle Sam will deny them any aid.

Institutional Forms

Some schools, particularly the most selective private schools, want even more information than the standardized forms provide because when giving out their own aid, they consider such things as the funds you have in a 401(k), IRA, or other retirement plan, which the other forms don't ask about. Usually, they will ask for that additional information in Section Q of the PROFILE form. But some schools will ask you to complete the school's own form, available from its financial-aid office, in addition to or in lieu of the others. Sometimes you'll also be asked to supply copies of your income-tax returns. (You may be asked for this even if a school requires only the FAFSA or the FAFSA and the PROFILE.)

State Forms

To be eligible for aid from your home state, you may need to send financial information to an educational agency in your state. Ask a high school guidance counselor or college financial-aid officer for details.

Timing Taxes and Aid Forms

You may wonder whether you can file the financial-aid forms before completing your income-tax returns. You can, and unless you're an early bird with your tax return, you probably should. The financial-aid forms ask for figures from the tax return most taxpayers file April 15. But most aid deadlines are in February or March, so if you wait until the April 15 tax deadline to apply, you may be too late.

The best route is to prepare your return early, even if you don't mail it to the IRS until April 15. That allows you to use numbers you know are accurate on the financial-aid forms. But if you don't have all the information you need to complete your tax return, or you can't get it done ahead of time, go ahead and file the financial-aid forms with your best estimates. On federal and institutional forms, you'll have an opportunity later to make corrections if your estimates turn out to be off by more than a small margin.

Note that if you do use estimates, the expected family contribution shown on the Student Aid Report you and the colleges receive will be annotated with an asterisk. That alerts financial-aid officers that you used estimates on the aid forms. You'll have a chance to amend those estimates when you get the SAR. At many schools, you will also be asked to supply a copy of your tax forms when they're completed.

> **The best route is to prepare your tax return early. That allows you to use numbers you know are accurate on financial-aid forms.**

The Financial-Aid Years

It's a mistake to wait until you must fill out the forms to think about how you'll fill them out. Planning ahead is critical, because the snapshot that financial-aid officers take of your finances begins about 20 months ahead of your child's first hour in a lecture hall. How so?

- **You complete financial-aid forms** typically in January or February for the school year your child starts the following September.
- **For the family income you report,** those forms ask you to look backward, to the prior calendar year.
- **But you report your assets** as of the day you sign and date the financial-aid form.

So for the 2004–2005 academic year, for example, what we'll call the "financial-aid year" actually started in January 2003 and ended sometime in the first two months of 2004. If your son or daughter will go to college beginning with the 2006–2007 academic year, your financial-aid years will work out as shown in the table below.

Keep this timetable in mind as you read about how the financial-aid number crunchers arrive at a figure representing your "ability to pay" the college bills. As you'll see, to take advantage of many of the aid-boosting strategies discussed in Chapter 6, you need to begin planning before your child is roughly halfway through high school.

THE FINANCIAL-AID CALENDAR

Applying for financial aid isn't a one-time chore; you will have to reapply each academic year, and your family's income and assets will be reconsidered each time. This table shows the corresponding periods of time from which those figures will be drawn. (The time frame for reporting assets shifts slightly after the first year because aid forms for upperclassmen are usually due a bit later than those for freshmen.) This calendar is for someone beginning college in the fall of 2006, but you can easily adapt it to your child's schedule.

Academic year	Income and assets considered
Freshman (2006–2007)	**Income:** Earned January to December 2005 (mid-junior to mid-senior year in high school) **Assets:** As of the day you sign and date the financial-aid forms early in 2006 (senior year in high school)
Sophomore (2007–2008)	**Income:** Earned January to December 2006 (senior year in high school to freshman year in college) **Assets:** As of early to mid-2007 (freshman year in college)
Junior (2008–2009)	**Income:** Earned January to December 2007 (freshman to sophomore year in college) **Assets:** As of early to mid-2008 (sophomore year in college)
Senior (2009–2010)	**Income:** Earned January to December 2008 (sophomore to junior year in college) **Assets:** As of early to mid-2009 (junior year in college)

If your child is headed off to college soon and you've already entered the first financial-aid year, you've missed some of the aid-boosting opportunities in Chapter 6, but not all of them. The most important thing, of course, is to get the aid forms in on time.

Estimate Your Expected Family Contribution Early

Seventh grade—and even earlier—isn't too soon to test-run the financial-aid formulas to get a rough idea of what your expected family contribution will be. Some financial-aid consultants advise parents of children of any age to know their EFC. If they track it as their children grow up, with each raise in salary, the accompanying rise in the EFC will wake them up as

---

THE FINANCIAL-AID PAPER TRAIL

In the fall of your child's senior year

■ Pick up a FAFSA from a high school guidance counselor or college financial-aid officer or register online to receive a copy (see page 102).

■ If any of the schools you're applying to requires the PROFILE aid form, also pick up a PROFILE registration form and mail it to the College Scholarship Service to request the PROFILE application materials, or register online. In response to your application, the College Scholarship Service will send you either the standard PROFILE form or a customized version as required by the school(s) to which you're applying.

As soon as possible after January 1

■ Send the completed FAFSA to the processor using the envelope that is supplied with the form, or complete the form online.

■ If PROFILE is required, send it by the earliest deadline (each college can set its own deadline) to the College Scholarship Service, which processes the forms.

What you'll receive

The FAFSA processor and the College Scholarship Service will send your information to the schools you name on the forms.

FAFSA processors will also send you notification of your expected family contribution, on a form called the Student Aid Report (see page 102).

The formulas used are often called the federal methodology, and they figure your expected family contribution from four sources.

to how tough paying for college is going to be, and therefore how crucial it is that they don't spend all their income now.

Tracking your EFC when you begin saving for college can help you know approximately how much you should save. Even if you're only a few years away from college bills, knowing your EFC can help you make the most of the time you've got. You can put yourself in the best position possible to qualify for aid or, if the numbers show you won't qualify for much aid, spend your energies elsewhere, such as applying for scholarships.

Uncle Sam's Math: The Federal Methodology

The financial-aid forms are about as nosy, and as tedious, as an income-tax return. And the mathematical gymnastics that convert the data you supply on your aid application into an expected family contribution are equally likely to remind you of the instructions that come with your tax forms. The formulas used are often called the federal methodology, and they figure your expected family contribution from four sources: your income, your assets, your child's income, and your child's assets. You won't see the calculations on the federal aid form you fill out; you supply the data, and the number crunching takes place behind the scenes. The best way to understand how the federal methodology determines your ability to contribute to college costs from those four sources is to take a look at the examples on the pages that follow. They show how three fictitious families— the Joneses, the MacDonalds, and the Browns— would fare under the federal methodology, using the federal aid formulas for the 2005–2006 academic year. In the Joneses' case, we devised an accompanying worksheet that will walk you through some sample calculations. (You can come up with an estimate of your own contribution using the worksheet, with the necessary instructions and tables, provided on pages 120–124.

You could also use one of the online calculators that were designed for this purpose, such as the one at http://apps.collegeboard.com/fincalc/efc_welcome.jsp or at www.finaid.org//calculators/finaidestimate.phtml.)

You might be tempted to just fill out the form and ignore the lengthy instructions and examples available to you. Don't. You might overlook a deduction that would lower your EFC by hundreds or even thousands of dollars. For more tips on filling out the forms to your best advantage, see pages 174–181 in Chapter 6.

Home Equity— an Important Exception

About $6,706 a year for a college education, as the Joneses will be expected to pay, may sound manageable—or at least not impossible—to a family earning $60,000 a year. But that "official" EFC can be misleading if you're planning to apply to private colleges. The reason? While private colleges use the federal methodology to determine what federal aid you qualify for, they use a modified formula—called the institutional methodology—to determine how much aid they'll offer you from their own coffers.

The chief difference is that the federal methodology excludes the equity in your home from assets, but many private colleges add it back in when giving out their own aid. (Public colleges generally follow the federal methodology even when awarding their own money.) That can lead to a big disappointment for the family that, based on the Student Aid Report, is expecting $17,000 in aid at a $25,000 school and gets far less—because in the eyes of aid officers at private schools, the home's value significantly boosts their ability to pay.

If you have significant assets, including home equity, prepare yourself ahead of time for the shock by running through the worksheet on pages 120–121

continued on page 112

> **DON'T MISS OUT**
>
> Want more information about financial aid and how it works? Here is an especially good resource: *Don't Miss Out: The Ambitious Student's Guide to Financial Aid,* published by Octameron Associates ($12 plus shipping; P.O. Box 2748, Alexandria, VA 22301; 703-836-5480; www.octameron.com), dissects the financial-aid process and is chock-full of financial-aid tips.

THE JONES FAMILY, A SUMMARY

The Joneses are a family of four with two children, one in college, the other age 15. Mr. Jones, age 47, is the older parent. They live in California.

Parents' income: $60,000

Both Mr. and Mrs. Jones work, and jointly they earned $56,000 last year, plus $4,000 in interest income (see line 1). They each contributed $2,000 to a 401(k) plan, which was tax-deductible.

Taxes: $14,390

Their tax allowances, including federal, state, and social security taxes, total $14,390 (see lines 2–4).

Parents' assets: $77,000
(line 9 plus equity in home)

The Joneses have $2,000 in checking and savings accounts. In addition to their 401(k)s, they have $25,000 in taxable mutual fund accounts (see line 9). They also own a $150,000 home, on which the mortgage balance is $100,000.

Student's income: $4,000

Jane Jones earned $4,000 working during the summer and school holidays and paid $506 in taxes (see lines 16–19).

Student's assets: $2,500

Jane has $2,500 in savings bonds in her own name (see line 24).

UNDER THE FEDERAL METHODOLOGY
The parents' contribution: $5,304

From income: $5,304. For tax purposes, the Joneses' adjusted gross income was $56,000. But for financial-aid purposes, the Joneses income was $60,000, because

the formulas add back their contributions to retirement accounts, including IRAs and 401(k)s.

From their income they can subtract their taxes, an income-protection allowance of $21,330 (the amount for a family of four with one child in college) and an employment-expense allowance of $3,000.

After the subtractions, the Joneses' "available income" for aid purposes is $21,280 (line 8). Think of your available income on financial-aid forms in the same terms as your taxable income on income-tax forms. In this case, the Joneses' contribution comes to about 25% of their available income. Because they are in a mid-range "bracket," however, 34% of each additional dollar of available income would be added to their EFC (see Table E on page 124).

From assets: $0. Because home equity is excluded from the federal aid formulas, the Joneses' net worth for aid purposes is $27,000 (line 9). But they get an asset-protection allowance of $39,600, the allowance for a two-parent family in which the older parent is age 47 (line 10), so they don't have to contribute anything from their assets (line 12; unless Jane attends a private college that adds home equity to its calculations, as discussed on page 109).

From the student's income: $527 From her $4,000 in earnings, Jane can subtract the $506 she paid in taxes and a $2,440 income-protection allowance. The remainder, $1,054, is her available income. Her contribution from income is 50% of that amount, or $527 (see line 23).

From the student's assets: $875
Students must contribute a flat 35% of their assets to the college bills each year. That's $875 of the $2,500 Jane has in savings bonds (see line 25).

Annual out-of-pocket expense: $6,706
The Joneses' total expected family contribution: $6,706 (see line 26).

THE JONESES' EXPECTED CONTRIBUTION WORKSHEET

Section 1: Parents' income

1.	Parents' income	$60,000
2.	Federal taxes	5,600
3.	State taxes	4,200
4.	Social security taxes	4,590
5.	Income-protection allowance	21,330
6.	Employment-expense allowance	3,000
7.	Add lines 2, 3, 4, 5, and 6	38,720
8.	Parents' available income (Subtract line 7 from line 1)	21,280

Section 2: Parents' assets

9.	Total assets	$27,000
10.	Asset-protection allowance	39,600
11.	Parents' available assets (Subtract line 10 from line 9)	−12,600
12.	Multiply line 11 by 0.12 (If result is negative, enter zero)	0

Section 3: Parents' contribution from income and assets

13.	Adjusted available income and assets (Add lines 8 and 12)	$21,280
14.	Parents' contribution (Table E, page 124)	5,304
15.	More than one child (Divide line 14 by the number of children you have in college)	NA

Section 4: Student's income

16.	Student's income	$4,000
17.	Federal taxes	0
18.	State taxes	200
19.	Social security taxes	306
20.	Income-protection allowance	2,440
21.	Add lines 17 through 20	2,946
22.	Student's available income (Subtract line 21 from line 16)	1,054
23.	Student's contribution from income (Multiply line 22 by 0.5)	527

Section 5: Student's assets

24.	Assets in student's name	$2,500
25.	Student contribution from assets (Multiply line 24 by 0.35)	875

Section 6: Expected family contribution

26.	If one child is in college (Add lines 14, 23 and 25)	$6,706
27.	If two or more children (Add lines 15, 23, and 25 for each student)	NA

twice, once excluding home equity and the second time including it among your assets. The second result will give you a ballpark picture of what you can expect from a typical private college.

Other Differences

There are other differences, too, between the federal and institutional methodologies, although none are likely to have as large an impact on your EFC as home equity:

- **The institutional methodology,** for instance, looks at assets you have accumulated in a student's siblings' names. If those are significant, at many private colleges your EFC could go up accordingly.
- **Income- and asset-protection allowances** are somewhat different (and there's an education-savings allowance for siblings that can offset some of the impact of having saved money in younger siblings' names).
- **Losses from a business or investments** do not reduce your income as they can under the federal methodology.

THE MACDONALD FAMILY, A SUMMARY

Anne MacDonald is a 41-year-old single mother. Her son, George, will begin college in the fall. They live in Ohio.

Income: $30,000
Anne earned $30,000 in wages last year and had no other income.

Taxes: $6,895
Her total tax bill, including federal, state, and social security taxes, was $6,895.

Assets: $12,500 total
She has $500 in a checking account, $2,000 in a certificate of deposit, and $10,000 in home equity.

Student's income: $3,000
George earned $3,000 last year at a summer job. He paid $380 in state and social security taxes.

Student's assets: $500
George has $500 in a savings account.

UNDER THE FEDERAL METHODOLOGY
The parent's contribution: $1,372
From income: $1,372. Anne can subtract her taxes, a $13,870 income-protection allowance (the amount for a family of two with one child in college), and a $3,000 employment-expense allowance from her income (allowed for single-parent families and for two-parent families in which both parents work). She's expected to contribute about 22% of the remainder.

From assets: $0. The asset-protection allowance for a 41-year-old single parent is $13,600. Because her assets are below that amount, Anne would have no contribution from assets.

■ **And, on the plus side,** students are expected to contribute 25% of their assets to college costs each year under the institutional methodology, rather than 35% under the federal methodology. Parents contribute 3% of the first $25,000 in assets (after allowances), 4% of the next $25,000, and 5% of available income over $50,000.

The worksheets in this chapter compute your EFC under the federal methodology. If you want a projection of your EFC under the institutional methodology that takes into account more of the nuances described above, the online calculators mentioned on page 109 are the best place to go.

How It Would Work for the Jones Family

For example, let's take another look at the Jones family's situation:

From the student's income: $90
After subtracting his taxes and a $2,440 income-protection allowance, George's contribution from income is 50% of the remainder.

From the student's assets: $175
George contributes a flat 35% of his assets.

Annual out-of-pocket expense: $1,637
The MacDonalds' total expected family contribution: $1,637.

UNDER THE INSTITUTIONAL METHODOLOGY
The MacDonalds are expected to contribute a bit more overall under the institutional methodology. Anne's contribution is $1,372 and George's is $1,435, for a total of $2,807.

The primary difference is a larger contribution from George's income, because the institutional formula does not shelter the first $2,440 in earnings.

THE AID FOR WHICH THEY'LL QUALIFY
Here's how much aid the MacDonalds might qualify for at public and private institutions.

At a high-priced private college:
$40,000 total cost – $2,807 EFC = $37,193 financial aid

At an average-priced private school:
$30,000 total cost – $2,807 EFC = $27,193 financial aid

At an average-priced public college:
$15,000 total cost – $1,637 EFC = $13,363 financial aid

Under the federal methodology, the Jones's family contribution is $6,706—that is, $5,304 from the parents and $1,402 from the student. Because the federal methodology excludes home equity, the Jones's assets are less than their asset-protection allowance, and thus the contribution from assets under that formula is zero.

Under the institutional methodology, their total contribution comes to $9,488—$7,116 from the parents and $2,372 from the student. The institutional methodology includes $50,000 in home equity among their assets. The student's contribution is higher because the federal formulas exclude the first $2,440 of student income, while there is no such income-protection allowance under the institutional formula.

Using the institutional methodology at private institutions (but not at the public college), the following shows how much aid the Joneses might qualify for at various colleges:

At a high-priced private college: $40,000 total cost – $9,488 EFC = $30,512 financial aid

---

DECLARE INDEPENDENCE?

Q. Years ago, I qualified as an independent student because I moved out of my parents' home and they stopped claiming me as a dependent on their income-tax return. As a result, I qualified for lots of financial aid. Why not encourage my children to do the same?

A. The government has since changed the criteria for independent students, on the notion that too many parents were exploiting the more-liberal rules to duck their responsibility to help with the college bills. Now it's much tougher to qualify as an independent student. In "documented unusual circumstances," a financial-aid officer can declare a student independent, but, generally speaking, your child must meet one of the following criteria:

- **Is age 24 or older** by December 31, 2005 (for the 2005–2006 academic year);
- **Is a veteran** of the U.S. armed forces;
- **Is married;**
- **Is a graduate student;**
- **Has a legal dependent,** other than a spouse; or
- **Is (or has been) a ward of the court.**

At an average-priced private school: $30,000 total cost – $9,488 EFC = $20,512 financial aid

At an average-priced public college: $15,000 total cost – $6,706 EFC = $8,294 financial aid

What if the Joneses had twice as much home equity? Using the institutional methodology, adding $100,000 to their assets, instead of $50,000, boosts the expected family contribution from $9,488 to $12,308, a $2,820 increase.

If You'll Have Two Kids in College at Once

Having two family members in college at the same time sounds like the ultimate budget buster. But two sets of tuition bills at once can actually qualify you for lots more aid than if your children attend college sequentially. That's because, under the federal need analysis, the parents' expected contribution is the same no matter how many family members are in school. If two are in college, the parents' contribution is divided in half for each student. If there are three sets of tuition bills, the parent contribution is split into thirds. Each student, of course, is responsible for his or her own contribution from income and assets.

In the Brown family example, shown in the box on pages 116–117, the parents' contribution from income and assets is $21,631 under the federal formulas. If both Janet and her brother Charles attend college at the same time, the parent contribution is half that, or $10,816 for each child. The total contribution for Janet, including her $627 from income and $875 from assets, is $12,318. For Charles, who has lower earnings and the same assets, the family contribution is $11,625.

Together the family still contributes almost $24,000 a year to college costs. But the aid packages Janet and Charles get are potentially much bigger than if they

Two sets of tuition bills at once can actually qualify you for lots more aid than if your children attend college sequentially.

attended school at different times because they report an expected family contribution of $11,625 or $12,318—instead of nearly double that amount—to the schools they attend.

The institutional methodology expects the Browns to contribute $12,226 for each child. Janet is expected to add $2,472, for a total of $14,698. And Charles is expected to add $1,780, for a total of $14,005.

There are exceptions. You can't divide the contribution by two if one of your two students:

■ **Attends a service academy,** such as West Point, where there are no fees for tuition and room and board.
■ **Is in graduate school.** Graduate students are considered independent, even if you're still footing the bills. But their independent status means your income

THE BROWN FAMILY, A SUMMARY

Mr. and Mrs. Brown are both 51 and both work. They have three kids, two in college, and the other age 14. They live in Texas.

Parents' income: $100,000
The Browns' combined income is $100,000.
Taxes: $21,650
Their federal, state, and social security taxes total $21,650.
Parents' assets: $128,000
The Browns have $3,000 in checking and savings accounts, $75,000 in mutual funds and stocks, and a $150,000 home, on which the mortgage balance is $100,000.
Students' income: $4,000 and $2,500
Janet Brown earned $4,000 last year and paid $306 in taxes. Charles Brown earned $2,500 and paid $191 in taxes.
Students' assets: $2,500 each
Janet and Charles each have $2,500 in a money-market mutual fund.

UNDER THE FEDERAL METHODOLOGY
Parents' Contribution: $21,631
From income and assets: $21,631. From their income and assets, the Browns subtract their taxes, a $22,790 income-protection allowance (the amount for a family of five with two children in college), a $43,900 asset-protection allowance, and a $3,000 employment-expense allowance. They're expected to contribute about 38% of the remainder.
Because they have two kids in college, the Browns can divide their contribution in two—that's $10,816 for each student.
From Janet's income: (She earned enough to have to make a contribution. Charles did not.) $627
After taxes and a $2,440 income-protection allowance, Janet contributes $627 from income, and Charles, nothing from income since he didn't earn enough.

and assets are excluded from their financial-aid forms.

For Divorced Parents

If you're divorced, you report the income and assets of the custodial parent (the parent the child lives with more than half the time) on the FAFSA. And if the custodial parent is remarried, the income and assets of the stepparent count, too. The federal need analysis does not include the financial resources of the noncustodial parent.

Whether you think it's fair or not, most colleges follow the federal methodology, including a stepparent's

---

From the students' assets: $875 each
Each contributes 35% of assets, or $875.

Annual out-of-pocket expense: $12,318 and $11,625
The Browns' total expected family contribution for Janet: $12,318. Their total contribution for Charles: $11,625.

UNDER THE INSTITUTIONAL METHODOLOGY
The Browns' expected parent contribution for each student is $12,226. However, the total EFC is higher because Janet and Charles are expected to use a larger portion of their earnings toward college costs. The formulas figure a total family contribution of $14,698 for Janet (including $1,847 from Janet's income and $625 from Janet's assets). The total contribution for Charles is $12,853 (including $1,155 from Charles's income and $625 from his assets).

THE AID FOR WHICH JANET WILL QUALIFY
At a high-priced private college:
$40,000 total cost – $14,698 EFC = $25,302 financial aid

At an average-priced private school:
$30,000 total cost – $14,698 EFC = $15,302 financial aid

At an average-priced public college:
$15,000 total cost – $12,318 EFC = $2,682 financial aid

Note that if Janet were the family's only student in college, she'd qualify for much less aid at most private colleges, with a total family contribution, under the institutional methodology, of $26,923.

Most colleges follow the federal methodology, including a stepparent's resources and excluding the resources of a noncustodial natural parent.

resources and excluding the resources of a noncustodial natural parent. Those requirements ignore any agreements you may have made in a divorce decree or privately with an ex-spouse. But just because the non-custodial parent's income and assets aren't included when calculating the family's expected contribution doesn't mean that parent can't actually help meet your child's college costs.

Divorced parents should know that many schools that deviate from the federal formulas often ask about a noncustodial parent's income and assets on their own aid forms, and consider the resources of both natural parents—as well as the custodial parent's spouse. (However, if the noncustodial parent is remarried, that person's income and assets probably would not be considered.) If that happens and you feel the aid package you're awarded is unfair, you can appeal to a financial-aid officer. You'd probably be able to make a good case for a lower expected family contribution if the step-parent is also contributing to the college costs of his or her natural children, or if the noncustodial parent has no contact with your child or has consistently failed to make child-support payments (something that you'd probably need to document with a statement from a social worker or a member of the clergy).

Be sure to ask about a school's policies as you visit campuses. Even if you can't do anything about it when filling out the forms, you'll have an idea ahead of time what you may be up against. If, for instance, the non-custodial parent has a high income, you're likely to qualify for much less aid at a school that includes that parent's resources—unless you can make a convincing case for why it should be excluded.

While it's not the usual practice, some schools depart from the federal methodology and completely recalculate the family contribution, using the income and assets of both natural parents and excluding stepparents, when giving out their own aid. Amherst is one such school. "We believe the responsibility lies with the two [natural] parents," says financial-aid dean Joe Paul Case. "If it's a fairly recent remarriage, especially, we think it's unfair to ignore the recentness of that occurrence." This doesn't seem to be a hard-and-fast policy, however. Case says if it's a long-standing remarriage or the stepparent has adopted the child, he'll follow the federal methodology, including the stepparent and excluding the noncustodial natural parent.

What if a stepparent refuses to provide the information necessary to complete the forms, much less any financial help? Aid officers say they encounter a few such objections every year, and in most cases stick to their guns on requiring the information and including the stepparent's resources. (They can deny you aid entirely if you don't supply the information.) But occasionally an exception is made. If you can make a persuasive case for why a stepparent's resources should be excluded, or perhaps replaced by those of the other natural parent, an appeal might be worth a try.

Calculate Your Contribution

You can calculate your own expected family contribution using the worksheet, with accompanying tables, on pages 120–124.

Keep in mind that, like the tax brackets on a tax return, the allowances and other numbers in the formulas tend to go up each year with inflation, so if your income is just keeping up with inflation, your EFC is likely to stay relatively level. But if it grows faster or slower than inflation, you'd expect less or more aid correspondingly.

After you complete the worksheet on pages 120–121 with your actual income and assets (or estimates), work through the calculations again with slightly more income and then with slightly higher assets. That will give you a feel for what will happen if your income rises faster than inflation and as you add to your savings. You can also rerun the calculations with a bit less income and assets to estimate the impact of some of the financial-aid strategies suggested in Chapter 6.

continued on page 122

FIGURING YOUR EXPECTED FAMILY CONTRIBUTION

Use this worksheet and accompanying tables to figure your expected family contribution, the amount your family will be expected to pay toward college costs before receiving aid. The worksheet reflects the federal need-analysis formula for the 2005–2006 academic year—private schools may deviate from this formula when giving out their own financial aid. These calculations are designed for families with dependent students; the federal government has separate calculations for independent students, which aren't included here. Independent students can obtain appropriate information from their guidance counselor or financial-aid officer.

SECTION 1: PARENTS' INCOME

1. Parents' income $_____

(From your 2004 tax return for the 2005–2006 academic year, for example. Include: wages, including payments made this year to IRA, Keogh, and 401(k) plans; social security benefits; interest and investment income; tax-exempt interest income; child support received; unemployment compensation; and housing or other living allowances.)

2. Federal taxes (paid in 2004)   _____

3. State taxes (see Table A on page 122)   _____

4. Combined social security taxes (see Table B on page 123) _____

5. Education tax credits claimed on your 2004 return, and child support that you paid   _____

6. Income-protection allowance (see Table C on page 123) _____

7. Employment-expense allowance   _____

(For two-income families, 35% of the smaller income, or $3,000, whichever is less. For one-parent families, 35% of earned income, or $3,000, whichever is less. For two-parent families with only one parent who earns an income, $0.)

8. Add lines 2, 3, 4, 5, 6, and 7   _____

9. Parents' available income $_____

(Subtract line 8 from line 1.)

SECTION 2: PARENTS' ASSETS

10. Total assets $_____

(If your adjusted gross income was less than $15,000 and both you and your children are eligible to file a 1040A or 1040EZ tax form or are not required to file any income tax return, your contribution from assets is zero.

Otherwise, include: cash, bank accounts, stocks, bonds, real estate other than your primary residence, trust funds, 529 savings plans, commodities, and precious metals. Exclude equity in your home, retirement accounts such as IRAs, Keoghs, or 401(k) plans, prepaid tuition plans, and any cash value in life insurance policies.

Business and farm assets are included at a discounted rate; use

Table F on page 124 to calculate how much to include.)

11. Asset-protection allowance (from Table D on page 124) _____

12. Parents' available assets _____
(Subtract line 11 from line 10.)

13. Multiply line 12 by 0.12 $ _____
(If result is negative, enter zero.)

SECTION 3: PARENTS' CONTRIBUTION FROM INCOME AND ASSETS

14. Adjusted available income and assets $ _____
(Add lines 9 and 13.)

15. Parents' contribution _____
(Using figure on line 14, see Table E on page 124.)

16. If you have more than one child in college $ _____
(Divide line 15 by the number of children you have in college.
The result is the contribution for each student.)

SECTION 4: STUDENT'S INCOME

17. Student's income $ _____
(Include wages, interest, and investment income. Exclude any
student aid that you had to report on last year's tax return.)

18. Federal taxes _____

19. State taxes (see Table A) _____

20. Social security taxes (see Table B) _____

21. Income-protection allowance _____

22. Add lines 18 through 21 _____

23. Student's available income _____
(Subtract line 22 from line 17.)

24. Student's contribution from income $ _____
(Multiply line 23 by 0.5.)

SECTION 5: STUDENT'S ASSETS

25. Assets in student's name $ _____
(Cash, savings, trusts, investments, and so on)

26. Student's contribution from assets $ _____
(Multiply line 25 by 0.35.)

SECTION 6: EXPECTED FAMILY CONTRIBUTION

27. If one child is in college $ _____
(Add lines 15, 24, and 26.)

28. If two or more children are in college $ _____
(Add lines 16, 24, and 26 for each student.)

TABLE A: STATE TAX ALLOWANCES

State	PERCENT OF TOTAL INCOME Parents only $0 to $14,999	$15,000 or more	Student only	State	PERCENT OF TOTAL INCOME Parents only $0 to $14,999	$15,000 or more	Student only
Alabama	3%	2%	2%	Missouri	4%	3%	3%
Alaska	2	1	0	Montana	5	4	3
Arizona	4	3	2	Nebraska	5	4	3
Arkansas	3	2	3	Nevada	2	1	1
California	7	6	5	New Hampshire	4	3	1
Colorado	4	3	3	New Jersey	8	7	4
Connecticut	7	6	4	New Mexico	4	3	3
Delaware	4	3	3	New York	8	7	5
District of Columbia	7	6	6	North Carolina	6	5	4
				North Dakota	2	1	1
Florida	2	1	0	Ohio	6	5	4
Georgia	5	4	3	Oklahoma	4	3	3
Hawaii	4	3	4	Oregon	7	6	5
Idaho	5	4	3	Pennsylvania	5	4	3
Illinois	5	4	2	Rhode Island	7	6	4
Indiana	4	3	3	South Carolina	5	4	3
Iowa	5	4	3	South Dakota	1	0	0
Kansas	5	4	3	Tennessee	1	0	0
Kentucky	5	4	4	Texas	2	1	0
Louisiana	2	1	2	Utah	5	4	4
Maine	6	5	4	Vermont	6	5	3
Maryland	7	6	5	Virginia	5	4	3
Massachusetts	6	5	4	Washington	2	1	0
Michigan	5	4	3	West Virginia	3	2	2
Minnesota	6	5	4	Wisconsin	7	6	4
Mississippi	3	2	2	Wyoming	1	0	0

Note: State tax allowances for American Samoa, Canada, Federated States of Micronesia, Guam, Marshall Islands, Mexico, Northern Mariana Islands, Palau, Puerto Rico, and the Virgin Islands are 3%, 2% and 2%, respectively, in the above categories.

You'll find that relatively small increases in income in a given year—perhaps from a bonus or from cashing in some investments—can make a big difference. Changes in assets, however, don't make that much of a difference.

TABLE B: SOCIAL SECURITY TAX

Calculate separately the social security tax of each parent and the student.

Income earned from work*	Social security tax
$0 to $90,000	7.65% of income
$90,000 or greater	$6,885 + 1.45% of amount over $90,000

*For the 2005 tax year (the 2006–2007 financial-aid year)

TABLE C: INCOME-PROTECTION ALLOWANCES

For each additional family member, add $3,320. For each additional college student, subtract $2,360.

Number of persons in parents' household including student	Number of college students in household				
	1	2	3	4	5
2	$13,870	$11,490			
3	17,270	14,910	$12,530		
4	21,330	18,950	16,590	$14,220	
5	25,160	22,790	20,430	18,060	$15,700
6	29,430	27,060	24,700	22,330	19,970

Let Your Computer Help

I f you would rather let a machine crunch the numbers, get online and use one of the several Web sites that allow you to come up with a rough estimate of your expected family contribution. To calculate your EFC online, try the College Board's Web site at http://apps.collegeboard.com/fincalc/efc_welcome.jsp. Or try the calculator available at a site called FinAid (www.finaid.org/calculators/finaidestimate.phtml). There is no charge to use these interactive Web sites. Web site addresses change from time to time, so if these don't work, try the home page of the main site (www.collegeboard.com or www.finaid.org) and navigate through the menus from there.

TABLE D: ASSET-PROTECTION ALLOWANCES

Older parent's age	ALLOWANCE		Older parent's age	ALLOWANCE	
	If two parents	If only one parent		If two parents	If only one parent
35	$22,200	$ 8,900	51	$43,900	$17,000
36	24,400	9,800	52	44,900	17,400
37	26,600	10,600	53	46,300	17,800
38	28,900	11,500	54	47,400	18,300
39	31,100	12,400	55	48,900	18,700
40	33,300	13,300	56	50,000	19,100
41	34,100	13,600	57	51,500	19,700
42	35,000	13,900	58	53,100	20,100
43	35,900	14,200	59	54,600	20,700
44	36,700	14,500	60	56,200	21,200
45	37,700	14,800	61	57,800	21,800
46	38,600	15,200	62	59,500	22,400
47	39,600	15,500	63	61,500	23,000
48	40,500	15,900	64	63,300	23,700
49	41,500	16,200	65 or older	65,400	24,300
50	42,800	16,200			

TABLE E: PARENTS' CONTRIBUTION FROM ASSETS AND INCOME

Available funds	Parent contribution
Less than $3,409	$750
$3,409 to $12,400	22% of available assets and income (AAI)
$12,401 to $15,600	$2,728 plus 25% of AAI over $12,400
$15,601 to $18,700	$3,528 plus 29% of AAI over $15,600
$18,701 to $21,900	$4,427 plus 34% of AAI over $18,700
$21,901 to $25,000	$5,515 plus 40% of AAI over $21,900
$25,001 or more	$6,755 plus 47% of AAI over $25,000

TABLE F: BUSINESS/FARM NET WORTH ADJUSTMENT

If the net worth of a business or farm is	Then the adjusted net worth is
Less than $1	$0
$1 to $100,000	40% of net worth of business and farm
$100,001 to $295,000	$40,000 + 50% of excess over $100,000
$295,001 to $495,000	$137,500 + 60% of excess over $295,000
$495,001 or more	$257,500 + 100% of excess over $495,000

How the Schools Build Your Aid Package

T he previous chapter explained how the federal government determines your expected contribution to college costs from income and assets. But that's only half the picture. Once college financial-aid officers receive your data, they often combine your "official" expected family contribution with the additional information you supply, on the PROFILE or institutional aid form, to come up with the package of aid you're offered in an award letter sometime in the spring. It may seem like hocus-pocus until you understand the method they use.

The Usual Process

H ere's the process that a financial-aid officer would typically use to put together a financial-aid package.

The Cost Comes First

As discussed in Chapter 1, tuition and room and board are just the beginning—and colleges recognize that. At most schools, the total cost also includes books, an allotment for living expenses, and sometimes travel costs. As shocking as the total may seem, the higher these estimates, the better, because high numbers create a bigger gap between your expected contribution and the total tab—and thus make you eligible for more aid.

Some schools are more generous on this point than others. Amherst (in Massachusetts), for instance, adds up to $2,000 in travel expenses for students who come

The financial-aid officer uses that "need" number to parcel out the first layer of the aid package— federal and state grants, loans, and work-study jobs.

from the West Coast. But at the University of California at Berkeley, the standard travel allowance is about $650, which isn't much help for a student from the Midwest or the East Coast. Wake Forest, which provides every freshman with a laptop computer and color printer, includes that cost in tuition, making students eligible for more financial aid to cover the expense.

Other schools use ridiculously low estimates for everyday living expenses—or omit them entirely. That's a sneaky form of "gapping," or not meeting a family's entire need (for more on gapping, see page 138). No matter how frugal your child is, he's got to buy toothpaste, laundry soap, paper, and pens.

Followed by the EFC

Next, the financial-aid officer looks at your "official" expected family contribution, as calculated by the federal methodology, and subtracts that figure from the total cost.

For instance, if Jane Jones (from the example on pages 110–111) attended an average-priced private college:

$30,000 total costs − $6,706 EFC = $23,294 "need"

The First Layer of Aid

The financial-aid officer uses that "need" number to parcel out the first layer of the aid package—federal and state grants, loans, and work-study jobs.

- **If your EFC were $3,850 or less for the 2004-2005 academic year,** you would probably qualify for a Pell Grant ranging from $400 to $4,050. (Most Pell Grant recipients have family incomes of $35,000 or less.) Otherwise the first piece of aid in the package is likely to be a federal loan—either a very-low-interest Perkins loan for low-income students who qualify or, more commonly, a subsidized Stafford loan of $2,625 for a freshman. (Upperclass students are eligible for larger Stafford loans.)
- **Next, the aid officer might parcel out state grants,** if any are available. (See the box on pages 132–134.)
- **A work-study job** might also be added to the pack-

age. Federal work-study awards are usually in the neighborhood of $1,500.

■ **If you have an outside scholarship,** the financial-aid officer may include it in your aid package, perhaps using it to replace loans or a work-study award. (See page 207 in Chapter 8.)

The School's Own Resources

After federal and state aid, the school, whether public or private, awards its own money.

Let's assume Jane Jones gets a $2,625 Stafford loan, a $1,000 state grant, and a work-study job worth $1,500. That still leaves $18,169 of need, right?

Not always. Colleges must use the federal need-analysis figures when giving out federal (and usually state) aid. But the next layer of the package consists of grants, scholarships, and loans made from the school's own funds. And while public schools will generally continue to use the federal methodology to calculate need when doling out their own money, private schools often recalculate your need using their own formulas for this purpose.

How and Why Schools Adjust the Federal Formula

H ere's where all that additional data on the PRO-FILE or institutional form comes into play. (If you're asked for those additional forms, you can generally assume the school makes adjustments to the federal need analysis.) By taking into account your home equity, for instance, or a greater portion of student earnings, the school can come up with a much higher expected contribution at this point, making you eligible for far less institutional aid than you might have expected. Some schools offset that factor by requiring a smaller contribution from parents' earnings, while others also take into account additional expenses that the federal formulas don't, such as unusual medical costs or tuition that you're paying for a younger

> **After federal and state aid, the school, whether public or private, awards its own money.**

WHAT KIND OF AID YOU MAY BE OFFERED

Almost as important as how much aid you will receive is what kind of aid you will receive. Clearly grants and scholarships, which neither you nor your child will have to repay, are more desirable than loans or work-study jobs. Most aid packages are a mixture of all three. This section gives an overview of the most common forms of financial aid. (Chapter 9 will discuss the various types of loans in more detail.)

Pell Grants

These federal grants, named after Senator Claiborne Pell, their creator, ranged from $400 to $4,050 in the 2004–2005 academic year. Pell Grants go to the neediest students—generally families whose expected family contributions are $3,850 or less.

Stafford Loans

These are low-interest loans to students. Freshmen can borrow up to $2,625, sophomores up to $3,500, and upperclassmen up to $5,500 a year. When banks make the loans, they're called Federal Family Education Loans and the federal government "guarantees" the loans, meaning that Uncle Sam is on the hook for the loan if the student defaults. The federal government also makes some Stafford Loans directly; those are called Federal Direct Student Loans. Whether you get a government-guaranteed bank loan or a direct government loan depends on the school. More important than the issuer is whether the Stafford Loan is subsidized or not.

- **If you qualify based on need,** the federal government pays the interest on the loan while your child is in school and for six months after graduation.
- **If you don't qualify for a subsidized Stafford,** your child can still borrow under the program, but interest begins accruing immediately. If your child chooses not to pay the interest while in school, it's added to the loan balance to be repaid after graduation. (The long-term cost of this option is discussed in Chapter 9.)

child at a private high school. So your EFC can go up or down at this point.

It's important to realize that each school will have different policies on recalculating the expected family contribution before giving out institutional aid. Most public colleges and universities and some private ones won't deviate from the federal formulas at all. Others will follow the College Board's institutional methodology, discussed in the previous chapter. And still others will make substantial adjustments of their own that may reflect the school's recruiting priorities, but most likely reflect what the school thinks is a fair way to distribute the funds; many aid officers think there are

Either way, you get a relatively low rate: 2.3 percentage points above the 91-day Treasury bill rate, but no more than 8.25%. (For the 2004–2005 academic year, the rate was 3.37%.)

Perkins Loans

These are federal loans doled out by the individual schools. The "pool" for making these loans comes mostly from previous students' loan repayments, so schools with low default rates will have the most to lend. The maximum loan for most undergraduates is $4,000 a year. The interest rate is 5%, and interest does not accrue while the student is in school.

Federal and state work-study

Work-study is usually an on-campus job that pays minimum wage, or something close to it. At a typical school, the work-study component of a financial-aid package is around $1,500. That's about eight hours a week at a $6-an-hour job for two 16-week semesters.

Supplemental Educational Opportunity Grants

These are grants of up to $4,000 a year in federal money. As with Pell Grants, they primarily go to the lowest-income students. Schools receive a pool of grant money from the federal government and award these grants until the funds run out.

State grants

Most states have grant, loan, and scholarship programs for residents who attend in-state schools, whether public or private. To find out what types of aid your state offers, consult the listing of state aid agencies beginning on page 132.

Institutional aid

This is money the college or university has available to award to students, in the form of grants, scholarships, or loans, based on need or merit. Schools can apply their own criteria to evaluate need when giving out their own need-based awards.

inequities in the formulas, and they take the opportunity to correct for those when they are allowed to do so.

As a general rule, the most prestigious schools do the most tinkering with the aid formulas. Amherst's aid policies, for instance, are typical of other elite northeastern schools, such as Harvard, Yale, and MIT, and we'll cite them by way of example throughout this discussion. To some extent, the fact that the private schools (especially the prestigious ones) have more institutional money to give out offsets the fact that their aid policies are less generous than the federal formulas to, say, people with lots of equity in their homes. And, in fact, some of the wealthiest schools have made

IVY LEAGUES LOOSEN THEIR WALLETS

Princeton University won headlines in 2001 when it announced that it would substitute outright grants for student loans in its financial-aid packages, saving a typical family from $4,000 to $6,000 a year. But that's only the latest in a series of changes that Princeton has made to make more money available, especially to families whose income is in the range of $60,000 to $120,000. The university's financial-aid formulas now completely ignore home equity when considering how much a family can afford to pay, plus the school doesn't ask a family to contribute more when assets are held in a student's name. (Normally, students must cough up 35% of any savings in their names each year, while parents contribute about 5% of their assets.)

The bottom line is that a student whose parents earn $100,000 and have $50,000 in nonretirement savings, $100,000 in home equity, and $10,000 saved in the student's name might receive $25,000 to $26,000 in grants. That's enough to more than offset half of the school's $43,900 sticker price for 2005–2006. Even a family earning $150,000

a year might get a small grant. (You can assess your own chances by visiting Princeton's Web site at www.princeton.edu/main/admission-aid/aid.)

Most private colleges don't have the wherewithal to match Princeton's generosity. But many other top-tier schools are heading down the same road. At least 30 colleges and universities, including Dartmouth, Duke, and Stanford, have adopted the 568 Consensus Approach to Needs Analysis. Created by the 568 Presidents' Group, this reformation of the institutional methodology is used to determine the ability of each student's family to support the annual costs of attendance. It features capping home equity at 2.4 and requiring a lower contribution from the student.

And most top private schools now allow students who win outside scholarships to use that money to replace loans rather than offsetting grants in the financial-aid package. Such policies generally benefit middle- and upper-middle-income families—those most likely to have accumulated significant savings in a child's name or significant wealth in the family home.

their policies even more generous in recent years. (See the box above.)

Here are some of the adjustments that the schools typically make.

Adjusting for Home Equity

Adding home equity to your assets is the most common adjustment. Until 1992 the federal formulas also included home equity as an asset. When that changed, colleges were suddenly confronted with "needier" families based on the federal need analysis, but no additional federal aid money to fill the gap. Most private schools' response was to simply add home equity back to the equation when doling out institutional money. Others chose to follow the federal formula and exclude home equity but to no longer meet 100% of need for every family.

Some schools put a twist on the home-equity figure. Dartmouth, Duke, Stanford, and Amherst, for instance, add home equity but cap the value at 2.4 times your income.

Adding home equity to your assets is the most common adjustment made by private schools.

Student Income

One big difference between the federal and institutional aid formulas is that the institutional formulas (and thus many private colleges) do not shelter the first $2,440 of a student's income from being rolled into the family contribution. Because students are expected to contribute 50% of their income, that means a student who earns at least $2,440 is asked to come up with $1,220 more from earnings under the institutional formulas.

Asset Protection Allowances

Under recent changes to the College Board's institutional methodology, the asset-protection allowances for families now differ significantly from those under the federal methodology. The new allowances are maddeningly complicated to calculate, but here's an example: A family of four with a college student and a 15-year-old would get an emergency-reserve allowance, plus an education-savings allowance for the 15-year-old's college education, resulting in a total asset-protection allowance that's similar to the asset-protection allowance provided under the federal formulas for a family with two parents (but any number of children and any income level). The big difference is that a family with no younger children at home gets only the emergency-reserve allowance and no education-savings allowance—and thus a much smaller asset-protection allowance overall than they do under the federal formula. Thus,

continued on page 134

STATE HIGHER EDUCATION AGENCIES

These agencies can provide information on grants, scholarships, and other financial aid offered by the states.

Alabama
Commission on Higher
    Education
334-242-1998
www.ache.state.al.us

Alaska
Commission on
    Postsecondary Education
907-465-2962
800-441-2962
www.state.ak.us/acpe/

Arizona
Commission for
    Postsecondary Education
602-258-2435
www.acpe.asu.edu

Arkansas
Dept. of Higher Education
501-371-2000
www.arkansashighered.com

California
Student Aid Commission
916-526-7590
www.csac.ca.gov

Colorado
Commission on Higher
    Education
303-866-2723
www.state.co.us/cche_dir
/hecche.html

Connecticut
Department of Higher
    Education
860-947-1800
www.ctdhe.org

Delaware
Higher Education Commission
302-577-3240
www.doe.state.de.us/high-ed

District of Columbia
State Education Office
877-485-6751
www.seo.dc.gov/

Florida
Contact individual schools
directly.

Georgia
Student Finance Commission
770-724-9000
www.gsfc.org

Hawaii
State Postsecondary
    Education Commission
808-956-8213
www.hern.hawaii.edu/hern

Idaho
State Board of Education
208-334-2270
www.idahoboardofed.org

Illinois
State Assistance Commission
847-948-8500
www.collegezone.com

Indiana
State Student Assistance
    Commission
317-232-2350
www.ssaci.in.gov

Iowa
College Student Aid
    Commission
515-281-3501
www.Iowacollegeaid.org

Kansas
Board of Regents
785-296-3421
www.kansasregents.org

Kentucky
Higher Education Assistance
    Authority
502-696-7200
www.kheaa.com

Louisiana
Office of Student Financial
    Assistance
225-922-1012
www.osfa.state.la.us

Maine
Finance Authority
207-623-3263
www.famemaine.com

Maryland
Higher Education
   Commission
410-260-4500
www.mhec.state.md.us

Massachusetts
Board of Higher Education
617-994-6950
www.mass.edu

Michigan
Higher Education
   Assistance Authority
517-373-3394
www.MI-StudentAid.org

Minnesota
Higher Education Services
   Office
651-642-0533
www.mheso.state.mn.us

Mississippi
Postsecondary Education
   Financial Assistance Board
601-432-6997
www.ihl.state.ms.us

Missouri
Department of Higher
   Education
573-751-2361
www.dhe.mo.gov

Montana
Montana University System
   Student Loan Program
406-444-6570
www.montana.edu
/wwwoche

Nebraska
Coordinating Commission
   for Postsecondary
   Education
402-471-2847
www.ccpe.state.ne.us
/PublicDoc/CCPE/Default.asp

Nevada
Contact individual schools
directly.

New Hampshire
Postsecondary Education
   Commission
603-271-2555
www.state.nh.us
/postsecondary

New Jersey
Higher Education Student
   Assistance Authority
609-292-4210
www.state.nj.us/
highereducation/index.htm

New Mexico
Commission on Higher
   Education
505-827-7383
www.nmche.org

New York
Higher Education Services
   Corp.
518-473-7087
www.hesc.com

North Carolina
State Education Assistance
   Authority
919-549-8614
www.cfnc.org

North Dakota
University System
701-328-4114
www.ndus.edu

Ohio
Board of Regents
614-466-7420
www.regents.state.oh.us/sgs

Oklahoma
State Regents for Higher
   Education
405-524-9120
www.okhighered.org

STATE HIGHER EDUCATION AGENCIES *continued*

Oregon
State Student Assistance
    Commission
541-687-7400
www.osac.state.or.us

Pennsylvania
Higher Education Assistance
    Agency
717-720-2800
www.pheaa.org

Rhode Island
Higher Education Assistance
    Authority
401-736-1100
www.riheaa.org

South Carolina
Commission on Higher
    Education
803-737-2260
www.che400.state.sc.us

South Dakota
Board of Regents
605-773-3455
www.ris.sdbor.edu

Tennessee
Higher Education
    Commission
615-741-3605
www.state.tn.us

Texas
Higher Education
    Coordinating Board
512-427-6101
www.thecb.state.tx.us

Utah
State Board of Regents
801-321-7100
www.utahsbr.edu

Vermont
Student Assistance Corp.
802-655-9602
www.vsac.org

Virginia
State Counsel of Higher
    Education for Virginia
804-225-2600
www.schev.edu

Washington
State Higher Education
    Coordinating Board
360-753-7800
www.hecb.wa.gov

West Virginia
Higher Education Policy
    Commission
304-558-2101
www.hepc.wvnet.edu

Wisconsin
Higher Education Aids Board
608-267-2206
www.heab.state.wi.us

Wyoming
Community College
    Commission
307-777-7763
www.commission.wcc.edu

such a family will qualify for less aid at a private college than they might have a few years ago.

Sibling Assets

Another difference is that the institutional methodology now includes a sibling's assets, such as savings in a custodial account or a prepaid college-savings plan, among the parents' assets. The education-savings allowance discussed above is meant to offset that some-

> ### SEMESTER ABROAD
>
> **Q.** My daughter is planning to spend a semester abroad next year, which means extra expenses for us. Will that affect our financial-aid package?
>
> **A.** It should. The cost of airfare and any additional living costs should increase the total cost of college for financial-aid purposes. Subtracting your expected contribution from that increased cost should mean you're eligible for additional aid.

what, but if you have large sums set aside in younger siblings' names, that may boost your family contribution from assets.

Student Assets

Here, the institutional formulas are now more generous than the federal. While the feds expect students to contribute 35% of their assets each year, private colleges that use the institutional methodology ask students to contribute 25% of assets per year.

Contributions from Income

The institutional formulas are significantly more generous than the federal formulas in the amount that parents are expected to contribute from their income. Depending on your income, you might find that the institutional formula requires about $1,000 less in contribution.

Private School Tuitions for Younger Siblings

Some schools will ask about this and automatically adjust your contribution from income downward to account for it. Others won't ask up front, but will make an after-the-fact adjustment to your aid package if you bring it up in an appeal. Often there's a cap on the private-school expenses the financial-aid office will recognize. At Princeton University, for instance, the cap is rather generous—from $7,000 to $10,000.

"Prize" students definitely have leverage, especially at so-called second-tier schools.

Unusually High Medical Expenses

As with private-school tuition, sometimes you will be asked up front about medical expenses, and sometimes you will have to bring them to the attention of the aid officer. Be prepared to document your unreimbursed expenses.

Extraordinary Debt

This is unusual, but some schools will lower your contribution from income to account for high loan payments. "This is not simply for a run-up of credit cards," says Amherst's Case, "but for long-term debt because of a past business failure, a past period of unemployment, or a significant medical episode."

How It Would Work for the Jones Family

Continuing with the example that begins on page 126, let's say the school uses the institutional methodology and recalculates the Jones family's expected family contribution to $9,488, reducing their need to $20,512. After the $5,125 in federal and state aid, their need from the school's standpoint is $15,387 (the $30,000 total cost, minus $9,488 out of the Joneses' pocket and $5,125 in federal and state aid). In the best case, the school would meet the entire $15,387 with a grant or scholarship. Less desirable is a mixture of grant money and loan money, or a package that doesn't meet their full need.

Preferential Packaging

The generosity of the institutional portion of the aid package may depend on how desirable your child is to the school. Many schools practice "preferential" or "targeted" packaging, which means that students at the top of the class academically and students with special talents (say, in sports or music) will receive a better aid package than those students who were lucky to be admitted. "Prize" students definitely have leverage, especially at so-called second-tier schools that want to attract students who would otherwise go to, say, Princeton or Duke. One student might be offered an enhanced financial-aid package—based on merit or need—because the school needs a hockey goalie, a trombone player, or more engineering majors; because home is 2,000 miles from campus; or even because he replied to a mailing rather than initiating contact with the school. Another applicant with similar credentials and need might be offered less because she lives nearby or wants a popular major—or because the college wants to boost its ratio of men to women. Even top schools, like Yale, MIT, and Princeton, are sweetening offers to attract more middle-income families.

Colleges have even turned to sophisticated software programs to help focus resources on the most desirable students with the minimal outlay of institutional grants and scholarships. These software programs will zero in on just how much financial aid is enough to win you away from a competing school.

Here are some examples of preferential packaging:

One university awards merit scholarships to recruit students who will boost its academic profile and uses preferential packages to meet other goals for the class, such as regional diversity. One prospect might receive a package that meets need with 60% grants and 40% loans, while a more desirable applicant might get 80% grants and 20% loans.

At a second university, high-ranking students get a better ratio of grants to loans. One student with $10,000 in need might get a $6,000 grant and a $4,000 loan from the school. A higher-ranking student might get a $6,500 grant and a $3,500 loan.

At a third university, the first $6,100 of most aid packages for in-state students is composed of loans and student work. But for 200 exceptionally strong students, as determined by the faculty after an invitation-only interview, the school meets the family's entire need with a scholarship.

> Try applying to a few colleges far from home or where you are likely to stand out, either academically or in some other way.

How do you become one of these sought-after students? Try applying to a few colleges far from home or where you are likely to stand out, either academically or in some other way.

Ask the admissions or financial-aid officer to estimate the need- or merit-based aid your child might qualify for. If he or she is an obvious candidate for a preferential package, that may enter into the estimate, even if you're not told why. Finally, scatter applications to a wide variety of schools. You might harvest a fat scholarship or financial-aid package or be offered one that you can use as a bargaining chip at another school.

Mind the Gap

The other practice that affects the institutional side of the package is "gapping," which means the school doesn't meet 100% of your need but instead leaves a gap. Schools generally set a standard gap, and some guidebooks even publish a figure for the percentage of need met. Many schools, public and private, meet only 80% or 90% of your need—and leave you to your own devices to make up the difference. In effect, the gap increases your expected family contribution. Often, colleges will suggest a federal PLUS loan (which is taken out by parents and is made or guaranteed by the federal government) or another loan to help you make up the gap—and to fund any part of your expected contribution you can't pay from income or assets.

How a Less-Expensive School Can Cost You More

Because of gapping, you can wind up paying less to attend a $30,000 college than you'd pay to go to a $15,000 one. How so? Say your expected family contribution is $10,000. You need another $5,000 to attend the public university, which gives you a $2,625 Stafford loan and that's all. So you have to come up with the $10,000 contribution plus something to bridge the

$2,375 gap, a total of $12,375. At the $30,000 college, your expected contribution is maybe $11,000, but the school covers every nickel of the rest. Result: You pay $1,375 less to go to the more expensive school—with the same loans at both schools.

What the Jones Family Gets—Best Case

In a best-case scenario the school meets 100% of the Joneses' need with a scholarship, after accounting for other resources and the expected family contribution. The $30,000 gets paid as follows:

Total cost of college:	**$30,000**
Minus grant from the state ($1,000), work-study job ($1,500), and Stafford loan, which Jane will begin repaying after graduation ($2,625):	− $5,125
Minus expected family contribution:	− $9,488
Equals remaining need:	= $15,387
Minus scholarship from the college (100% of remaining need):	− $15,387
Equals gap:	= 0
Plus expected family contribution:	+ $9,488
Equals total cost from the family's resources:	= $9,488

What the Jones Family Gets—Worst Case

In a less-favorable scenario, the school meets only 80% of the Jones family's remaining need. The $30,000 gets paid as follows:

Total cost of college:	**$ 30,000**
Minus grant from the state ($1,000), work-study job ($1,500), and Stafford loan, which Jane will begin repaying after graduation ($2,625):	− $5,125
Minus expected family contribution:	− $9,488
Equals remaining need:	= $15,387
Minus scholarship from the college (80% of remaining need):	− $12,310
Equals gap:	= $3,077
Plus expected family contribution:	+ $9,488
Equals total cost from the family's resources:	= $12,565

Many schools, public and private, meet only 80% or 90% of your need—and leave you to your own devices to make up the difference.

Except at superelite colleges, discounts from the sticker price—in the form of merit scholarships and other nonneed-based awards—are widespread.

Aid That Isn't—and How to Recognize It

Of course, if the Joneses are typical, they'll wind up borrowing a good portion of that $9,488 or $12,565. And there are a number of sources for parent loans, which are discussed in Chapter 9. But any school that claims to meet your "need" with an unsubsidized Stafford loan, a PLUS loan, or other parent loan is playing games. Those loans aren't financial aid— they're ways to help you meet your family contribution, and you or your student will pay the full cost. If this is what you're offered, you might confront the school, but don't hold your breath; it simply may not have any more money to give. You'll have to determine how much your child wants to go there and whether you're willing to spend the extra money.

No Need-Based Aid? Target a "Discount"

Need-based financial aid can seem like a cruel joke to families in the netherworld between being needy enough to get a hefty aid package and wealthy enough not to care. Though it might be clear to you that you need help, what really matters is how you fare under the federal and college financial-aid formulas. If your expected family contribution based on the formulas comes close to or exceeds total costs at the school, you'll receive no aid—or perhaps just a loan.

There is another route. Except at superelite colleges, discounts from the sticker price—in the form of merit scholarships and other nonneed-based awards— are widespread. According to the College Board, more than 50% of undergraduates were receiving some form of institutional grant that reduced college tuition. Many of those grants were nonneed awards targeting students who might not otherwise enroll.

Those students are not all superstars, and your child doesn't have to be, either. At some schools, students in the top half of the entering class academically receive nonneed scholarships. Most colleges also ante up for good musicians, thespians, writers, athletes, and others with special accomplishments.

As you would expect, merit discounts don't exist at colleges so flooded with applicants that they can afford to turn away straight-A students who score 1400 on their SAT exams (see the box on the following page). If your child gets into one of those prestigious schools, you might decide that a $170,000 diploma is worth every gold brick. But you and your child might decide that two-thirds that amount—or less—also buys a fine education. Applying to a few lesser-known schools may at least give you a choice.

The Physics of Discounting

A 4.0 grade point average and a score of 31 on the ACT college-entrance exam was enough to get one young woman into the highly selective University of Notre Dame. But at the South Bend, Indiana, school, even stellar students pay full freight—$41,970 for tuition and room and board in 2005–2006—unless they show financial need. "That would have been kind of expensive," says the student, who chose Rhodes College, in Memphis, over the home of the Fighting Irish. Even though the standards for admission—and the costs—are nearly as high at Rhodes, her credentials earned the business and computer-science major an $8,600 scholarship, renewable for four years. Because she would not have qualified for need-based aid, the award saved her family $34,400.

Balancing Merit and Need

What if you have both merit and need? Usually the college selects students for nonneed awards before considering them for need-based aid. So some or all of an award could preempt a need-based grant the student would otherwise receive. But many schools use a merit award to replace "self-help" aid—loans and work-study jobs—with money the student doesn't have to earn or repay. And if a student has need that exceeds the amount of a merit award, he or she will receive

Merit discounts don't exist at colleges so flooded with applicants that they can afford to turn away straight-A students who score 1400 on their SAT exams.

financial aid to fill the gap—occasionally an enhanced aid package.

If You Can't Negotiate, Appeal

The aid package you receive on paper still may not be the final word. You may be able to do some old-fashioned bargaining. Most colleges don't broadcast the fact that they will sweeten financial-aid packages for students they want. In some cases, experts say, marketing a four-year college education resembles marketing airline tickets: Schools charge full price to those students who can afford to pay, then offer discounted "fares" to everyone else to fill their

---

WE DON'T DISCOUNT (WE DON'T HAVE TO)

These colleges have enough students who are willing to pay in full for annual tuition, fees, and room and board that they don't have to offer merit scholarships, which rep-

resent an off-the-top discount from sticker price. (The annual costs given here include tuition, room and board, fees, and books for the 2004–2005 school year.)

	Annual cost		Annual cost
Amherst College (Mass.)	$42,729	Middlebury College (Vt.)	$40,400
Barnard College (N.Y.)	39,257	Mount Holyoke College (Mass.)	41,998
Bates College (Me.)	41,950	Pomona College (Cal.)	39,750
Bowdoin College (Me.)	39,780	Princeton University (N.J.)	41,380
Brown University (R.I.)	42,303	Reed College (Ore.)	39,920
Bryn Mawr College (Pa.)	40,330	St. John's College (Md.)	38,660
Bucknell University (Pa.)	38,000	Sarah Lawrence College (N.Y.)	41,818
Colgate University (N.Y.)	40,820	Thomas Aquinas College (Cal.)	24,850
Columbia University (N.Y.)	41,538	Union College (N.Y.)	40,200
Connecticut College	40,775	University of Pennsylvania	40,464
Cornell University (N.Y.)	40,760	Vassar College (N.Y.)	40,730
Dartmouth College (N.H.)	41,000	Wellesley College (Mass.)	39,800
Harvard University (Mass.)	42,450	Wesleyan University (Conn.)	40,124
Haverford College (Pa.)	42,232	Williams College (Mass.)	38,900
MIT (Mass.)	42,700	Yale University (Conn.)	41,379

classrooms. The discounts appear as extra financial aid from the school.

Many schools—including the California Institute of Technology, Harvard, and Johns Hopkins—flatly deny that they negotiate financial-aid packages. Others justify increased awards by saying that they underestimated a family's financial need. Whatever the reason, the fact remains that schools are increasingly willing to beef up their offers.

Bargaining Chips

When you receive a financial-aid offer, don't assume that the numbers are written in stone. Some colleges have gone so far as to tell students in their acceptance letters that the school will be more than happy to compare financial-aid awards, and will make up the difference so that their award will be as high as a competing school's.

Of course, if you're going to bargain, it helps to have a few chips. If your child is an A student, class president, and a tennis star or violin virtuoso, she will probably have her pick of schools and a leg up in negotiating an aid package. Likewise, you'll be in a stronger position if you have a competing offer from a school with a comparable academic reputation.

But your child doesn't have to be a potential superstar for you to successfully negotiate a better financial-aid offer. Part of the art of bargaining is making your child attractive to a school. That may mean choosing a good school that's shy of Ivy League status, where your student has a better chance of standing out.

One young man was accepted both to Dartmouth College, in New Hampshire, and to St. Lawrence University, in New York. Both schools received the same financial-aid forms from the student, but St. Lawrence offered him $7,000 more in assistance. Dartmouth would have been happy to have him, but he didn't stand out among its applicants. St. Lawrence really wanted him. And that's where he decided to go.

Many schools are actively recruiting good students. Here are just a few examples:

Most colleges don't broadcast the fact that they will sweeten financial-aid packages for students they want.

Albertus Magnus College, in New Haven, Connecticut, gives a four-year full-tuition scholarship to all students who were a high-school valedictorian or salutatorian.

Lebanon Valley College, in Pennsylvania, offers a 50% discount on its $22,920 tuition to any student who graduates in the top 10% of his or her class.

WHAT COLLEGES WILL REALLY COST

Once you've received financial-aid offers from the schools you're considering, use this worksheet to compare costs after taking financial aid into account. Your real cost is line 11, the cost after financial aid you don't have to repay (grants, scholarships, and work-study). But a low-cost loan—especially a subsidized Stafford loan on which the government pays the interest during the college years—also eases the burden. The amount on line 13 allows you to compare what you have to come up with out of pocket for a year to afford each of the colleges.

	School A	School B	School C	School D
COSTS				
1. Tuition	_____	_____	_____	_____
2. Room and board	_____	_____	_____	_____
3. Books	_____	_____	_____	_____
4. Transportation	_____	_____	_____	_____
5. Personal expenses	_____	_____	_____	_____
6. Total cost (add lines 1 through 5)	_____	_____	_____	_____
FINANCIAL AID				
7. Grants	_____	_____	_____	_____
8. Scholarships	_____	_____	_____	_____
9. Work-study job	_____	_____	_____	_____
10. Total direct aid (add lines 7, 8, and 9)	_____	_____	_____	_____
11. Your cost after direct aid (line 6 minus line 10)	_____	_____	_____	_____
12. Loans	_____	_____	_____	_____
13. Your cost after direct aid and loans (line 11 minus line 12)	_____	_____	_____	_____

Washington College, in Chestertown, Maryland, offers automatic scholarship awards of up to $40,000 over four years to students who were members of their high school's National Honor Society. (More than 50% of the college's student body qualifies.)

The Art of the Deal

Don't begin your negotiations by barging into a financial-aid office with both guns blazing, demanding more aid because you can't pay for your only child's education on a salary of $100,000 a year. You're more likely to get better results by adopting a diplomatic approach, such as one of the following two strategies:

CAN YOU TOP THIS? Ask financial-aid officers whether they'll match another school's offer and most will tell you "no." Ask financial planners who specialize in college aid and most will tell you about clients who have succeeded with this strategy. One planner's client, whose first-choice school was Carnegie Mellon, received an aid offer from Cornell that was $2,500 richer. The father explained to a Carnegie Mellon financial-aid officer that the better aid package might tip the decision to Cornell. Carnegie Mellon reviewed its offer and improved it by $2,500. Another client persuaded Brandeis to add $4,000 to a financial-aid package to match one offered by Amherst.

This kind of negotiating works best when the two schools are almost equally matched in reputation and admission standards. You're not going to get a top university to match an aid offer from a lesser-rated one.

You also have more pull when your child is high in the applicant pool or has a special talent that makes him or her attractive to the school. (Compare your child's SAT score and class rank with the average of students attending the school you're looking at, figures that are available from the school or a guidebook.)

If you're going to try the "top this" route, you should negotiate before you've accepted an offer of admission—you have little leverage once you've committed to a school.

> Asking one school to match another's aid package works best when the two schools are almost equally matched in reputation and admission standards.

Even those aid officers who say that they won't play "let's make a deal" do say they'll reconsider an aid package if the family believes something has been overlooked.

If the idea of negotiating with a school causes you discomfort or appears a little unseemly, take heart. It's common for students to let one school know what the other has offered. It's not blackmail or muscling. The student is just looking for the best opportunity.

WILL YOU RECONSIDER? Even those aid officers who say emphatically that they won't play "let's make a deal" do say they'll reconsider an aid package if the family believes something has been overlooked. While the methodology for calculating federal aid tends to be cut-and-dried, financial-aid officers have a lot more leeway in doling out money and other assistance that comes directly from the school. An appeal is your chance to bring to the aid officer's attention any unusual circumstances that affect your ability to pay the college bills. Are you paying nursing-home expenses for an elderly relative, graduate-school tuition for an older child, or debts from uninsured medical expenses? Those costs might be used to reduce your available income. Will it cost your child more than other students to attend a particular school because you live far away, need special equipment, or have to accommodate a disability? Those are persuasive reasons for a school to increase the student's budgeted cost of attendance. Some other examples include:

Medical expenses and private-school expenses. Until a few years ago, the federal formulas reduced your contribution if you had high medical bills or if you sent younger children to private elementary or secondary schools. Some colleges, on their own forms, ask about these two expenses and take them into account automatically. But others adjust your contribution for them only if you bring them up on appeal, so don't neglect to ask.

Graduate school for another child. The federal formulas don't consider a graduate student a dependent, and therefore don't make adjustments for graduate school bills you're paying for another child. But you may be

TAXABLE OR TAX-FREE

Q. Are scholarships and fellowships taxable?

A. First, the good news: For students who are taking courses toward a degree, the value of grants for tuition and course-related expenses for books, supplies, and equipment is tax-free. Now, the bad news: Any part of a grant that goes for room, board, or incidental expenses is taxable income for the student. And nondegree students (those who are taking courses but aren't pursuing a degree) are taxed on the full value of any scholarship, including the amount that covers tuition.

Also taxable are amounts received for teaching, research, or other services, whether the student is paid in cash or via a tuition-reduction program. If tuition is discounted in exchange for a graduate student's work as a teaching assistant, for example, the amount that's shaved off tuition counts as taxable income.

able to persuade an aid officer to take them into account, and perhaps even to split your parent contribution between the two children.

An unusually high-income year. Maybe you received an unusually large bonus last year, sold some stock and reinvested the proceeds, or had to declare large capital-gains distributions from your mutual funds on your tax return, even though you didn't sell any shares. (This could have happened, for example, during the soaring stock market of the mid-1990s, when many funds made large capital-gains distributions that wound up boosting the adjusted gross income of many taxpayers. That, in turn, would have boosted the contribution from income for a parent applying for financial aid.)

You won't be able to do anything about the higher "official" expected family contribution that will result from the extra income. But once you start receiving aid offers from colleges, take the opportunity to explain that this year—and typically—your income is lower,

Financial-aid officers are generally prepared to make adjustments for hardship circumstances.

and be prepared to prove it with your past years' tax returns.

Depending on the circumstances, some aid officers might lower your expected contribution. And even if it's not lowered, you may put yourself in a better position to qualify for aid next year. That's because some—but not all—schools give out all the "continuing" aid money first and then meet the need of "new" upperclassmen. If the aid officer is aware ahead of time that you'll need money next year, you won't automatically be placed at the back of the line with the new applicants.

High levels of debt. Not all aid officers will be sympathetic, but if large debt payments take a big bite out of your income, let the financial-aid office know in an appeal. Particularly if the debt is the result of a recent period of financial hardship, an aid officer might see fit to adjust your family contribution. Be prepared to document your case, perhaps with tax returns showing a reduced level of income if you've been laid off, with medical bills if that's the source of the debt, or with documentation of the loan.

A financial downturn. Several months may elapse between the time you complete the aid forms and the time you receive an aid offer from the college. You shouldn't be too proud to ask for a break if:

- **you're laid off in the meantime,**
- **your business takes an ugly turn,**
- **you suddenly face a long illness,**
- **there's a death in the family that affects your finances,**
- **there's any other bad news.**

Financial-aid officers are generally prepared to make adjustments for hardship circumstances. What breaks through is evidence of genuine need, not a parent with a beat-the-system or let's-make-a-deal attitude. Financial-aid officers are put off when families that don't really need the help manipulate the system to get it, which leaves less money for the families that are truly in need.

EXTENDING DEADLINES FOR RESPONSE

Q. We got an attractive aid offer from my son's second-choice college, which wants a $500 deposit within ten days. But we haven't yet heard from his first-choice school. What should we do?

A. Write back and ask the school to extend the admissions deadline but go ahead and accept the aid package. Most schools will extend the deadline to May 1, by which time most schools have notified students of their aid awards. This is routine—you won't lose your aid package by delaying the admissions decision to May 1. The deposit is to hold the student's place in the class, and the extension accomplishes the same thing. If the answer is no, then $500 is the price of keeping your options open. You'll have to decide whether you're willing to forfeit the deposit if the first choice comes through with an acceptable aid package.

Back Up Your Appeal

In addition to a good argument, you also need good documentation. Aid officers have a lot of discretion, but they also have to justify their decisions to federal auditors. You want to have written documentation they can put in their files, so they don't have to write up a justification You have to make it easy for them to say yes.

Bear in mind, too, that by asking for a review of your aid package, you're asking for additional scrutiny. One financial-aid director says he will look more closely at the finances of a family that has asked for special consideration. At that point, for instance, he'd ask how much equity the parents have in their home, even though he doesn't consider that resource otherwise. Also, be aware that you may not get a lot of sympathy if a closer examination of your finances reveals that you've aggressively shifted income or assets to qualify for more aid (see Chapter 6).

Increasing Your Eligibility for Aid

Armed with an understanding of the financial-aid process, you can take steps to boost your eligibility for aid. In some circles this is controversial stuff. There are those who argue that arranging their finances to maximize their eligibility for aid is akin to tax planning, where it's perfectly acceptable to take advantage of legal maneuvers that reduce your tax. Others argue that parents who file their forms with an eye on boosting their eligibility for aid are cheating less savvy—and possibly needier—families out of limited aid dollars. One school's financial-aid director put it this way: "Manipulating the need-analysis system may be legal, but it's of questionable ethics. The fact that some people have found ways to disguise their ability to pay drains resources from others."

We don't advocate cheating or turning your finances inside out to look "needy" on the financial-aid forms. But consider this example: When you include a younger child's investment income on your tax return, it boosts your adjusted gross income, which in turn increases your expected contribution from income for your prospective college student. But if you file a separate tax return for the younger child, the income is excluded from your AGI for financial-aid purposes. Why shoot yourself in the foot by including it on your return?

Another caution: Don't put the financial-aid cart before the smart-money-management horse. Locking up every spare cent in an annuity you can't touch until

Parents' income usually has the largest impact on the family's expected contribution.

you're age 59½ to exclude that money from your assets for aid purposes, for instance, doesn't make sense if it will leave you cash-poor and force you to borrow more than necessary to pay the tuition bills. As you peruse the following discussion of aid-boosting strategies, consider only those moves that are also beneficial to you financially or, at worst, are financially neutral.

Accelerate or Defer Income

As the calculations in Chapter 4 show, parents' income usually has the largest impact on the family's expected contribution. Any income you can accelerate into the year before the first financial-aid year (the calendar year spanning the junior and senior years of high school) or defer until after the last financial-aid year (the calendar year spanning the sophomore and junior years of college) will reduce your expected contribution at least in the first and last years of college. If you're an employee, you probably don't have much control over when you receive your salary or even a bonus. (It can't hurt to ask if a January bonus could be paid the last day of December or vice versa, but you may find that the company wants to time the bonus to minimize its own taxes.) But there are several other income-shifting opportunities, especially for investors and self-employed people.

Stocks and Mutual Funds

If you are planning to use the proceeds from mutual funds or stocks to pay the college bills, consider selling all the shares you plan to use for college expenses before January of your child's junior year in high school, especially if the sale will produce a large profit, which is likely if you've held the shares for many years. That maneuver will keep the gain out of your income for all of the financial-aid years. And it won't boost your assets because you're simply shifting the money from an investment asset to cash, both of which are included in financial-aid calculations. Selling the shares is normally a wise investment move as well, since money you need in the short term for tuition and other college-related expenses should be protected from the fluctuations of the stock market. For more on this, see Chapter 3.

If you must take investment gains, take a good look at your portfolio to see whether there are investment losses you can take to offset those gains. (If you sold a stock with a $2,000 loss, for instance, you'd wipe out $2,000 in gains on a stock you sold at a profit.) You can offset all your gains, plus up to $3,000 of ordinary income, such as wages, with investment losses. Don't sell just for tax reasons, but if you have a loser you've lost faith in, why not pull the plug now, when it will save you taxes and possibly gain you more financial aid?

Savings Bonds

The same logic holds for U.S. savings bonds you or your child has held for many years. Unless you elected otherwise when you bought the bonds, all the interest will be paid to you on redemption, which will boost

---

A CHILD'S INCOME

Q. My daughter, a high school senior, works part-time during the school year and full-time during the summer. Should she cut back on her hours to qualify for more financial aid?

A. Under the federal aid formulas, students get a $2,440 income-protection allowance, which means that the first $2,440 they earn doesn't affect how much financial aid you will receive. After that, under the federal need analysis, your daughter will be expected to contribute 50% of her income to college costs.

That doesn't mean that she should stop working once she hits the $2440 mark. For one thing, some colleges, when awarding their own, institutional money (as opposed to federal funds), will expect her to contribute a minimum of around $1,000 to $2,000 from a summer job, even if she earned less.

The most important thing is that she save some of her earnings to go toward college bills instead of spending it all on clothes she doesn't need or movies. Otherwise, not only does her income increase your family contribution, but the extra money winds up coming out of your pocket.

To the extent that it's practical, take full advantage of any set-aside accounts available to you.

the income you report on your tax return and thus the financial-aid forms. Cash the bonds in early or hold them until after the financial-aid years, so the lump-sum interest payment won't boost your contribution from income. (See page 57 in Chapter 3 for details on cashing in savings bonds.)

Don't redeem your bonds early if you qualify to receive the interest tax-free to pay college bills. Generally, the interest is tax-free if your income is $91,850 or less on a joint return, or $61,200 or less on a single return. (See page 55 for the complete requirements.) In that case, you'd want to wait until the year your child is actually in college to cash in the bonds, because to receive the interest tax-free, you must have tuition bills in the same calendar year in which you redeem the bonds.

Business Income and Expenses

If you're self-employed, you probably have much more control than an employee over when you receive income. In the year before the first financial-aid year, for instance, think about ways to accelerate income you might otherwise receive during the first financial-aid year:

- **Can you bill customers a little earlier** to pull some income into the earlier year?
- **Can you schedule a project to end** in November or December, instead of January?
- **Can you offer customers a small discount** to stock up on supplies late in the year?

Take Advantage of Set-aside Accounts

Many employers allow their employees to contribute to so-called "flexible spending" or "set-aside" accounts that allow you to use before-tax income to pay for medical and dependent-care expenses. For financial-aid applicants, these accounts have a double benefit. Not only do you avoid paying tax on the earnings you allocate to a set-aside account, but because the income never finds its way to your tax return, it also doesn't count toward your contribution from income on the Free Application for Federal Student Aid (FAFSA).

YOUR RETIREMENT ACCOUNTS

Q. How do the financial-aid formulas treat contributions to retirement accounts?

A. Remember that while contributing to retirement accounts, such as a SEP–IRA, Keogh, or 401(k) plan (and for most people, an IRA), reduces your adjusted gross income for tax purposes, it does not reduce your income for financial-aid purposes. The federal aid formulas don't count as an asset funds you've accumulated in retirement accounts in prior years, but they do add back to your income any retirement-plan contributions made in the financial-aid years. The reasoning, whether you agree or not, is that during the college years, income you don't need for everyday living expenses should go toward college bills, not retirement.

To the extent that it's practical, take full advantage of any set-aside accounts available to you. In other words, if you have dependent-care or medical expenses and can use these accounts to cover your expenses, fund them to the full amount of the expenses you expect to incur (or to the maximum allowed—typically $5,000—if your expenses will be higher). That saves you money even if it doesn't help you qualify for more financial aid. But be careful not to overfund a set-aside account: In some types of accounts, you forfeit any money left in the account at the end of the year.

Unfortunately, PROFILE forms, used by many private colleges when giving out their own aid, take these accounts into consideration.

Postpone IRA Distributions

If you're over age 59½ while your child is in college, you can tap your IRA or other retirement accounts without incurring the 10% early-withdrawal penalty to pay college bills. That's not a bad way to meet the bills, but bear in mind that the distributions add to your adjusted gross income. (If you took a tax deduction for the original contribution, the entire distribution is included as

If you're self-employed, consider putting your children on the payroll.

income and is taxed. If you made nondeductible contributions, only the portion that represents earnings on your original contribution counts as income.) If you have other assets you can tap, such as investments in nonretirement accounts, consider using those resources first so you don't boost your income unnecessarily in a financial-aid year.

Hire Your Kids in the Family Business

If you're self-employed, either full-time or part-time, consider putting your children on the payroll if there's work they can do for you in the evenings and on weekends during the school year or summer. The move brings you several tax and financial-aid advantages. First and most important, any wages you pay your child are a deductible business expense to you. That reduces your income, saving you taxes and possibly gaining you extra financial aid. In addition, assuming you operate your business as a sole proprietorship rather than a corporation and your child is under age 18, your child is not subject to the 7.65% social security tax on the earnings.

To deduct the wages as a business expense, they must be reasonable and for real work your child performs for your business. Claiming a deduction for paying your 8-year-old $100 an hour to clean your office on Saturday mornings would be asking for IRS scrutiny. But it's legitimate to pay a reasonable wage for performing such necessary services as:

■ **cleaning,**
■ **taking phone messages,**
■ **filing documents,**
■ **making deliveries, or**
■ **acting as your resident computer whiz.**

To protect the deduction, keep careful records of the work done, the hours worked, and the hourly wage paid, and pay with a check drawn on your business account. At the end of the year, you will need to file a form W-2 to report your child's earnings to the IRS.

Won't the earnings increase your college student's contribution from income? Yes, but assuming your child would work anyway, you may as well take advantage of the opportunity to deduct the wages from your income. And remember that wages you pay a younger sibling reduce your income, too.

Purchase Business Equipment You Need

If you own your own business and need to buy business equipment, a computer, or office furniture, can you postpone the expense until the first financial-aid year, which would reduce your business income for that year? You can take up to $100,000 (in 2005, 2006, and 2007) as a deduction in the year you buy the equipment, instead of depreciating it over several years. By "expensing," you'll not only reduce your income for financial-aid purposes but you'll also enjoy the total tax benefit now instead of spreading it out over time.

Pay Your Taxes Early

If you expect to owe the IRS money with your tax return in April, normally you'd want to wait until the last minute to pay—to earn interest on that money as long as you can. But the reverse may make sense for financial-aid purposes. Sending in your return with a check before you send off your financial-aid form will reduce the balance in your checking or savings account, which you report on the financial-aid form.

Avoid Big State and Local Tax Refunds

Some people treat their income taxes as a form of forced saving—they allow a little too much to be withheld from each paycheck and look forward to big refunds from Uncle Sam and their state treasury each spring. Applicants for financial aid should break that habit. Withholding too much and getting a refund is basically a wash from a tax standpoint (except that you give up the opportunity to earn a bit of interest by letting the government hold your money for you). But if you must report last year's state or local income-

You could postpone the purchase of business equipment until the first financial-aid year, which would reduce your business income for that year.

tax refund as income on this year's federal tax return, it can make a difference in your eligibility for financial aid. (You never have to report your federal refund as income.)

Say you receive a refund check from your state in 2006, reimbursing you for having too much withheld from your paychecks in 2005. If you itemized deductions on your 2005 return—and therefore took a tax deduction for the state taxes you paid, including the overpayment—you'll have to report part or all of the refund you receive in 2006 as income on your 2006 return. How much you report depends on the extent to which you got a tax benefit for it in the previous year:

- **If your itemized deductions** minus the standard deduction for your filing status ($10,000 for married couples filing jointly; $5,000 for singles) exceeds the amount of the refund, you must report all of it.
- **If your deductions** minus the standard deduction is less than your refund, you report only the difference between your itemized deductions and the standard deduction.

Either way, you'll have increased your all-important contribution from income.

If you got a fat refund from your state last spring, chances are you're well on your way to another big check next year. To get off the pay-too-much-and-get-a-refund carousel, file a revised W-4 form with your employer. You can get the form and instructions for filling it out from your payroll office, or from the IRS at 800-829-3676 or www.irs.gov.

If You Can't Reasonably Avoid Out-of-the-Ordinary Income

You certainly wouldn't want to turn down a big bonus from your employer just because it falls during a financial-aid year. Or suppose the future doesn't look so rosy for a stock you've held through many good years: It wouldn't be wise to keep the shares just to avoid a big capital gain. But are there ways to minimize the impact of that one-time income boost on your financial-aid package? Sometimes, yes.

You'll have to include the income on your financial-aid forms, of course, and the resulting expected family contribution figure will be higher than it would have been otherwise. But don't pass up the chance to explain to the financial-aid officer that last year's income was not typical, and that you don't expect to have the same income next year—or in future years. As proof, you might even send or bring copies of prior years' income-tax returns.

Some aid officers will only reassure you that, based on a lower income, next year's aid package will be more generous. But others will consider an adjustment for the extra income in the current financial-aid year. A financial-aid officer's response can run a continuum all the way from not taking the extra income out at all to removing it entirely, depending on the circumstances. If, for instance, gains from the sale of stock were used to make a down payment on vacation property, it would be more likely to be included in your assets than if the money went to pay for something like medical expenses not covered by insurance. (For more about negotiating with financial-aid officers, see Chapter 5).

Explain that last year's income was not typical, and that you don't expect to have the same income next year— or in future years.

Should You Shift Assets?

We've already mentioned that the federal aid formulas exclude your home (or family farm) equity and the money you've accumulated in tax-deferred retirement accounts. Also protected in the calculations is any cash value you have built up in a life insurance policy. (Standard whole life, universal life, and variable life are all forms of cash-value insurance.) Money you hold inside a fixed annuity or variable annuity is excluded, too. So should you shift money into retirement accounts, annuities, or insurance to qualify for more aid? You should certainly take advantage of those vehicles if they make sense for your retirement savings or insurance needs—and enjoy

It almost never makes sense to put more money into protected investments than you would otherwise, simply to qualify for more aid.

the fact that those assets are protected. But it almost never makes sense to put more money into those protected investments than you would otherwise, simply to qualify for more aid.

The reasons are threefold.

It's Hardly Worth It

First, notice in the Jones example (Chapter 4, pages 110–111) how little of the family contribution comes from assets even after home equity is taken into account. Because of the federal financial-aid formula's asset-protection allowance, and on top of that the relatively low levy of up to 5.6% on assets that exceed the allowance, most families wind up being asked to put only a very small portion of their assets toward the expected family contribution. Only when assets reach into six figures do they have much impact at all on the expected family contribution, and then it's still relatively modest (see pages 116–117 for an example of this). For most families, asset-shifting strategies have a very humble payoff—if any.

You'll Lose Penalty-free Access to Your Funds

Second, when you put money into tax-deferred investments like retirement accounts or annuities, you generally can't touch the money before age 59½ without paying a penalty. Unless you'll reach that age while your child is in college, investing more than you would otherwise in such accounts could leave you retirement-account rich but with no cash to help with the family contribution—or other family needs. (Even though the formulas derive much of the contribution from income, most parents find themselves using assets or loans to actually pay the bills.) Put money into an annuity or other tax-deferred account only if you're confident you won't need it until age 59½.

You'll Pay to Borrow Your Own Money

What about life insurance? If you've had a cash-value life policy for many years, it has probably accumulated some equity and is a resource you can borrow against if necessary. But dumping extra money into the policy to shelter it from financial aid could, once again, leave you without the cash you need to pay college bills or meet other family needs. Yes, you can borrow the money back to pay college costs, but why pay interest to the insurance company to tap that money—especially when the financial-aid benefit is likely to be so small? And buying a new policy solely to shelter assets makes no sense because first-year commissions are usually very high, and it can take as long as ten years to build up significant cash value.

The bottom line on asset shifting: Make such moves only if they make financial sense regardless of whether you'll get more aid.

How About Reducing Assets?

Sometimes it can make sense to reduce assets, especially your child's assets, which are assessed much more heavily in the financial-aid formulas.

Spring for Big-Ticket Purchases

Spending down some of your savings for a big-ticket item, such as a computer or a car, before you sign and date your financial-aid application can make sense assuming it's a purchase you were going to make anyway. But don't get carried away because, as with asset shifting, the impact probably won't be very large. Besides, if your child has some savings tucked away and the purchase is for him or her (such as a computer or a car to take to college), you're better off spending down your child's savings, which are assessed more heavily in the financial-aid formulas.

What to Do with Kids' Assets

Money held in a child's name, whether in a bank or investment account, savings bond or trust, is depleted by 35% a year under the federal aid formulas (25% per year under the institutional aid formulas). So if a student has $10,000 as a high school senior, he or she

> Sometimes it can make sense to reduce assets, especially your child's assets, which are assessed much more heavily in the financial-aid formulas.

will be expected to use $3,500 toward the freshman-year bills; $2,275 (35% of the remaining $6,500) toward the sophomore-year bills; $1,479 toward the junior-year bills; and $961 toward the senior-year bills—leaving $1,785 from the original $10,000. (This assumes for simplicity's sake that the $10,000 does not continue to grow.)

PROVE IT

Don't be tempted to "forget" about an asset when you're filling out the aid forms. Most schools randomly validate a certain percentage of their financial-aid applications, asking you to supply tax returns and other back-up documentation. (And some schools ask for 1040s from every family, as a matter of course.) If your 1040 shows interest or dividends, for instance, financial-aid officers know to look for corresponding assets. You'll be asked to explain discrepancies.

If your aid application is selected for verification, you may also be asked for other documentation, such as proof of marriage, birth certificates, divorce records, or proof that a sibling is enrolled at another college.

When the same $10,000 is held in the parents' name, it is reduced by no more than 5.6% a year (5% under the institutional formulas). In the worst case (which assumes the $10,000 is not sheltered by the allowance that excludes assets ranging up to $75,100 from the aid formulas), the parents would be expected to tap $2,059 of that $10,000 over the four college years, leaving $7,941.

So, if you consider all the money to be coming from one family pot, it's far better for financial-aid purposes to have the money in your name than in your child's. If you expect to qualify for aid, you should certainly put any additional college savings in your own name.

But what about money that's already been saved in the child's name? You can't simply take it back. Money that's placed in a custodial account for a child is an irrevocable gift and it legally belongs to the child. Once the child reaches a certain age (usually 18 or 21), adult supervision ends and the child may do anything he or she wants with the money. In the meantime, however, the custodian of the account (often the parent) may use the money to pay for things that are exclusively for the child's benefit. The mortgage payment or heating bill doesn't count. But things like tuition at a private high school or fees for summer camp do. So would a computer or car your child would take to college. In the years leading up to the financial-aid years, it may make sense to look for opportunities to spend down the child's savings on expenses you would incur anyway for him or her.

There's no custodial-account police force that's going to monitor your expenditures. But raiding a child's custodial account is the kind of thing that occasionally leads to intrafamily legal disputes later on—for example, if the child believes his or her money was ill-spent. It doesn't happen often, but it happens. If you're cautious, you'll document that you're spending the money for the child's benefit.

And, of course, during the college years the money can be spent on the college bills. Using all the student's savings toward tuition and other expenses in the freshman year will in most cases increase the family's eligibility for aid in the subsequent years. But not always. A few schools have gotten hard-nosed about this and now factor the student's assets into the financial-aid equation as though they're drawn down over the four years—even if the money is actually spent in the first year.

> Giving your parents a "gift" of money is the kind of asset-hiding that sends financial-aid officers into orbit—and probably does step over the ethical line.

What About Giving Money to Your Parents?

Yes, it's legal. You can give any individual up to $11,000 a year without having to worry about gift-tax consequences. So, for example, you and your spouse could give each of your parents as much as $22,000 a year on the presumption that they will later help pay the college bills with the money or hold it for you until after the financial-aid years. But that's the kind of asset-hiding that sends financial-aid officers into orbit—and probably does step over the ethical line. Plus, there's a practical caveat to this strategy: The money is a gift, and there's no guarantee the recipient will spend it or keep it as you intend.

But there's nothing wrong with reversing this strategy: If your parents want to help with the college bills, thank your lucky stars—then ask them if they'd mind keeping the "college money" they'd otherwise give to

At schools that include home equity in the financial-aid calculations (most public colleges don't), home-equity debt will reduce that asset.

your kids over the years in an account in their own name. When financial-aid eligibility is no longer an issue, they can hand the money over then to help pay the last year's bills or help pay off student and parent debt. (While it's not likely anyone would know if they gave you the money during the college years, the FAFSA and PROFILE do ask you to disclose contributions of family members to college costs, and such a disclosure would reduce your aid eligibility.)

If your parents don't agree—they may not want to pay the taxes on the interest or dividends that money produces over the years, for instance—the next best idea is probably for them to give the money to you, rather than to your kids, because your assets are assessed much more gently than your kids' in the need analysis.

Most Debt Doesn't Count

You may already have noticed that the financial-aid worksheet asks very little about your debt. That's because most debt has no impact on your eligibility for aid. Generally speaking, a family with a $50,000 income, a $900 mortgage payment, and a $300 car-loan payment each month will make the same contribution from income as a family that has no mortgage and no car loan. And, under the federal methodology, the car loan doesn't reduce your assets, either. Credit card debt also has no bearing on aid.

There are exceptions:

Home-Equity Debt

At schools that include home equity in the financial-aid calculations (most public colleges don't), home-equity debt will reduce that asset. And since it's most families' largest asset, the numbers can be large enough to have a significant impact. In the case discussed in the following section, adding $130,000 of free-and-clear home equity to the Lassiter family's assets added about $7,300 to their expected family contribution. Were they to borrow $20,000 on a home-equity line of credit to buy a car, that would reduce their contribution from assets by around $1,000.

A Margin Loan

Another form of debt that will reduce your assets is a margin-account loan secured by your investments. That's because the federal aid formulas subtract investment debt from the value of your investments. For that reason, it may make sense to use a margin loan for a big-ticket purchase—or to pay the college bills, which would reduce your assets in subsequent financial-aid years.

Margin loans make sense when:

- **You have significant investment assets against which to borrow.** As discussed in Chapter 9, you generally want to keep your borrowing in a margin account to no more than 25% of the value of your investments. That protects you from a "margin call" if your investments drop in value.
- **You need to borrow anyway.** In that case, why not choose a loan that reduces your assets rather than one that doesn't? Another plus: Because margin loans are secured by your investments, the rate you pay is relatively low—around 8.5%.

Get Rid of It

Another way to make debt count, so to speak, is to use savings or investments to pay it off, thereby decreasing your assets and your expected family contribution. That's not a bad idea, anyway, especially if that debt is on a high-interest-rate credit card. You'll save the interest and eliminate a payment from your monthly burdens.

Can You Save Too Much?

Is there such a thing as saving too much for college? Mary Ann and Bob Lassiter, supersavers by anyone's standard, wondered.

The Lassiters, both in their 40s, have always been savers. Their first goal was to pay off the $40,000 mortgage on their home in Sandwich, Massachusetts,

> **Another way to make debt count, so to speak, is to use savings or investments to pay it off, thereby decreasing your assets.**

Even though income weighs far more heavily than assets in determining eligibility for aid, assets in the six figures do trigger a higher expected family contribution.

which they accomplished in six years. Then they began redirecting the $350 mortgage payment into mutual funds, and added even more whenever Bob's video-production business had a flush month. The result: a $170,000 nest egg, about half-sheltered inside Bob's SEP–IRA (a retirement account for self-employed taxpayers), ordinary IRAs, and Mary Ann's 401(k) tax-deferred retirement plan.

Their prodigious saving gives them "a great sense of accomplishment and pride and security," says Bob. But they worry that their thrift will mean they'll have to pay college bills for their older daughter, Katie, and younger son, Andrew, without the benefit of financial aid—a process that could decimate their retirement nest egg. "It's frustrating that the guy down the street has two Mercedes in the driveway, and he'll get more aid than I will because he doesn't have any assets," Bob says.

Those fears aren't totally unfounded. Even though income weighs far more heavily than assets in the formulas that determine how much aid families are eligible for, assets in the six figures do trigger a higher expected family contribution—the amount parents must cough up each year before they're eligible for any aid.

Public schools generally stick to the federal aid formulas, which exclude home equity. But many private schools would expect the Lassiters to tap the $130,000 of equity they have in the home they own free and clear. That might boost their contribution by $7,300 a year.

Already in their favor for financial-aid purposes is that all of their savings is in Bob's or Mary Ann's name. Colleges would generally expect the family to contribute 25% to 35% of any assets in Katie's or Andrew's name each year, but only up to 5.6% of parents' assets go into the pot.

Some financial planners who specialize in college-aid issues suggest a few other moves the Lassiters could make between now and Katie's junior year of high school to keep down the family's expected contribution:

Buy an Annuity

Since they're already contributing as much as possible to retirement accounts (which are excluded from most financial-aid calculations), in the future they might put some of their nonretirement savings into an annuity, which also would be excluded. However, since they can't tap an annuity until after age 59½, they'd need to be confident they wouldn't need the money until then. Also, they'd have to be sure they wouldn't incur a surrender penalty, which many annuities charge for withdrawals during the first five or seven years.

Buy More Business Equipment

Bob could hold down family income in the years that count for financial aid (beginning halfway through Katie's junior year of high school) by waiting until then to purchase business equipment he might otherwise buy a year or two sooner, or by accelerating such purchases toward the end of Katie's college career so they'll be included in the last financial-aid year (which ends halfway though a student's junior year).

Buy Your Child's Computer

If the Lassiters have big-ticket expenses they're going to incur during the college years, such as a computer for Katie, they might as well spend the money toward the end of her high school years, which would reduce family assets for aid purposes.

Take Out a Home-Equity Loan

If they need to borrow to buy a car, a home-equity loan would reduce their available assets at schools that include home equity in their aid calculations.

Move Up?

One question on Bob's mind: Would moving up to a bigger house—with a bigger mortgage—help the family qualify for more aid? Probably not. For financial-aid purposes, having $130,000 of equity in a home you own free and clear is the same as having $130,000 of equity in a $200,000 house with a $70,000 mortgage.

Only if they spent down some of the equity—say, to cover closing costs or to remodel—would the Lassiters have fewer assets to report, and then only at schools that count home equity in their calculations. "To do it strictly to get more aid seems kind of silly," Bob concludes. We agree.

Encourage More A's

Another strategy the Lassiters can pursue, regardless of their savings, is to aim for merit-based aid by applying to colleges where Katie, an A student so far, would be in the top 20% of her class. A 3.5 GPA student with 1200 SATs has a good chance of getting a super merit-based award at a pretty good college.

Don't Bother Trying to Beat the System

It's best not to spend a lot of time trying to feint and jab and beat the system. If the Lassiters keep saving at the same rate, they'll have $150,000 to $200,000 outside of retirement accounts by Katie's freshman year. At that time, they could set up an automatic distribution from their mutual funds to pay them the earnings each month, generating perhaps $11,000 to $15,000 a year toward college bills. If they also diverted the $10,000 to $15,000 they're saving annually, their nest egg wouldn't grow during their kids' college years, but it would still be intact.

While the neighbors who prefer a Mercedes to mutual funds may get more aid, a good chunk of that aid is likely to be in the form of loans that somebody has to pay back. They'll have a significant loan burden when they want to be saving for retirement, or their kids will graduate laden with debt.

What About a Parent in School?

Until recently, when a parent went back to school (half-time or more) at the same time as his or her child, the family's expected contribution was split in two, one-half for each student, allowing the family to qualify for more financial aid. But the rules have changed, and parents in school no longer count toward the two-in-school bonus. So, no longer do you come out ahead by timing your continuing education to coincide with your child's.

Completing the FAFSA

The Free Application for Federal Student Aid (FAFSA) is available in paper and electronic formats. It is a good idea to obtain a current paper version for the year in which you apply and fill that out and use our tips to check it. (We've reproduced the 2005–2006 version on the following pages.) When you are satisfied that it is complete, you can either mail it in or transfer your answers to the Web-based version.

You can get the paper version from your child's high school, the financial-aid office at any college or university, the public library, or by calling 800-4-FEDAID.

You can fill out the Web-based version of the form at www.fafsa.ed.gov. Step-by-step instructions are provided on the site. FAFSA on the Web offers several benefits, including:

- **You will get your Student Aid Report (SAR)** sooner than with the paper form.
- **Your FAFSA will be more accurate** than a paper application because the form on the Web has built-in edit checks to catch simple errors.
- **You will save the federal government money** by reducing its processing costs.

Whether or not you've planned ahead to maximize your eligibility for financial aid, it's essential to carefully complete the FAFSA, required by most colleges (and the PROFILE, required by many private schools, which is discussed in the next section). The line-by-line tips for the FAFSA beginning on page 174 will help you avoid mistakes that could cost you financial aid. Plus, while most aid-boosting strategies require long-range planning, we've flagged a few last-minute opportunities to maximize your eligibility.

continued on page 174

It's essential to carefully complete the FAFSA, required by most colleges, and the PROFILE, required by many private schools.

FREE APPLICATION FOR FEDERAL STUDENT AID

FAFSA

July 1, 2005 — June 30, 2006
FREE APPLICATION FOR FEDERAL STUDENT AID
We Help Put America Through School

OMB # 1845-0001

Step One: For questions 1–30, leave blank any questions that do not apply to you (the student).

1-3. Your full name (as it appears on your Social Security card)

1. LAST NAME	2. FIRST NAME	3. MIDDLE INITIAL
FOR INFORMATION ONLY	DO NOT SUBMIT	

4-7. Your permanent mailing address

4. NUMBER AND STREET (INCLUDE APT. NUMBER)

5. CITY (AND COUNTRY IF NOT U.S.)

6. STATE

7. ZIP CODE

8. Your Social Security Number

XXX – XX – XXXX

9. Your date of birth

MM DD 19 YY

10. Your permanent telephone number

( ) –

11-12. Your driver's license number and state (if any)

11. LICENSE NUMBER

12. STATE

13. Your e-mail address

WE WILL USE THIS E-MAIL ADDRESS TO CORRESPOND WITH YOU. YOU WILL RECEIVE YOUR FAFSA INFORMATION THROUGH A SECURE LINK ON THE INTERNET, SENT TO THE E-MAIL ADDRESS YOU PROVIDE. LEAVE BLANK TO RECEIVE INFORMATION THROUGH REGULAR MAIL. WE WILL ONLY SHARE THIS ADDRESS WITH THE SCHOOLS YOU LIST ON THE FORM AND YOUR STATE. THEY MAY USE THE E-MAIL ADDRESS TO COMMUNICATE WITH YOU.

@

14. Are you a U.S. citizen? Pick one. **See page 2.**

a. Yes, I am a U.S. citizen. **Skip to question 16.** ○ 1
b. No, but I am an eligible noncitizen. **Fill in question 15.** ○ 2
c. No, I am not a citizen or eligible noncitizen. ○ 3

15. ALIEN REGISTRATION NUMBER

A

16. What is your marital status as of today?

I am single, divorced or widowed ○ 1
I am married/remarried ○ 2
I am separated ○ 3

17. Month and year you were married, separated, divorced or widowed

MM YYYY

18. What is your state of legal residence?

STATE

19. Did you become a legal resident of this state before January 1, 2000?

Yes ○ 1 No ○ 2

20. If the answer to question 19 is "**No**," give month and year you became a legal resident.

MM YYYY

21. Are you male? (Most male students must register with Selective Service to get federal aid.)

Yes ○ 1 No ○ 2

22. If you are male (age 18–25) and not registered, answer "Yes" and Selective Service will register you.

Yes ○ 1 No ○ 2

23. What degree or certificate will you be working on during 2005–2006? **See page 2** and enter the correct number in the box.

24. What will be your grade level when you begin the 2005–2006 school year? **See page 2** and enter the correct number in the box.

25. Will you have a high school diploma or GED before you begin the 2005–2006 school year? Yes ○ 1 No ○ 2

26. Will you have your first bachelor's degree before July 1, 2005? Yes ○ 1 No ○ 2

27. In addition to grants, are you interested in student loans (which you must pay back)? Yes ○ 1 No ○ 2

28. In addition to grants, are you interested in "work-study" (which you earn through work)? Yes ○ 1 No ○ 2

29. Highest school your father completed   Middle school/Jr. High ○ 1 High School ○ 2 College or beyond ○ 3 Other/unknown ○ 4

30. Highest school your mother completed   Middle school/Jr. High ○ 1 High School ○ 2 College or beyond ○ 3 Other/unknown ○ 4

31. **Do not leave this question blank.** Have you ever been convicted of possessing or selling illegal drugs? If you have, answer "Yes," complete and submit this application, and we will send you a worksheet in the mail for you to determine if your conviction affects your eligibility for aid.

No ○ 1 Yes ○ 3

DO NOT LEAVE QUESTION 31 BLANK

Page 3

For Help – www.studentaid.ed.gov/completefafsa

Step Two: For questions 32–45, report your (the student's) income and assets. If you are married as of today, report your and your spouse's income and assets, even if you were not married in 2004. Ignore references to "spouse" if you are currently single, separated, divorced or widowed.

32. For 2004, have you (the student) completed your IRS income tax return or another tax return listed in question 33?

   a. I have already completed my return. ○ 1   **b.** I will file, but I have not yet completed my return. ○ 2   **c.** I'm not going to file. **(Skip to question 38.)** ○ 3

33. What income tax return did you file or will you file for 2004?

   a. IRS 1040 .... ○ 1
   b. IRS 1040A, 1040EZ, 1040TeleFile .... ○ 2
   c. A foreign tax return. **See page 2.** .... ○ 3
   d. A tax return with Puerto Rico, Guam, American Samoa, the U.S. Virgin Islands, the Marshall Islands, the Federated States of Micronesia, or Palau. **See page 2.** .... ○ 4

34. If you have filed or will file a 1040, were you eligible to file a 1040A or 1040EZ? **See page 2.**   Yes ○ 1   No ○ 2   Don't Know ○ 3

For questions 35–47, if the answer is zero or the question does not apply to you, enter 0.

35. What was your (and spouse's) adjusted gross income for 2004? Adjusted gross income is on IRS Form 1040—line 36; 1040A—line 21; 1040EZ—line 4; or TeleFile—line I. $ ⎕⎕⎕,⎕⎕⎕

36. Enter the total amount of your (and spouse's) income tax for 2004. Income tax amount is on IRS Form 1040—line 56; 1040A—line 36; 1040EZ—line 10; or TeleFile—line K(2). $ ⎕⎕⎕,⎕⎕⎕

37. Enter your (and spouse's) exemptions for 2004. Exemptions are on IRS Form 1040—line 6d or on Form 1040A—line 6d. For Form 1040EZ or TeleFile, **see page 2.**   ⎕⎕

38-39. How much did you (and spouse) earn from working (wages, salaries, tips, etc.) in 2004? Answer this question whether or not you filed a tax return. This information may be on your W-2 forms, or on IRS Form 1040—lines 7 + 12 + 18; 1040A—line 7; or 1040EZ—line 1. TeleFilers should use their W-2 forms.   **You (38)** $ ⎕⎕⎕,⎕⎕⎕   **Your Spouse (39)** $ ⎕⎕⎕,⎕⎕⎕

Student (and Spouse) Worksheets (40–42)

40-42. **Go to page 8** and complete the columns on the left of Worksheets A, B, and C. Enter the student (and spouse) totals in questions 40, 41 and 42, respectively. Even though you may have few of the Worksheet items, check each line carefully.

   Worksheet A (40) $ ⎕⎕⎕,⎕⎕⎕
   Worksheet B (41) $ ⎕⎕⎕,⎕⎕⎕
   Worksheet C (42) $ ⎕⎕⎕,⎕⎕⎕

43. As of today, what is your (and spouse's) total current balance of **cash, savings, and checking accounts**? Do not include student financial aid. $ ⎕⎕⎕,⎕⎕⎕

44. As of today, what is the net worth of your (and spouse's) **investments**, including real estate (not your home)? *Net worth* means current value minus debt. **See page 2.** $ ⎕⎕⎕,⎕⎕⎕

45. As of today, what is the net worth of your (and spouse's) current **businesses and/or investment farms**? Do not include a farm that you live on and operate. **See page 2.** $ ⎕⎕⎕,⎕⎕⎕

46-47. If you receive veterans' education benefits, for how many months from July 1, 2005, through June 30, 2006, will you receive these benefits, and what amount will you receive per month? Do not include your spouse's veterans' education benefits.   **Months (46)** ⎕⎕   **Monthly Amount (47)** $ ⎕,⎕⎕⎕

Step Three: Answer all seven questions in this step.

48. Were you born before January 1, 1982? ....   Yes ○ 1   No ○ 2

49. At the beginning of the 2005–2006 school year, will you be working on a master's or doctorate program (such as an MA, MBA, MD, JD, PhD, EdD, or graduate certificate, etc.)? ....   Yes ○ 1   No ○ 2

50. As of today, are you married? (Answer "Yes" if you are separated but not divorced.) ....   Yes ○ 1   No ○ 2

51. Do you have children who receive more than half of their support from you? ....   Yes ○ 1   No ○ 2

52. Do you have dependents (other than your children or spouse) who live with you and who receive more than half of their support from you, now and through June 30, 2006? ....   Yes ○ 1   No ○ 2

53. Are both of your parents deceased, or are you (or were you until age 18) a ward/dependent of the court? ....   Yes ○ 1   No ○ 2

54. Are you a veteran of the U.S. Armed Forces? **See page 2.** ....   Yes ○ 1   No ○ 2

If you (the student) answer "No" to every question in Step Three, go to Step Four.
If you answer "Yes" to any question in Step Three, skip Step Four and go to Step Five on page 6.

(Health Profession Students: Your school may require you to complete Step Four even if you answered "Yes" to any Step Three question.)

For Help – 1-800-433-3243

FREE APPLICATION FOR FEDERAL STUDENT AID *continued*

Step Four: Complete this step if you (the student) answered "No" to all questions in Step Three. Go to page 7 to determine who is a parent for this step.

55. What is your parents' marital status as of today?

Married/Remarried.............. ○ ₁ Divorced/Separated.............. ○ ₃

Single .... ○ ₂ Widowed .... ○ ₄

56. Month and year they were married, separated, divorced or widowed

M M Y Y Y Y

57-64. What are the Social Security Numbers, names and dates of birth of the parents reporting information on this form? If your parent does not have a Social Security Number, you must enter 000-00-0000.

57. FATHER'S/STEPFATHER'S SOCIAL SECURITY NUMBER

☐☐☐ – ☐☐ – ☐☐☐☐

58. FATHER'S/STEPFATHER'S LAST NAME, AND

☐☐☐☐☐☐☐☐☐☐☐☐☐☐☐ ,

59. FIRST INITIAL

☐

60. FATHER'S/STEPFATHER'S DATE OF BIRTH

M M D D 1 9 Y Y

61. MOTHER'S/STEPMOTHER'S SOCIAL SECURITY NUMBER

☐☐☐ – ☐☐ – ☐☐☐☐

62. MOTHER'S/STEPMOTHER'S LAST NAME, AND

☐☐☐☐☐☐☐☐☐☐☐☐☐☐☐ ,

63. FIRST INITIAL

☐

64. MOTHER'S/STEPMOTHER'S DATE OF BIRTH

M M D D 1 9 Y Y

65. Go to **page 7** to determine how many people are in your parents' household.

☐

66. Go to **page 7** to determine how many in question 65 (exclude your parents) will be college students between July 1, 2005, and June 30, 2006.

☐

67. What is your parents' state of legal residence?

STATE ☐☐

68. Did your parents become legal residents of this state before January 1, 2000?

Yes ○ ₁ No ○ ₂

69. If the answer to question 68 is "**No**," give month and year legal residency began for the parent who has lived in the state the longest.

M M Y Y Y Y

70. For 2004, have your parents completed their IRS income tax return or another tax return listed in question 71?

a. My parents have already completed their return. ○ ₁

b. My parents will file, but they have not yet completed their return. ○ ₂

c. My parents are not going to file. **(Skip to question 76.)** ○ ₃

71. What income tax return did your parents file or will they file for 2004?

a. IRS 1040 .... ○ ₁

b. IRS 1040A, 1040EZ, 1040TeleFile .... ○ ₂

c. A foreign tax return. See page 2. .... ○ ₃

d. A tax return with Puerto Rico, Guam, American Samoa, the U.S. Virgin Islands, the Marshall Islands, the Federated States of Micronesia, or Palau. See page 2. .... ○ ₄

72. If your parents have filed or will file a 1040, were they eligible to file a 1040A or 1040EZ? See page 2.

Yes ○ ₁ No ○ ₂ Don't Know ○ ₃

For questions 73-83, if the answer is zero or the question does not apply, enter 0.

73. What was your parents' adjusted gross income for 2004? Adjusted gross income is on IRS Form 1040—line 36; 1040A—line 21; 1040EZ—line 4; or TeleFile—line I.

$ ☐☐☐ , ☐☐☐

74. Enter the total amount of your parents' income tax for 2004. Income tax amount is on IRS Form 1040—line 56; 1040A—line 36; 1040EZ—line 10; or TeleFile—line K(2).

$ ☐☐☐ , ☐☐☐

75. Enter your parents' exemptions for 2004. Exemptions are on IRS Form 1040—line 6d or on Form 1040A—line 6d. For Form 1040EZ or TeleFile, see page 2.

☐☐

76-77. How much did your parents earn from working (wages, salaries, tips, etc.) in 2004? Answer this question whether or not your parents filed a tax return. This information may be on their W-2 forms, or on IRS Form 1040—lines 7 + 12 + 18; 1040A—line 7; or 1040EZ—line 1. TeleFilers should use their W-2 forms.

Father/Stepfather (76) $ ☐☐☐ , ☐☐☐

Mother/Stepmother (77) $ ☐☐☐ , ☐☐☐

Parent Worksheets (78-80)

78-80. Go to **page 8** and complete the columns on the right of Worksheets A, B, and C. Enter the parents' totals in questions 78, 79 and 80, respectively. Even though your parents may have few of the Worksheet items, check each line carefully.

Worksheet A (78) $ ☐☐☐ , ☐☐☐

Worksheet B (79) $ ☐☐☐ , ☐☐☐

Worksheet C (80) $ ☐☐☐ , ☐☐☐

81. As of today, what is your parents' total current balance of **cash, savings, and checking accounts**?

$ ☐☐☐ , ☐☐☐

82. As of today, what is the net worth of your parents' **investments**, including real estate (not your parents' home)? *Net worth* means current value minus debt. **See page 2.**

$ ☐☐☐ , ☐☐☐

83. As of today, what is the net worth of your parents' current **businesses and/or investment farms**? Do not include a farm that your parents live on and operate. **See page 2.**

$ ☐☐☐ , ☐☐☐

Now go to Step Six.

Page 5

For Help – www.studentaid.ed.gov/completefafsa

Step Five: Complete this step only if you (the student) answered "Yes" to any Step Three question.

84. **Go to page 7** to determine how many people are in your (and your spouse's) household.

85. **Go to page 7** to determine how many people in question 84 will be college students, attending at least half time between July 1, 2005, and June 30, 2006.

Step Six: Please tell us which schools may request your information, and indicate your enrollment status.

Enter the 6-digit federal school code and your housing plans. Look for the federal school codes at **www.fafsa.ed.gov**, at your college financial aid office, at your public library, or by asking your high school guidance counselor. If you cannot get the federal school code, write in the complete name, address, city and state of the college. For state aid, you may wish to list your preferred school first.

	1st FEDERAL SCHOOL CODE		NAME OF COLLEGE	STATE		HOUSING PLANS
86.		OR	ADDRESS AND CITY		87.	on campus ○ 1 / off campus ○ 2 / with parent ○ 3
88.	2nd FEDERAL SCHOOL CODE	OR	NAME OF COLLEGE / ADDRESS AND CITY	STATE	89.	on campus ○ 1 / off campus ○ 2 / with parent ○ 3
90.	3rd FEDERAL SCHOOL CODE	OR	NAME OF COLLEGE / ADDRESS AND CITY	STATE	91.	on campus ○ 1 / off campus ○ 2 / with parent ○ 3
92.	4th FEDERAL SCHOOL CODE	OR	NAME OF COLLEGE / ADDRESS AND CITY	STATE	93.	on campus ○ 1 / off campus ○ 2 / with parent ○ 3
94.	5th FEDERAL SCHOOL CODE	OR	NAME OF COLLEGE / ADDRESS AND CITY	STATE	95.	on campus ○ 1 / off campus ○ 2 / with parent ○ 3
96.	6th FEDERAL SCHOOL CODE	OR	NAME OF COLLEGE / ADDRESS AND CITY	STATE	97.	on campus ○ 1 / off campus ○ 2 / with parent ○ 3

98. **See page 7.** At the start of the 2005-2006 school year, mark if you will be: Full time ○ 1   3/4 time ○ 2   Half time ○ 3   Less than half time ○ 4   Not sure ○ 5

Step Seven: Read, sign and date.

If you are the student, by signing this application you certify that you (1) will use federal and/or state student financial aid only to pay the cost of attending an institution of higher education, (2) are not in default on a federal student loan or have made satisfactory arrangements to repay it, (3) do not owe money back on a federal student grant or have made satisfactory arrangements to repay it, (4) will notify your school if you default on a federal student loan and (5) will not receive a Federal Pell Grant for more than one school for the same period of time.

If you are the parent or the student, by signing this application you agree, if asked, to provide information that will verify the accuracy of your completed form. This information may include your U.S. or state income tax forms. Also, you certify that you understand that **the Secretary of Education has the authority to verify information reported on this application with the Internal Revenue Service and other federal agencies.** If you sign any document related to the federal student aid programs electronically using a Personal Identification Number (PIN), you certify that you are the person identified by the PIN and have not disclosed that PIN to anyone else. If you purposely give false or misleading information, you may be fined $20,000, sent to prison, or both.

99. Date this form was completed.

MMDD   2005 ○   or   2006 ○

100. **Student** (Sign below)

Parent (A parent from Step Four sign below)

If this form was filled out by someone other than you, your spouse or your parents, that person must complete this part.

Preparer's name, firm and address

101. Preparer's Social Security Number (or 102)

102. Employer ID number (or 101)

103. Preparer's signature and date

SCHOOL USE ONLY: Federal School Code

D/O ○ 1

FAA Signature

DATA ENTRY USE ONLY: ○ P   ○ *   ○ L   ○ E

Page 6

For Help—1-800-433-3243

Taxes reduce the amount of income considered available for college expenses, so underreporting could shortchange you of aid.

Step 1 (page 170) asks for personal information and enrollment plans and is generally self-explanatory. Because your EFC will be based predominantly on your income, Steps 2 through 4 (pages 171 and 172) are the heart of the FAFSA. You'll be asked for your student's and your own adjusted gross income (AGI)—basically, income before subtracting exemptions and deductions—and other data from your tax returns.

Not all families need to supply information about their assets. If parents have a combined income of less than $15,000 and both parents and student are eligible to file a 1040A or 1040EZ, or are not required to file any income tax return, assets are excluded from the aid formulas.

Lines 27–28

On lines 27–28, be sure to indicate that you want to be considered for work-study and student loans. Marking "no" won't increase the grants you are offered, and you can always turn down a loan or work-study job if you decide that a home-equity loan or other employment is a better choice.

Lines 35 and 73

On line 35 you report the student's AGI (if any) and on line 73, your own AGI, which will be used to determine your family contribution from income. If you are no longer living with your spouse due to death, divorce, or separation but will file a joint return, you should show only your portion of the joint AGI— ditto for taxes paid and untaxed income, discussed below.

Lines 36 and 74

Lines 36 and 74 ask for federal income tax paid. Be sure to report your total federal tax liability for the year, not just what was withheld from your pay or the balance due in April. Taxes reduce the amount of income considered available for college expenses, so underreporting could shortchange you of aid.

Lines 38–39 and 76–77

Income earned from work (lines 38–39 and 76–77) is used to compute your social security tax (which also reduces available income) as well as an extra allowance for two-income couples. Don't overlook income that isn't part of your AGI but on which you pay social security taxes, such as earnings you divert to a 401(k) plan.

Lines 40–42 and 78–80
(Worksheets A, B, and C)

Lines 40–42 and 78–80 refer to three worksheets that ask about tax credits, untaxed income and benefits, and other more-obscure items that may impact your aid eligibility. For most families, Worksheet B, on which you report untaxed income and benefits, is the most significant. These are considered additional resources even if you can't really tap the money for tuition and other college costs. Contributions you made for last year to a tax-deductible IRA, 401(k), or other tax-deferred pension plan, for instance, are added back to your AGI and assessed as income, even though you've locked the money away for retirement. (Contributions you made in prior years are considered assets and sheltered from the aid formulas.)

LAST-MINUTE STRATEGY: One item not included in untaxed income is money set aside in an employer-sponsored flexible spending account for child care or medical expenses. If you have access to such a plan at work, take maximum advantage of it for the year ahead.

OTHER ITEMS ADDED TO INCOME. Other items added to income include any social security benefits or pension income not tallied in your AGI, child support (only what you actually received), tax-exempt interest, foreign income, veterans' benefits, and living allowances for military or clergy. You're also asked to report "cash or any money paid on your behalf," which is where you'd disclose that Grandpa chipped in $11,000 toward educational expenses last year. However, if he

Consider drawing down cash to pay off a debt that won't count against assets, or pay off consumer debt with a margin loan.

gave your child a car or computer, rather than cash, you don't have to include its value.

Lines 43 and 81

On lines 43 and 81 you report cash and savings and checking-account balances, excluding any student aid that's been deposited.

LAST-MINUTE STRATEGY: These accounts are fluid, and you must report their value on the day you sign and date the form. Before you do, pay any outstanding bills—maybe even next month's bills—to reduce your account balances.

Lines 44 and 82

Lines 44 and 82 address your real estate and investments. Your primary home or family farm is excluded, as are cash value in a life insurance policy and assets in your retirement plans. But you must include the value of a vacation home or investment property, along with money-market funds, mutual funds, stocks, bonds, and CDs outside retirement accounts. In the student's column, include custodial or trust accounts even if the student can't touch the money yet (unless a trust fund is set up exclusively for noneducational expenses, such as an accident settlement). You can omit an asset if its ownership is contested, as in a divorce.

Lines 45 and 83 should reflect the net worth of these assets—their current value less any outstanding debt. You should account for, say, the mortgage on an investment property or a margin-account loan you have with your broker. You can't include the mortgage on your primary home, loans from your retirement plan, or consumer debt (such as an auto loan or credit card balances) in order to reduce the value of your assets.

LAST-MINUTE STRATEGY: Consider drawing down cash to pay off a debt that won't count against assets, or pay off consumer debt with a margin loan.

Lines 45 and 83

On lines 45 and 83, you report the net worth of any business you own (value minus debt). Include hard assets like inventory, but not intangibles like goodwill. If you're a part owner of the business, show only your share of net worth.

Lines 60 and 64

Line 60 asks for the father's date of birth. Line 64 asks for the mother's date of birth. These dates will determine the age of the older parent, which is used to determine the parents' asset-protection allowance.

LAST-MINUTE STRATEGY: It won't make a huge difference, but if the older parent will have a birthday in January or early February, waiting until after the birthday to complete the form can shield an extra $1,000 to $2,000.

Line 65

On line 65, the more household members you include, the higher your income-protection allowance, which shelters a modest portion of your income from the aid formulas. You can include any children who get more than half their support from you, even if they're living on their own or with your former spouse. The instructions don't say so explicitly, but you can also include a child who will be born during the coming academic year. The number of household members reported here does not have to match the number of exemptions you'll take on your tax return. But if they differ, you'll probably be asked to explain.

Line 66

If you indicate on line 66 that your household will have more than one college student, your expected family contribution will be divided among them, boosting aid eligibility for each. To be included, a member of your household (excluding a parent) must be enrolled at least half-time and working toward a degree at an institution that's eligible for federal aid.

If your household will have more than one college student, your expected family contribution will be divided among them, boosting aid eligibility for each.

The FAFSA asks nothing about how much you expect to earn in the coming year, but the PROFILE wants details.

Lines 73 and 76–77

Lines 73 and 76–77, where you report your family income, are a bone of contention for many parents who have divorced and remarried. If you are the parent with whom the child lived for most of the year, you'll be the one completing the form. And you must include your new spouse's income and assets, even if he or she isn't helping with college expenses. The aid formulas do not recognize legal agreements that absolve the stepparent from college expenses or make the noncustodial parent responsible. Sometimes you can persuade a financial-aid officer to make adjustments later. But for now you have to report the joint data—and cross your fingers.

Preparing the PROFILE

If you must also complete the PROFILE, here's some "nitty-gritty" assistance with the areas where this form differs from the FAFSA.

Your Home Equity

When you add home equity to the equation, as most private colleges do, your EFC can jump significantly. Value your home at what you think you could net if you sold it now, after transaction costs. The figure plugged into the aid formula is your home's value, minus the balance on your mortgage and other loans secured by the home.

LAST-MINUTE STRATEGY: Convert consumer debt, such as a credit card balance, to home-equity debt to reduce total equity.

The Family Farm

If your farm qualifies for this special designation, only roughly half of the first $495,000 of equity is added to your assets, and no more than 5% of that is considered available each year. You qualify if the farm is your principal residence and you participate in its operation.

Other Assets

Parents must report savings in the names of the student's siblings. This is meant to deter parents from hiding assets by shifting them among children. Students must report the value of any retirement accounts they have, such as an IRA set up with summer earnings. Some students get a break on trust funds, however. Rather than including them with other assets, the PROFILE asks you to report them separately and indicate whether any principal or income is currently available. If not, some schools may assess trust funds at the parents' 5% rate or exclude them completely.

Income and Benefits

In contrast to the FAFSA, parents must report how much they contribute to flexible spending accounts for child care and medical costs. Parents must also report their previous year's income and tax data, which may raise questions if they are significantly higher than the current year's.

Expected Income and Resources

The FAFSA asks nothing about how much you expect to earn in the coming year, but the PROFILE wants details. Students must also divulge outside scholarships they expect, employer-provided tuition benefits, and relatives' contributions—which may reduce your aid package dollar for dollar.

LAST-MINUTE STRATEGY: Ask relatives to hold off on gifts to help you pay for college. Gifts given after college can help pay off student loans.

Unusual Expenses

Most of the probing questions on the PROFILE might increase your tab, but the "Special Circumstances" section gives you a chance to reduce it. Students and parents should report child support paid and unreimbursed medical and dental expenses. Parents can report their own student-loan payments and private-school tuition for younger siblings. Some schools

> Most of the probing questions on the PROFILE might increase your tab, but the "Special Circumstances" section gives you a chance to reduce it.

Even if you didn't qualify for aid in your child's freshman year, you should reapply in subsequent years. You never know when the federal government, or a school, may change its policies.

automatically adjust your available income for such expenses; others use their discretion.

Divorced and Separated Parents

The PROFILE asks how much the noncustodial parent plans to contribute to the student's education. Most colleges, however, ask separately for the noncustodial parent's income, assets, and expenses—plus data from that parent's spouse. Policies differ, so ask ahead of time whose income and assets will count.

Business Owners

Many private colleges require yet another form from business owners asking for detailed financials for the previous two years, plus projections for the coming year. Business assets are assessed lightly, using the same formula as for family farms. But aid officers may disallow business losses or depreciation expenses—something you can dispute on appeal.

After Freshman Year

Unfortunately, you will go through the process of applying for financial aid not once, but four times for each child. Even if you didn't qualify for aid in your child's freshman year, you should reapply in subsequent years. You never know when the federal government, or a school, may change its policies.

Gird yourself, however, for a less-generous ratio of grants to loans in the sophomore, junior, and senior years, because grants tend to shrink as the lending limits for Stafford loans rise. A freshman is eligible for a $2,625 loan. But a sophomore can borrow up to $3,500 under the Stafford loan program, and juniors and seniors can borrow up to $5,500. At schools that put Stafford loans into the aid package before institutional aid (which is fairly typical), a bigger loan can reduce the "remaining need" that is filled with institutional money. If the institutional award you received last year was a grant or scholarship, the bigger Stafford loan winds up shrinking the grant or scholarship in the upper-class years.

Your best defense?

- **Each financial-aid year, review this chapter** and look for reasonable ways to trim your adjusted gross income or your assets.
- **Consider using up some of your child's savings first,** since they're assessed more heavily than your assets, even though the college bills will probably diminish some of your assets anyway.
- **Consider accelerating the purchase of needed items,** such as a car, major appliance, or computer, if you think it may boost your eligibility for aid.
- **And if your financial situation changes**—because of a job change, a layoff, a divorce, or a death in the family—be sure to let a financial-aid officer know. If you're fortunate, you'll get an immediate change in your aid package. If not, the school will be aware that it needs to carve out additional aid for you next year.

Hire a College-Aid Helper? Study First

College financial-aid forms are a lot like income-tax returns: They're time-consuming and detail-intensive, and a little planning and strategy can save you hundreds or even thousands of dollars. While you can hire an accountant to file your taxes, parents have traditionally been on their own to tackle aid forms. But now you can hire a private financial-aid consultant to do the job for you.

For a flat fee of $250 to $700, aid consultants typically help parents fill out the Free Application for Federal Student Aid (FAFSA) and other aid forms, conduct scholarship searches, negotiate financial-aid awards with colleges, and advise the family on strategies to lower the expected family contribution.

But guidance counselors and financial-aid administrators caution that some consultants promise more than they can deliver.

And it's important to recognize that there's no specific training or certification to become an aid counselor, as there is for accountants. Some financial-aid counselors are certified financial planners (CFPs), while others are former guidance counselors, teachers, or just entrepreneurs. A CFP won't necessarily be trained in financial-aid matters, but that credential at least makes it easier to check on a counselor's background (ask for the planner's ADV disclosure form, which details his or her education, business practices, and ethical conduct).

Even if you do find good help, you won't learn anything you couldn't find out on your own, with guides such as this book. As with taxes, it comes down to whether you want to learn the ropes and wrestle with the forms or spend the money to have someone else take on the task.

The Financial Side of Choosing a College

Chapter 7

There are about as many reasons to choose a particular college as there are students.

My dad went there.
I love the football team.
It has a soccer team I'd like to play for.
It has a great theater company.
It has a great campus newspaper.
It has a great academic reputation.
It has a great [fill in the field of study] department.
It has a fine liberal-arts program—or great
technical or professional programs.
There are a lot of students of my own religion.
It's close to home—or far from home.
It's in a warm climate—or in ski country.
It's in a small town—or a big city.
It has a Greek system—or it doesn't.
It's conservative—or countercultural.
It's small and intimate—or big and bustling.

Those are all reasonable criteria to consider. But once your child has narrowed the list from the universe of more than 3,000 schools—in the U.S., that is—to perhaps half a dozen that might be a good fit, the final selection often comes down to family finances. Are you willing to foot the bill for your child's school of choice, whatever the cost? Or will the final decision balance all those other fine points against the expense? There are probably as many answers to that question as there are parents:

Are you willing to foot the bill for your child's school of choice, whatever the cost? Or will the final decision balance the fine points against the expense?

Some parents are willing to foot the bill for undergraduate education at their children's school of choice, but that's where they draw the line. Graduate or professional school would be the kids' responsibility.

When many parents map out college plans for their children, they decide all they are willing to pay for is a public university. If the kids want to go to a private school, they have to get a scholarship or find some other way to finance it.

A few parents might restrict their children's choices based on their religious beliefs.

Still other parents decide they'll pay for tuition—at whatever college their child chooses—and expect their kids to cover room, board, and living expenses with part-time and summer job earnings and student loans.

Maybe your answer to who'll pay for what will be more free-form: You expect that you and your child will contribute as much as possible, share in the borrowing, and somehow patch together the resources to afford the best college your child can get into. That's a common approach, but don't leave the patchwork to the last minute or you'll end up in a mad scramble to decide what's possible in the few weeks in which you have to accept an offer of admission. A financial checkup before you've begun applying to colleges can help you select a school that's a good financial fit for the family as well as a good educational fit for your child. (And, even if you're starting late, you can still take advantage of many of the suggestions and resources provided in this chapter.)

Step One: Complete a Need Analysis

More than 50% of students at four-year colleges receive some financial aid toward college costs. That means more than 50% don't pay the full sticker price. If you haven't done so already, use the worksheet on pages 120–121 of Chapter 4 to get a rough idea of how much you'll be counted on to ante up wherever your child goes. Whatever the resulting figure is, consider it an estimate of what you'll have to pay, whether your child attends State U. or prestigious Private U. If the sticker price is higher than your expected contribution, you'll be eligible for financial aid to make up the difference.

As Chapter 4 shows, your official expected family contribution only approximates what you'll have to pay out of pocket. Many private colleges use their own need-analysis formulas, which may boost what you're expected to pay, when awarding aid from their own coffers. And some schools won't meet all your need. Nonetheless, your official EFC is a good place to start when you're sizing up what college will cost and where the money will come from.

Ninth grade isn't too early to walk through this exercise. "It's better to have three or four years to know that you're not going to get much aid, than to find out with three months to go," says one independent admissions counselor. If you wait too long you won't have time to bolster your savings or to apply to more schools where the financial-aid picture might be brighter. Instead, you will have just two choices: pick the less-expensive school, or borrow to afford the more-expensive school.

> **Ninth grade isn't too early to walk through the exercise of estimating what you'll be expected to pay out of pocket and to assess where the cash is going to come from.**

Step Two: A Financial Checkup

Once you know approximately how much you will have to contribute, it's a good idea to take stock of your cash flow and assets, and determine what's available for college and what's off-limits. You can take inventory at any time in the years leading up to college and will probably want to take stock again just before you have to make a final choice.

For starters, how much of your monthly income will you be able to allocate toward saving for or paying for college bills?

WHAT ASSETS ARE AVAILABLE FOR COLLEGE?

Use this worksheet to calculate your current assets, liabilities, and net worth. Once you have a good picture of your resources, you can decide what you're willing or able to tap for college expenses—or perhaps you'll have fresh motivation to boost your savings.

Assets

Cash in savings accounts	$ _____	Other investments	_____
Cash in checking accounts	_____	Collectibles	_____
Cash on hand	_____	Precious metals	_____
Certificates of deposit	_____	Estimated market value of:	
Money-market funds	_____	Household furnishings	_____
U.S. savings bonds	_____	Automobiles and trucks	_____
Market value of home	_____	Boats, recreational vehicles	_____
Market value of other real		Furs and jewelry	_____
estate	_____	Loans owed to you	_____
Cash value of life insurance	_____	Other assets	_____
Surrender value of annuities	_____	**Total assets (A)**	$ _____
Vested equity in pension plans	_____		
Vested equity in profit sharing	_____	**Liabilities**	
401(k) or 403(b) plans	_____	Balance owed on mortgages	$ _____
Individual retirement accounts	_____	Auto loans	_____
Keogh plans	_____	Student loans	_____
Stocks (individually owned)	_____	Home-equity credit line	_____
Bonds (individually owned)	_____	Other credit lines	_____
Mutual funds	_____	Credit card bills	_____
State-sponsored college-		Other bills	_____
savings plans	_____	**Total liabilities (B)**	$ _____
Real estate investment trusts	_____	**Current Net Worth**	
		(A minus B)	$ _____

- **Perhaps you'll be finished** paying for a car next year and can redirect car payments toward college bills.
- **Maybe you can temporarily suspend** retirement-plan contributions to boost cash flow.
- **If you're divorced,** will you be able to count on a contribution from your ex-spouse?

You'll find budget-trimming suggestions in Chapter 2. The point here is to assess how much of your monthly income you can devote to paying college bills when the time comes. Now's the time to find out.

Extra Income May Not Help

Some parents also look for ways to bolster income during the college years. A stay-at-home mom might decide to go back to work. Or maybe it's a good time to launch a sideline business or try to get a few articles published in a trade magazine in your field. Before you do, though, rerun the needs analysis, factoring in the extra income. If you will be a candidate for significant financial aid, you may find that the extra income will reduce the amount you're eligible for and boost the amount you will be expected to contribute—leaving you not much further ahead toward covering the college bills. Tough as it may be to trim expenses, many families find that an extra dollar saved is more valuable than an extra dollar earned.

What Assets Will Be Available?

- **Are you willing to tap retirement accounts,** such as a 401(k) plan? The answer may depend on your age and ability to replenish those assets. (See page 44 in Chapter 2 for more on this issue.)
- **How much equity** do you have in your house, and are you willing to borrow against it?
- **Do you have cash-value life insurance** that you can borrow against?
- **Any stocks, bonds, or mutual funds** you can cash in?
- **How about a small cache of savings bonds** your child has received as gifts over the years?
- **Are grandparents or other relatives willing to help** out? If Grandma or Uncle Jim has hinted that there's some college money tucked away for your youngster, now's the time to find out (as delicately as you can) if it's really there and how much this generous help may amount to.

What Will Your Son or Daughter Be Able to Contribute?

About a third of all teenagers work regularly—collectively earning billions of dollars a year, most of it dis-

Tough as it may be to trim expenses, many families find that an extra dollar saved is more valuable than an extra dollar earned.

> A clear goal to work toward will probably be more motivating for your son or daughter than a vague appeal to "save something for college."

cretionary income. With a little prodding, your child may be able to save a percentage of his or her earnings from a summer job or part-time work to chip in toward the bills. But if you don't set that expectation now, all the money is likely to get spent on blue jeans and fast food. Many schools require their students to contribute a certain amount annually to their education, such as $1,500 or $2,000.

One way to encourage your child to save is to establish ahead of time how much you'll expect your child to contribute to college costs, whether it's a flat dollar amount per year of college or a percentage of his or her earnings during high school. A clear goal to work toward will probably be more motivating than a vague appeal to "save something for college."

How Much Are You Willing to Let Your Child Borrow?

The ideal is that any family should be able to afford the best school their child can get into. Unfortunately, the ideal often boils down to how much debt that family is willing to bear. Why? Because the amount of money the federal need analysis determines you can afford is usually impossible to squeeze out of your monthly cash flow. The formulas consider only your income and, to a lesser extent, your assets; they don't take into account your fixed expenses—say, how big your mortgage payment is, or whether you're making car payments or other loan payments. So most parents wind up depleting assets or borrowing just to meet the expected family contribution. You'll find some specific guidelines for parent and student borrowing in Chapter 9, but ultimately you have to decide for yourself how much debt is reasonable.

Weighing the Options

The point of a financial checkup isn't to lock you into—or out of—any choices beforehand. Remember, unless your child chooses a school that costs less than your expected family contribution, you must come up with that sum regardless of where he or she winds up. But knowing where you stand ahead of time will help you shop intelligently and ask the right questions as you begin choosing from among the possibilities. Fortunately, the possibilities might be greater than you had imagined. Here are some of them.

Public versus Private:
An Outcome You Might Not Expect

Some parents emerge from a "where do we stand?" exercise relieved. They have a much better picture of how they'll manage to bring numerous resources together to finance what previously seemed like an impossibly large sum of money. Others emerge frustrated and make up their minds that "a public college is all we can afford." Not so fast. While there's absolutely nothing wrong with a public-university education, the idea that it's the best value isn't always true.

WITH FINANCIAL AID, A PRIVATE SCHOOL MAY COST ONLY SLIGHTLY MORE. In the ultimate college-cost irony, affluent families may find that public colleges provide the best value, but the neediest students may get the most for their money at private schools. A family with a $3,000 expected family contribution, for instance, might qualify for as much as $32,000 in financial aid at a private college that costs $35,000 a year. But a family earning $100,000 a year and qualifying for little or no aid will probably nonetheless find it difficult, after taxes, to swing that $35,000 a year at the same pricey private school.

If you're somewhere in between—say, with an estimated family contribution of around $14,000—you'll probably pay the full cost at a public college but might qualify for a sizable financial-aid package at a private school. Say the public school costs $12,000 a year. You might decide that sending your child to the private college she prefers is well worth an extra $2,000 a year out of pocket, the difference after financial aid is factored in.

> While there's absolutely nothing wrong with a public-university education, the idea that it's the best value isn't always true.

If getting that sheepskin takes extra time, the additional costs may well eat up the savings from having chosen a public college over a private one.

PRIVATE SCHOOL MAY TAKE LESS TIME. Another point to consider in the public-private debate: Less than half of college graduates finish their degree in four years, according to the Center for Education Statistics. It can be especially difficult to finish in four years at a large public university, where required classes fill up quickly. If getting that sheepskin takes an extra semester, or an extra year, the additional tuition, room and board, and other costs may well eat up the savings from having chosen a public college over a private one.

A PUBLIC SCHOOL OUTSIDE YOUR STATE MAY COST PLENTY. When you're paying all or most of the tab, the public university in your state may well be a good value. But an out-of-state public school often is no bargain at all. Besides slapping out-of-staters with huge additional tuition charges, many state universities also make far less financial aid available to those students. At the University of California at Berkeley, for instance, out-of-state students pay a tuition surcharge of $8,478 (in 2004–2005). For the most part (excluding athletic scholarships), the only financial aid available to cover the surcharge is a loan or a student job. Berkeley is not a particularly good deal for needy out-of-state students. Other state universities have similar policies.

Honors Colleges

As with all generalizations, there are exceptions. An honors program at a top-notch, out-of-state (or in-state) public college—like Berkeley, Indiana University, the University of North Carolina at Chapel Hill, and the University of Virginia, to name a few—might offer the stellar student, who'd otherwise be accepted at the most competitive private colleges, a quality education at a cut-rate price.

The most selective private colleges, such as Harvard, Amherst, and Northwestern, don't give merit scholarships because, they say, everyone who's good enough to get in is good enough to deserve a merit award. Students without financial need applying to the schools listed on page 142 should plan on paying the full sticker price. But those same students typically do qualify for merit awards—sometimes substantial ones—at other private and public universities. Merit-award winners typically also have the opportunity to enroll in the college's honors program, which puts them in classes with the school's best professors, as well as other conscientious students. In some cases, these programs also let them enroll in courses ahead of other students, which helps honors students avoid the "five-year plan."

One family took this route after being admitted to Harvard, Duke, Stanford, and Northwestern. The expected family contribution was $8,000, and the student was offered no merit scholarships at those four schools. But she was also accepted to the Honors College at Ohio State, which offered a merit scholarship that brought the family's total costs to $2,000 a year.

Of course, top students are also good candidates for merit awards from less-prestigious—but still good—private colleges. Many private schools also have honors programs.

Public or private, weigh any financial benefit against the likelihood that your child will be challenged and that the school is strong in the departments in which your child hopes to concentrate his or her studies.

An honors program at a top-notch, out-of-state (or in-state) public college might offer the stellar student a quality education at a cut-rate price.

Good Values in Specific Fields

A prestigious school that's renowned for its physics and chemistry programs is probably just the right pick for the future scientist. But a lesser-known school with an excellent music program is probably a better choice for an aspiring violinist—regardless of the school's price tag or name recognition. In other words, spending $36,000 for your child to study at a prestigious university is no bargain if he or she concentrates his or her studies in one of the school's weaker departments.

If your child already has a well-developed interest in a specific field, how do you find out which schools are strong in your child's area of interest?

Ask professionals in the field what colleges they look to for new hires, or what schools have produced the most successful hires where they work.

GUIDEBOOKS ARE A START. Guidance counselors recommend these two books, and may even have them on hand for reference:

- *Rugg's Recommendations on the Colleges* ($23.95), which is organized by college major, lists schools that are strong in each field.
- *Index of Majors and Sports* ($49) is designed to complement the College Admissions Data Source Books (CADS). This resource profiles the same 1,700 institutions by major, intercollegiate sports, and 14 other areas, including tuition, cooperative education programs, honors and internship programs, religious affiliation, ROTC, and accreditations. To order, phone 978-692-9708, or go online to www.wgoh.com/index/html.

TALK TO EMPLOYERS. But admissions counselors warn that no one should take the guidebooks as gospel. A better way, many believe, is to ask professionals in the field what colleges they look to for new hires, or what schools have produced the most successful hires where they work. When that question was posed to an executive who works in hotel and restaurant management, he quickly named four schools he thinks produce the best-qualified graduates in the field: Michigan State, Cornell, Penn State, and the University of Nevada at Las Vegas.

NO CLUE. Of course, when your child's intended major is "undecided" (which is common), or if you simply want your child to get a first-class liberal-arts education, your best bet is to concentrate on the school's overall academic reputation. That way, your child will have plenty of strong options, even if he or she changes majors during college, as many students are prone to do.

Go International?

Many college students look for a college with a good study-abroad program so they can spend a semester or a year learning the language, culture, and history of another country. But how about spending all four years abroad?

One woman's two children both attended The University of St. Andrews in St. Andrews, Scotland. Her son, now graduated, chose St. Andrews because he was impressed with a representative of the college who visited his high school. Her daughter followed because she wanted to study languages, one of the college's strong suits. She's getting a $40,000 education for $20,000, plus the benefit of studying abroad to prepare her for today's international world, says her mother. Of course, an American student overseas won't be eligible for financial aid, and he or she will have to be pretty independent, given the improbability of the occasional weekend trip home.

A PROSPECTIVE COLLEGE STUDENT'S BOOKSHELF

The general guides

On bookstore shelves, you'll find numerous fat college guides, packed with comprehensive facts and statistics about virtually every college in the U.S. You need only one such guide to find out about application deadlines, average SAT scores, size of the student body, and so forth—and using one at the library or a guidance counselor's office is probably sufficient. Two such guides are:

- *College Board's College Handbook*
- *Peterson's Four-Year Colleges*

But what's it really like?

It's also helpful to read some subjective evaluations. One good resource:

- *The Fiske Guide to Colleges* (Sourcebooks, $29.95). A former education writer for the *New York Times*, Edward Fiske provides a thorough, subjective description of the 330 "best and most interesting colleges in America," with essays on each school's academics, social life, and overall "quality of life."

Making a good match

Aside from guides to the schools themselves, these resources can help students and parents evaluate what kind of school might be the best fit:

- *College Match* (Octameron Associates, $10). Through a series of worksheets and questionnaires, the first half of this workbook helps students determine what kind of college may be suitable—big or small, competitive or laid-back, and so on. The second half provides tips on campus visits, interviews, and essays.

- MyRoad offers personalized guidance online (www.myroad.com) to help students research college majors, colleges, and careers. This Web-based college and career planning program from the College Board is useful for high schoolers determining the right college and students already there with their career choices.

Select a School with Aid in Mind

It should be apparent by now that the school your child chooses can have a big impact on how much financial aid you will receive. Few families give financial aid much thought while they're helping their child figure out which schools to apply to. But unless the aid package will make no difference at all in the decision, take the time to find out about a school's financial-aid policies as well as its reputation, special academic programs, and social life. Here are some specific items to inquire about.

THE SCHOOL'S ENDOWMENT. Colleges with large endowments (money from donations, much of which traditionally funds student financial aid) naturally have the most money to award to students with financial need. Generally speaking, they're also the schools that don't "gap" (give you less than the full amount of financial aid you're eligible for; see page 138) and that have more-generous financial-aid policies. Harvard, Yale, the University of Texas, Princeton, and Stanford are among the richest, with more than $8 billion each in endowments (see the boxes on this page and the next).

SCHOOLS WITH ENDOWMENTS OVER $1 BILLION

	In billions		In billions
Harvard University	$22.1	Texas A&M University system	$4.3
Yale University	12.7	University of Michigan	4.1
University of Texas system	10.3	University of Pennsylvania	4.0
Princeton University	9.9	Washington University	4.0
Stanford University	9.9	Northwestern University	3.6
Massachusetts Institute of Technology	5.8	University of Chicago	3.6
University of California	4.7	Duke University	3.3
Emory University	4.5	Rice University	3.3
Columbia University	4.4	Cornell University	3.2
		University of Notre Dame	3.1

Source: National Association of College and University Business Officers

THE AVERAGE CLASS RANK AND SAT OR ACT SCORES OF ADMITTED STUDENTS. Consider applying to at least a couple of schools where your child ranks in the top 20% or 25% of the student body. That will improve your chances of getting a more generous aid package at a school that factors both need and merit into the financial-aid process (see the discussion of "preferential packaging" in Chapter 5, on page 136). You can get these average scores and class rankings from the school, or consult any of numerous college guidebooks, such as *U.S. News Ultimate College Guide,* a special guide published annually by *U.S. News & World Report,* or *The College Handbook,* published by the College Board.

THE SCHOOL'S "COMPETITORS." You may or may not be able to "negotiate" over your financial-aid package, asking an aid officer to improve his or her school's package to match another school's offer. (For more on negotiating an aid offer, see page 142 of Chapter 5.) But when you can negotiate, your odds are best when the schools you're playing against one another are close in admis-

LARGEST ENDOWMENTS PER STUDENT

	Per student		Per student
The Rockefeller University	$7,226,611	Swarthmore College	$724,850
Franklin W. Olin College		Webb Institute	712,314
of Engineering	2,080,020	Rice University	694,377
Princeton University	1,475,654	Stanford University	686,454
Princeton Theological Seminary	1,240,237	Williams College	612,614
Harvard University	1,161,786	Amherst College	612,087
Yale University	1,130,969	California Institute of	
Grinnell College	862,237	Technology	580,627
Marine Biological Laboratory	802,311	Massachusetts Institute of	
Academy of the New Church	786,175	Technology	569,438
The Curtis Institute of Music	757,255	Columbia Theological Seminary	553,524
Baylor College of Medicine	753,760		
Pomona College	750,470	Source: National Association of College and University Business Officers	

sions standards and reputation. You will have no chance of getting Duke to match a package from West Georgia College, but you might get it to match one from Cornell University. (*The Fiske Guide to Colleges* includes a listing of close "competitors" for each college; see page 193.) If you want to be sure you have a bargaining chip when the time comes, pair off schools by academic reputation as you apply. In other words, apply to:

■ **two so-called reach schools,** those your child may or may not get into;

■ **two schools where admission is probable;** and

■ **two so-called safety schools,** where you're virtually certain your child will get in.

COLLEGE RESOURCES ON THE INTERNET

With a little computer know-how, you can tap into some of the best and most up-to-date resources on college financial aid. Here are some excellent starting points.

The College Board Web Site
(www.collegeboard.com)
This is a rich Web site, with lots of helpful advice on financial aid and student loans. Especially handy are the online calculators for figuring out your expected family contribution and the monthly payment on a student loan.

The Financial Aid Information Page
(www.finaid.org)
This site was founded by Mark Kantrowitz, a computer-science graduate student at Carnegie Mellon University. The site provides lots of information about financial aid, student loans, scholarships, and other topics of interest to college students and their parents—with links to college financial-aid

offices, state aid agencies, instructions for filling out financial-aid forms, and much more. (The "site map" there is the best way to find all the resources available to you.)

The Sallie Mae Web site
(www.salliemae.com)
If you have a student loan, there's about a one-in-three chance you'll eventually be making your payments to Sallie Mae, the largest buyer of student loans on the secondary market, where banks sell their loans to investors. Here you'll find a list of lenders who sell their loans to Sallie Mae (making borrowers eligible for discounts when they pay on time; see page 243), plus information on student loans and several financial-aid and loan calculators. You can project future college costs and figure out, for example, how much you need to save and borrow, and how much it will cost you to defer loan payments while your child is in school.

Applying to six schools will run you several hundred dollars in application fees. (These days, many students apply to ten or more schools.) If that seems excessive, at least try to come up with a close match for your "safety" school. That's where your child is most likely to be an attractive candidate to the school, and therefore where you'd have the most leverage in negotiating a better aid package.

THE SCHOOL'S FINANCIAL-AID POLICIES. Don't skip the financial-aid office when you're touring college campuses. Be sure to ask which forms you'll have to fill out, and get a copy of the school's institutional financial-aid form, if it has one. The questions there will give you some insight into the school's aid policies, such as whether its formulas take home equity or retirement assets into account (if so, that policy is likely to increase what the school thinks you can afford to contribute). And if the school's literature doesn't address the following questions, ask someone in the financial-aid office to answer them:

Do you meet 100% of financial need? Schools that do will offer better aid packages than schools that leave a gap.

What's included in the cost of attendance? Some schools include books, commuting and transportation expenses, and spending money in the total cost, and they increase the aid package accordingly. Stanford University, for instance, includes about $1,815 for personal expenses in its annual estimate of total cost. Schools that exclude these expenses, or use stingy estimates, are gapping—even if they claim to meet 100% of need—because your actual college costs will exceed the total that's used for purposes of allocating financial aid.

What's your expected student contribution from earnings? Regardless of the federal needs analysis, which allows students a $2,440 income protection allowance, some schools expect students to contribute a mini-

> Don't skip the financial-aid office when you're touring college campuses. You can ask questions there that the school's literature may not answer.

mum sum toward costs, which you'll pay if your child can't.

How do you treat outside scholarships? Some schools use them to reduce, dollar for dollar, grants they would otherwise have offered. Others allow you to use them to reduce the required family contribution, at least in part. (For more on this, see Chapter 8.)

Do you include as financial aid unsubsidized Stafford loans (student loans on which the students pay interest while in college) and PLUS loans (parent loans for undergraduate students)? The answer should be no. Those loans are meant to help you finance your expected family contribution, and colleges that award them to meet your financial need are practicing another sneaky form of gapping.

For divorced parents: Whose finances do you consider when awarding aid? Do you include the income and assets of both natural parents? What about the custo-

---

FINANCIAL QUESTIONS TO ASK ON YOUR CAMPUS VISIT

- **What's the school's endowment?** The endowment per student?
- **What is the average SAT score and class rank?**
- **Do you meet 100% of financial need,** or do you leave a gap?
- **What expenses are included in the cost of attendance?** What are the allowances for transportation, books, and personal expenses?
- **Do you expect students to contribute** a certain amount of earnings toward college costs?
- **If my child is receiving financial aid,** will an outside scholarship replace a loan or a grant I would otherwise receive from the school?
- **Do you include unsubsidized Stafford loans or PLUS loans** in financial-aid packages?
- **For divorced parents:** Whose income and assets are included in financial-aid calculations?
- **Do you help students find paid internships or co-op jobs?**
- **Can my child finish early** if he or she has enough advanced-placement credits?
- **Do you have an accelerated-degree program?**
- **Can I pay tuition in installments?**

dial parent and any stepparent? Or is there some other combination?

You shouldn't necessarily eliminate a school based on its answers to these questions, but if you learn that its aid policies will likely be unfavorable to your circumstances, you can choose a more favorable backup. That will give you an alternative if you decide you really can't afford your first choice once you know exactly what it will cost you. (For more on these issues, see Chapters 4 and 5.)

IS THE SCHOOL NEED-BLIND OR NOT? Colleges have begun to stray from the once-cherished ideal of "need-blind" admissions—the policy of considering all students on their academic merits, regardless of their ability to pay. Instead, many private institutions have begun to look at a family's need for financial aid—and in certain cases to give the edge to those students who need the least.

Under a "need-sensitive" or "need-conscious" admissions policy, a typical college might rank candidates on a scale of 1 to 10, based on their academic credentials. All students rated, say, 1 to 5 would be admitted regardless of financial need. Students ranked lower might be chosen to fill out the remaining 5% to 15% of the class, but for them, ability to pay would be a consideration.

Colleges blame the shift in policy on swelling financial-aid demands in the wake of cutbacks in state and federal grants. So far, the practice has primarily been limited to the most selective and expensive private schools, including Bryn Mawr, in Pennsylvania, and Carleton College, in Minnesota, which have more applicants than openings. About 200 colleges in the country fall into that category.

Many schools are reluctant to disclose a need-sensitive admissions policy ahead of time. So what should your approach be? Students with financial need who apply to need-sensitive schools should apply to at least one backup school that they can afford without much financial aid. Don't refrain from

Colleges have begun to stray from the once-cherished ideal of "need-blind" admissions.

Parents of high school seniors are often shocked by the number and size of the fees and expenses they must pay just to earn the right to write tuition checks.

applying for financial aid in the hope that you will have an edge over students who do apply. Many colleges estimate a student's ability to pay without ever seeing a financial-aid form, simply by looking at the family's address and the parents' occupations. And if a student does get in, he or she faces a choice between borrowing heavily to cover costs or having to reject the school anyway.

A better strategy for families with financial need is to apply to a couple of schools where the student's grades and test scores are above average. Strong students tend to have their pick of colleges, and they often get a richer aid package than marginal students as an inducement to enroll.

The Cost of Getting into College

Parents of high school seniors are often shocked by the number and size of the fees and expenses they must pay just to earn the right to write tuition checks. One New Jersey father shelled out more than $4,000 to help his daughter get into college—and that didn't include the week he took off from work to visit campuses. The tally:

prep course
for the Scholastic Achievement Test (SAT) $900
the SAT $41.50
food and lodging
during a weeklong tour of East Coast campuses $2,000
several trips
to nearby campuses $100 to $150 each
applications
to eight colleges at $50 each $400
books
on paying for college and applying for financial aid   about $100

In the end, his daughter decided to study nursing at the University of Pennsylvania, at a total cost of $42,100 a year.

The parents of most college-bound students spend a lot less than this father. Even so, the costs are often unexpectedly high and come at the worst possible time—in a year when the family budget will also be nickel-and-dimed to death for such senior-year extras as the class ring, cap and gown, a fancy dress or tux for the prom, and the senior trip. But choosing a college needn't drain your savings. All too often parents believe they must buy a small library of books or sign up for special courses when all the assistance they need is available free or at a reasonable cost, says Joyce Smith, associate executive director of the National Association of College Admission Counselors, in Alexandria, Virginia.

SAT Preparation

A growing number of high schools offer weekend or after-school SAT preparation courses and provide students with computer programs designed to improve SAT scores. A graduate of Concord High School, in Concord, New Hampshire, says he used his school's free software and boosted his SAT scores by 170 points over the first time he took the test.

If your child can't borrow test-prep software or books through the school library, you can purchase them on your own.

- *The Official SAT Study Guide for the New SAT* ($19.95), the program of the College Board, the nonprofit association that sponsors the SAT.
- *Cracking the New SAT* (Princeton Review, $31.95 for book and CD-ROM)
- *Kaplan's SAT* (Kaplan, $32.00 for book and CD-ROM)

Campus Visits

Once a student zeros in on a particular school, at least one on-site visit is desirable—and often that is the most expensive part of the selection process. When a New Hampshire high school senior and his father visited his first-choice school, Oberlin College, in Ohio, the trip cost more than $1,500, including round-trip airfare to

Once a student zeros in on a particular school, at least one on-site visit is desirable—and often that is the most expensive part of the selection process.

QUESTIONS AND RESOURCES FOR CAMPUS TOURS

College officials are the best people to address questions about admissions and financial aid. But the campus tour, usually conducted by a student, is your chance to get the inside skinny on what campus life is really like. You might want to ask:

- **Is the campus secure?** Is there an escort system? Do you walk alone at night?
- **How big are classes**—freshman year and later on?
- **What do students do on weekends?** Does the school's social life revolve around fraternities and sororities? Can you comfortably be an independent?
- **Who are the best professors?**
- **What are the most popular classes?**
- **Who's teaching introductory classes,** professors or graduate students?

- **What's the campus housing like?** Do most students stay on campus in their junior and senior years?
- **How's the food?**

While you're on campus, also get a copy of the current course catalog if you don't have one already. That will give you a vivid picture of what your child's selection of courses will be like.

A book that may be helpful as you prepare to embark on college tours is *Visiting College Campuses* (Princeton Review, $20). This guidebook tells you how to get to 250 U.S. campuses by plane, train, or automobile and lists local hotels, regularly scheduled tour dates and times, and local attractions—in case you have some spare time.

Cleveland, a rental car, and a hotel for Dad. (The prospective freshman stayed in the dorm.) A lot of families would find ways to make the trip for less, but this father takes a sanguine view of all the money he has spent getting his son into college. "Money is always an issue, but if you're talking about spending four years at a place and shelling out close to $140,000 to do it, it's worth investing some money up front to make sure you make a good decision."

If you can't make the trip, many colleges and universities provide videotape programs about their schools to prospective students who ask for them. But another, less-biased choice for armchair "screening" tours is Collegiate Choice Walking Tours, videotaped at both U.S. and international college campuses (Collegiate Choice, 41 Surrey Lane, Tenafly, NJ 07670; www.collegiatechoice.com; $15 each plus $8 shipping per order). These aren't as slick as the free promotional tapes schools provide. Instead, the camera records a student-led tour of the campus, including questions from members of the tour group. "You'll see what you'd see if you went on the tour yourself," including the blemishes, says Cliff Kramon, who tapes most of the tours.

The Great Scholarship Quest

Your kid is a science whiz, a gifted writer, or a future Chopin or Matisse. So you skipped straight to this chapter to find the organizations that will reward his or her talents with big-bucks scholarships. Wishful thinking.

First, go back to Chapters 4 and 5 and spend most of your time there, getting to know how financial aid works. The fact is that 96% of college assistance is in the form of financial aid from federal and state governments and need- and merit-based aid from the schools themselves, and only about 4% is in private scholarships from organizations other than the schools.

There's money out there, to be sure, and someone has to win it. But finding and winning scholarships is an extra-credit project—with the emphasis on project. Filling out applications, getting recommendations, writing essays, and otherwise competing for scholarship money is time-consuming work for the applicant. And it's not always as rewarding as you might hope.

Most scholarships fall into one of three categories:

1. The incredibly narrow. Know anyone who would qualify for a scholarship for left-handed Lithuanians studying horticulture? Okay, that's a slight exaggeration, but consider some real awards:

- **From the American Pomological Society,** stipends for the best research or historical paper on fruit breeding.
- **From the Harness Horse Youth Foundation,** $1,500 to $3,500 scholarships to students interested in pursuing horse-related careers.

> **The competition itself can be a great experience for young people. Just be aware that lots of superbright, supertalented kids don't win.**

■ **From the Rocky Mountain Coal Mining Institute,** 15 $2,000 scholarships for students from Western states interested in a career in mining or geology.

Most of the time, the glass slipper just doesn't fit.

2. The supercompetitive. Some scholarship competitions could make you want to head for the lottery window instead.

■ **Thousands of high school seniors** apply for an ESPN Scholastic Sports America Scholarship, but only a limited number receive one. Winners receive a year's tuition for junior or senior year, a 12-week summer internship, and a visit to ESPN's Connecticut headquarters.

■ **More than 1,500 science prodigies** compete in the Intel Science Talent Search for 40 awards of $5,000 to $100,000.

■ **Another 7,000 dependents** of public or private school employees apply for 12 awards of $2,500 to $15,000 in the Horace Mann Scholarship competition.

Admittedly, many of the scholarships listed on pages 216–223 fall into this category. We've included them because they're some of the best-known and most prestigious awards. There's nothing wrong with competing for them—the competition itself can be a great experience for young people. Just be aware that lots of superbright, supertalented kids don't win. (Although people may scoff at Miss America, Miss Teenage America, and Junior Miss pageants as scholarship competitions, they are just as competitive as many of the more "serious" competitions—and they award a lot more money.)

3. The drop in the bucket. A huge number of scholarships you'll find listed in aid directories, available at your public library (see page 210) are for $500 or less, which maybe buys a semester's books. Yes, money is money. And the award itself adds an extra spark to the college application. But your kid might have an easier time earning $500 than meeting the entry requirements for a half-dozen scholarship competitions that might yield a $500 prize.

The Scholarship Mirage

Despite all the hurdles, say that your college-bound student wins a fantastic private scholarship. It's a proud moment. But be prepared for a rude surprise: The financial award might not help you as much as you might think with the college bills. Why not? When giving out financial aid, some colleges subtract the value of an outside scholarship from need-based grants they would have awarded, freeing up the funds for other students. Their view: You now have additional resources to cover the bills, so you need that much less help from the school. The result: Your out-of-pocket contribution to college costs remains as great as before the scholarship.

There is good news on this front, however. Many of the more-prestigious private colleges have softened their policy on outside scholarships, so that such awards replace student loans and work-study first. Then, if there's still scholarship money remaining, it replaces need-based grants. If, for instance, your child won a $10,000 outside scholarship, the first $4,000 or so might replace a $2,600 student loan and $1,400 in work-study. But the remaining $6,000 would replace an equivalent amount in grants from the college (if you were awarded that much). Thus the money may not be available to help you meet your expected parent contribution.

What if the school is one of an increasing number of schools that "gap," or leave families with a certain amount of unmet need (see the discussion in Chapter 5)? Most colleges that gap will allow an outside scholarship to cover that unmet need, which is only fair. Let's say, for instance, that you have $10,000 of need at a $20,000 college that meets just 90% of your need with a $9,000 aid package. Such a school would allow the first $1,000 of any outside scholarship to go toward

When giving out financial aid, some colleges subtract the value of an outside scholarship from need-based grants they would have awarded.

Scholarship seekers who stand to benefit most are those who don't expect to qualify for any financial aid or whose aid packages will consist mostly of loans.

meeting the gap, before using any additional scholarship money to replace grants, work-study, or loans in your aid package.

How will schools know that your child has received the scholarship? Most scholarship sponsors make the check out to both your child and the school. When the bursar's office receives such a check from a company or foundation, they typically flag it as scholarship money and notify the financial-aid office.

Before your son or daughter scouts out and applies for scholarships, ask a financial-aid officer at each college you're considering how the school treats outside awards.

- **If the school uses scholarships only to replace its own aid,** it probably doesn't make much sense to spend a lot of effort applying for scholarships.
- **If the college lets some or all of the scholarship go to replace loans** rather than grants (or, even better, to reduce your own contribution), then finding outside money is worth the effort.

Who Should Seek Scholarships?

Now that we've knocked the idea of scrambling after scholarship money, we're going to spend the rest of this chapter telling you how to do just that. Why? Because not everyone qualifies for financial aid. And some students (and parents) don't mind expending the time and effort to seek scholarships even if the gain might be small.

Here's who stands to benefit the most:

- **Families who don't expect to qualify for any financial aid** or whose aid packages will consist mostly of loans.
- **Families who do expect aid but are applying to schools that gap,** leaving students with unmet financial need.
- **Families who expect aid but are applying to colleges that have favorable policies toward scholarships**—for example, they use outside scholarships to replace loans and work-study in your financial-aid package, which your child would otherwise have to earn or

repay, rather than using them to replace their own institutional grants.

■ **Students who enjoy the thrill of competing and the prestige of winning,** even if the award doesn't reduce college costs.

Where to Look

The listing on pages 216–223 provides a sampling of big-dollar national scholarships and competitions. They're worth a look, and an entry if you think your child has a shot. Wherever possible, we've included an indication of the odds of winning.

To find local awards that are probably less of a long shot, prepare to do some detective work. Here's a list of leads to get you started.

Your High School Guidance Counselor

Most guidance counselors maintain a bulletin board or keep a folder of scholarship opportunities. That's an excellent place to find out about local groups sponsoring scholarships. Many national organizations, such as those listed at the end of the chapter, also distribute scholarship applications through high school guidance counselors, which saves you the trouble and wait of sending away for materials.

College Financial-Aid Officers

Drop in at the financial-aid office as you're touring college campuses, or pick up the phone and call if you're unable to make the trip. Ask whether the schools offer merit-based scholarships, and what grades, SAT scores, or other criteria would make your child eligible. The University of Massachusetts at Amherst, for instance, awards $6,000 scholarships to Massachusetts residents who have earned a 3.8 or better grade-point average and a score of 1,400 or better on the SAT, and $10,000 per year to students who rank first or second in their high-school class and have a score of 1,200 or more on the SAT. And the University of Central Oklahoma encourages Oklahoma residents who have been admitted

To find local awards that are probably less of a long shot, prepare to do some detective work.

Computerized services that you see advertised in newspapers or online are sometimes poor values— and sometimes outright rip-offs.

to apply for awards, some for full tuition. Applicants must be enrolled for a minimum of 12 credit hours, have a minimum composite ACT score of 27, and a minimum 3.25 GPA.

Find out whether you must apply and submit recommendations for such awards or whether the school awards them automatically based on information you've supplied on your child's application for admission. Also ask about departmental scholarships in your child's intended major.

Scholarship Directories

A rainy Saturday afternoon is a perfect time to hit the library and page through a couple of scholarship guides. There are dozens, each with page after page of scholarships—the small and obscure along with the big and prestigious. One good choice is the *Chronicle Financial Aid Guide* (check the reference section of your library or contact Chronicle Guidance Publications, www.chronicleguidance.com, 800-899-0454; $24.98).

Search Services Versus Free Databases

Should you use a computerized service to help you find scholarships? Those you see advertised in newspapers or online are sometimes poor values—and sometimes outright rip-offs. The $40 to $200 or more you spend may turn up awards with narrow eligibility or ones your child has only a remote chance of winning. Sometimes the search companies even claim that their services are "guaranteed" and offer a refund or a $200 savings bond to students who don't receive any scholarship money. But the Council of Better Business Bureaus has warned that such refunds are "difficult, if not impossible, to obtain," requiring, for instance, that you prove you applied for every scholarship on the list and were turned down. Besides, you don't need to pay a lot of money for someone else to do a computerized scholarship search when you can do it just as well or better yourself with the following resources.

FUND FINDER. You can probably tap into one of the best searches around in your high school guidance counselor's office—at no charge. One thousand high schools subscribe to the College Board's MyRoad, a database of thousands of private grants and scholarships.

THE COLLEGE BOARD'S WEB SITE. If your high school doesn't have Fund Finder, you can search the database at the College Board's Web site (http://apps.collegeboard .com/cbsearch_ss/welcome.jsp).

OTHER FREE SEARCHES. Other free search programs can be accessed on the Web, including fastWeb (www .fastweb.com) and (www.collegenet.com). To use fastWeb, for example, students complete a questionnaire that asks about their major subject, grade-point average, special interests, and ethnic origin, among other things. Within 15 minutes the program searches its database of financial-aid resources and returns via e-mail a customized listing of scholarships, grants, and loans your child may be eligible for, along with addresses, deadlines, and form letters that you can print out and mail to scholarship sponsors to request details. As new financial-aid listings are added to the database, fastWeb will alert students by e-mail to any that fit their profile.

High School Clubs

If your child belongs to the Latin club, Thespian club, National Honor Society, or other high school club, or a national scouting organization, he or she might be eligible for a scholarship or learn of scholarship competitions. Encourage your child to ask the club advisor to watch for awards he or she might want to apply or compete for. If the advisor or teacher chooses the nominees, your child's expression of interest might tip the scale in his or her favor.

Your Employer

Since 1969, Wal-Mart Stores Inc. has given more than $80 million in scholarships to children of employees and to the general public. Similarly, hundreds of other

Hundreds of large employers have generous grants and scholarships available to children of employees.

Every state has scholarships, grants, or loans available only to its residents.

large employers have generous grants and scholarships available to children of employees. Usually the programs are well publicized, and your company's human resources office will have details.

Professional Associations

Your child wants to study engineering? Nursing? Journalism? There's probably an association—like the National Society of Professional Engineers, National Student Nurses Association, or National Press Club— that wants to support the education of a potential member. The *Encyclopedia of Associations*, available in libraries, can help you pinpoint possibilities. Also check with any associations to which you belong; some award scholarships to children of members.

Unions

Scores of unions award scholarships to the college-bound children of members—from the American Postal Workers Union (five $4,000 awards, renewable for four years) to the Utility Workers Union of America (two awards, ranging from $500 to $2,000, renewable for four years). If your local chapter can't provide information, write to the union's national headquarters (often in Washington, D.C.) for an application.

Local Community and Civic Groups

Elks, Jaycees, Kiwanis, Lions, and similar civic groups often have funds earmarked for local college-bound students. The Elks, for instance, award more than $3 million annually nationwide. Call around to groups in your area to see what's available and how to apply.

State Agencies

Every state has scholarships, grants, or loans available only to its residents. In one of the more-generous state programs, any Georgia high school student with a 3.0 GPA or better receives a full waiver of tuition at any public college, university, or technical institute in the state or $3,000 to help offset tuition costs at any private school in the state. The program, called HOPE (Helping Outstanding Pupils Educationally), is funded by a state lottery. Many states provide grants to students willing to spend a few years in teaching or law enforcement after graduation (see page 241 of Chapter 9 for information about similar loan programs).

To find out what's available in your state, contact one of the state grant agencies listed on pages 132–134.

Advocacy Organizations for Ethnic Groups

There is an especially large group of scholarship programs for:

- **African-American students** (from numerous groups, including the NAACP, www.naacp.org; the National Urban League, www.nul.org; and others),
- **Hispanic students** (from, among others, the National Hispanic Scholarship Fund, www.hsf.net; the National Association of Hispanic Journalists, www.nahj.org; and the National Association of Hispanic Nurses, www.thehispanicnurses.org),
- **Indian/Alaskan students** (from the Bureau of Indian Affairs, www.doi.gov/bureau-indian-affairs.html; the Native American Scholarship Fund; and the Indian Health Service, www.ihs.gov), and
- **Italian-Americans** (primarily from the National Italian American Foundation, www.niaf.org).

But a little digging turns up scholarships for many other ethnic groups, including students of Albanian, Armenian, Asian, Chinese, Danish, Greek, Haitian, Japanese, Mexican, Nicaraguan, Norwegian, Polish, Portuguese, Swiss, and Welsh extraction.

These guidebooks (published by the Reference Service Press, 5000 Windplay Dr., Suite 4, El Dorado Hills, CA 95762; 916–939–9620; www.rspfunding.com; also in libraries) are a good place to start looking, although for most ethnic groups that aren't traditionally considered underprivileged, general scholarship directories are probably a better bet:

- *Financial Aid for African Americans* ($40.00)
- *Financial Aid for Asian Americans* ($37.50)
- *Financial Aid for Hispanic Americans* ($40.00)
- *Financial Aid for Native Americans* ($40.00)

> A little digging turns up scholarships for many other ethnic groups.

A little creative thinking about your child's recreational interests or hobbies might lead you to an offbeat scholarship.

Advocacy Groups for Disabled People

The National Federation of the Blind and the Alexander Graham Bell Association for the Deaf and Hard of Hearing are among the organizations that offer scholarships for disabled students. Here's a directory to try: *Financial Aid for the Disabled and Their Families* ($40; the Reference Service Press; see above).

Religious Groups

The Presbyterian Church in the USA, United Methodist Church, Aid Association for Lutherans, and Knights of Columbus are among the religious organizations with nationally organized scholarship programs.

Military Groups

Dozens of scholarship programs target children of military personnel whose parents may be active members of the armed forces, war veterans, deceased or disabled service personnel, MIAs and former POWs, retired officers, and members of specific branches or divisions of the military.

One guide to consult is an American Legion publication: *Need a Lift?* ($3.95; *Need a Lift?*, National Emblem Sales, P.O. Box 1050, Indianapolis, IN 46206; 888-453-4466).

Hobby or Other Connections

A little creative thinking about your child's recreational interests or hobbies might lead you to an offbeat scholarship. For instance, Columbia 300 Inc., a marketer of bowling balls, gives the $500 John Jowdy scholarship each year to a high school senior active in bowling. The National Scholastic Surfing Association awards scholarships in varying amounts to high school members who are surfing competitors and have good grades.

Special Advice for Athletes

If your child is the next Michael Jordan or Mia Hamm, colleges will come courting. But otherwise, students who are good athletes or excel in a more-obscure sport will need to put some effort into pursuing a scholarship or preferential aid package—and realize that the competition will probably be stiff.

Students who don't earn an athletic scholarship sometimes receive financial assistance in the form of an enhanced financial-aid package. These tips can help your child be in the running for either kind of help.

- **Write letters to the coaches at colleges to which you plan to apply.** Include a résumé of your athletic accomplishments, a letter of recommendation from your high school coach, and a video of up to five minutes showing off your skills.
- **Send your letter in advance of your final season in the sport you play,** in case a recruiter wants to catch a game. You may also want to include a schedule.
- **When you visit colleges, make an appointment to meet with the coach in your sport** to reinforce the message that you're interested. Don't be shy about mentioning that you need financial aid, because coaches often have influence over admissions and financial-aid decisions for athletes.

> **FOR BOY SCOUTS ONLY**
>
> Current and former Boy Scouts may want to send for a free copy of *Scholarship Information for Scouts and Explorers* from the Boy Scouts of America (1325 W. Walnut Hill Lane, Bin Item #99-052, Irving, TX 75015).

For more detailed advice, consult any of the following books:

- *The Winning Edge: The Student Athlete's Guide to College Sports,* by Frances and James Killpatrick (Octameron Associates, $6; 703-836-5480; www.octameron.com)
- *NCAA Guide for the College-Bound Student-Athlete* (available on the Internet at www.ncaa.org/eligibility/cbsa)

Tips for Scholarship Seekers

Thousands of bright students compete each year for scholarships. How can you improve your chances of coming away with a coveted prize?

continued on page 224

SCHOLARSHIPS OF BROAD INTEREST

From the thousands of available awards, we chose a representative sampling that reflects the range of talents and interests that might qualify a student for a scholarship. While many of these competitions are very competitive, we strove to include as many as possible with high-dollar prizes or a large number of winners.

ACADEMICS AND LEADERSHIP

Coca-Cola Scholars Foundation Inc.
Awards: 250 awards from $4,000 to $20,000 per year
Criteria: Character, personal merit, leadership in school and community, academic achievement
Deadline: October 31
Contact: High school counselor or e-mail scholars@na.ko.com

Educational Communications Scholarship Foundation
Awards: 127 awards from $1,000 to $6,000 per year
Criteria: Grades, SAT/ACT test scores, and leadership activities of high school students who are U.S. citizens
Deadline: May 15
Contact: Educational Communications Scholarship Foundation, 721 N. McKinley Rd., Lake Forest, IL 60045, or high school counselor or e-mail scholars@ecsf.org

Elks Most Valuable Student Scholarship
Awards: 500 four-year scholarships, from $1,000 to $15,000 per year
Criteria: Scholarship, leadership, and financial need. Must be U.S. citizen.
Deadline: Mid-January
Contact: Local Elks Club will provide state association address or www.elks.org

National Honor Society Scholarship Program for National Honor Society Members
Awards: 200 $1,000 scholarships
Criteria: Scholarship, character, service, leadership. For high school seniors who are National Honor Society members; each school that is a member of NHS may nominate two students.
Deadline: Late January
Contact: National Honor Society advisor or call 1-800-253-7746

National Merit Scholarship Program
Awards: 2,500 $2,500 scholarships, as well as corporate- and college-sponsored scholarships
Criteria: Top scorers on PSAT/NMSQT admission exams
Deadline: October of junior year
Contact: High school counselor or www.nationalmerit.org

Sam Walton Community Scholarship
Awards: Two scholarships of $1,000 from each community with a participating Wal-Mart store
Criteria: High school records, SAT or ACT scores, financial need, and school involvement
Deadline: February 1
Contact: High school counselor; www.walmartfoundation.org/scholarship

William Randolph Hearst Foundation United States Senate Youth Program

Awards: 104 $5,000 college scholarships for high school juniors and seniors who hold elected student office and who pledge to study government or a related field. Winners participate in an all-expenses-paid trip to the Senate Youth Program's Washington Week.

Criteria: Must be nominated by High School principal; based on merit and community service; most hold an elected school office.

Deadline: Varies by state; usually early fall

Contact: Guidance counselor or United States Senate Youth Program, William Randolph Hearst Foundation, 90 New Montgomery St., #1212, San Francisco, CA 94105 (800-841-7048; or e-mail: www.ussenateyouth.org)

THE ARTS

Annual Glenn Miller Scholarship Competition

Awards: Four $1,000 to $2,400 awards for instrumentalists and vocalists who "intend to make music a central part of their future life." Winners perform at the Glenn Miller Festival Stage show.

Criteria: Applicants send a screening tape and statement of musical intention. Finalists audition live.

Deadline: March 15

Contact: Glenn Miller Scholarship Committee, 107 E. Main St., Clarinda, IA 51632 (717-542-2461)

National Federation of Music Clubs Competitions and Awards

Awards: Offers more than $750,000 in competition and award prizes on the local, state, and national levels

Criteria: Selected based on auditions

Deadline: Varies by competition

Contact: Request a copy of the Scholarships and Awards chart from the National Federation of Music Clubs, 1336 N. Delaware St., Indianapolis, IN 46202. Application fees vary depending on award. (www.nfmc-music.org)

National Foundation for Advancement in the Arts Arts Recognition and Talent Search

Awards: Hundreds of cash grants, from $100 to $10,000

Criteria: Students submit samples of their work on videotape, audiotape or slides, or in writing. Those accepted compete in dance, music, theater, visual arts, writing, photography, and voice.

Deadline: Early deadline is June 1; regular deadline is October 1.

Contact: Arts Recognition and Talent Search, NFAA, 444 Brickell Ave., P-14, Miami, FL 33131 (800-970-2787; www.nfaa.org)

Scholastic Art Awards

Awards: Seven $10,000 awards (five in art, two in photography). More than 60 schools offer additional tuition scholarships; amounts vary with each school, ranging from $1,000 to full tuition.

Criteria: Outstanding ability based on portfolios

SCHOLARSHIPS OF BROAD INTEREST *continued*

Deadline: Varies
Contact: Request a portfolio entry form from Scholastic Visual Awards, Portfolio Entry Form, 555 Broadway, New York, NY 10012. Enclose an SASE. (212-343-6493; www.artandwriting.org)

VFW National Auxiliary Young American Creative Patriotic Art Awards

Awards: Three prizes, from $2,500 to $10,000, to further winners' education
Criteria: Students compete at local and state levels to be eligible for national awards.
Deadline: Changes each year
Contact: Local VFW Auxiliary or Administrator of Programs, Ladies Auxiliary, VFW, 406 W. 34th St., Kansas City, MO 64111 (816-561-8655)

ATHLETICS

Western Golf Association/Evans Scholars Foundation Chick Evans Caddy Scholarship

Awards: 200 full tuition-and-housing scholarships, renewable for up to four years, for students who have caddied for at least two years at a Western Golf Association member club and who are in top 25% of their class
Criteria: Outstanding character, integrity, leadership, financial need, academics, and two years as an outstanding caddy
Deadline: September 30 of senior year
Contact: Sponsoring golf club or Scholarship Committee, Western Golf Association/Evans Scholars Foundation, 1 Briar Rd., Golf, IL 60029 (847-724-4600; www.westerngolfassociation.com)

Women's Western Golf Foundation

Awards: 18 to 21 $2,000 annual scholarships, renewable for four years, for high school senior girls with involvement in golf (skill isn't a criterion)
Number of applicants: 400
Criteria: High academic achievement, financial need, and excellence of character
Deadline: April 5; preliminary application form due March 1
Contact: Send SASE to Mrs. Richard Willis, Director of Scholarships, 393 Ramsay Rd., Deerfield, IL 60015 (847-945-0451; www.wwga.org)

BUSINESS

Distributive Education Clubs of America (DECA) Scholarship

Awards: More than 20 scholarships of $1,000 each for students planning to major in management, marketing, marketing education, or entrepreneurship
Criteria: Must be an active member of DECA and rank in top one-third of class. Selection based on merit, club participation and accomplishments, leadership, responsibility, and character.
Deadline: Second Monday of March, but must first meet state deadline, usually January or February
Contact: DECA, 1908 Association Dr., Reston, VA 20191 (703-860-5000; www.deca.org)

Karla Scherer Foundation
Scholarship Program

Awards: Varying number of scholarship awards and amounts, depending on available funds and number of applicants, for women who are accepted into the Master of Arts in the Humanities at the University of Chicago

Criteria: Applicant must send a statement that includes his or her particular area of interest and detailed description of career plan.

Deadline: March 1. SASE required

Contact: Karla Scherer Foundation, 737 N. Michigan Ave., Suite 2330, Chicago, IL 60611 (www.comnet.org/kschererf)

ETHNICITY
National Italian American Foundation

Awards: Varying number of scholarships, from $2,500 to $10,000, for Italian American students or students of any ethnic background who are majoring or minoring in Italian language or Italian studies

Criteria: Need, academics, field of study interest, and career objectives. Applications are available online and must be submitted electronically at www.niaf.org/scholarships.

Deadline: April 30

Contact: Send e-mail to scholarships@niaf.org or write to the National Italian American Foundation, 1860 19th St., N.W., Washington, DC 20009

United Negro College Fund

Awards: More than 400 awards ranging from $500 to full tuition at 38 member colleges and universities, mostly historically black schools; $60 million in scholarships awarded each year.

Criteria: Students are considered without regard to race, creed, color, or ethnic origin. Must take SAT and file for financial aid.

Deadline: Varies

Contact: Send SASE to Program Services, 8260 Willow Oaks Corp. Dr., P.O. Box 10444, Fairfax, VA 22031-8044 (800-331-2244; www.uncf.org)

GOVERNMENT
Washington Crossing Foundation
National and Regional Awards

Awards: National awards range from $1,000 to $4,200. Varying awards of up to $20,000 for residents of Pennsylvania for students planning a career in government service

Number of applicants: NA

Criteria: U.S. citizen, purpose in career choice, understanding of career requirements, leadership qualities, sincerity, historical perspective

Deadline: January 15

Contact: For application, send SASE to Washington Crossing Foundation, P.O. Box 503, Levittown, PA 19058-0503 (215-949-8841; www.gwcf.org)

SCHOLARSHIPS OF BROAD INTEREST *continued*

HISTORY
National History Day
Awards: Three winners ($250 to $1,000) in each of 17 categories
Criteria: Students submit research papers, projects, live performances, and media presentations. Local and state winners compete at a national competition. Work judged on historical quality, quality of presentation, adherence to theme and rules.
Deadline: Fall
Contact: State history day coordinators or National History Day Inc., 0119 Cecil Hall, University of Maryland, College Park, MD 20742 (www.nationalhistoryday.org)

National Society of the Daughters of the American Revolution NSDAR American History Scholarships
Awards: One $8,000 first-place award ($2,000 per year), several second-place awards of $4,000 ($1,000 per year) given as funds are available.
Number of applicants: NA
Criteria: Seniors planning to major in history. Commitment to study of history, financial need, academic excellence, and a letter of sponsorship from a local DAR chapter
Deadline: February 1
Contact: Local DAR chapter or www.dar.org

MILITARY AFFILIATION
American Legion Auxiliary National President's Scholarship
Awards: Five $2,500, five $2,000, and five $1,000 scholarships for children of veterans who served in U.S. armed forces in WWI, WWII, Korea, Vietnam, Grenada, Lebanon, Panama, or Persian Gulf conflicts
Criteria: Character, leadership, scholarship, need, plus 50 hours of community service
Deadline: March 10
Contact: Local American Legion Auxiliary unit or state headquarters (www.legion-aux.org)

AMVETS National Scholarships
Awards: Undetermined number of $4,000 awards ($1,000 per year) to high school seniors and veterans. Seniors who are members of the Junior ROTC are also eligible for one $1,000 scholarship.
Criteria: Membership in AMVETS or have one parent or grandparent who is a member (or deceased parent or grandparent who would have been eligible). Academic achievement and financial need
Deadline: April 15
Contact: Send an SASE to AMVETS National Headquarters, 4647 Forbes Blvd., Lanham, MD 20706 (www.amvets.org)

Daughters of the Cincinnati Scholarship
Awards: Varying number of scholarships and amounts, up to $3,000
Criteria: High school senior and daughter of a career officer commissioned in the regular Army, Air Force, Navy, Coast Guard, or Marine Corps
Deadline: Postmarked March 15
Contact: Daughters of the Cincinnati, 122 E. 58th St., New York, NY 10022 (212-319-6915)

PUBLIC SPEAKING

American Legion National High School Oratorical Contest

Awards: Three national winners ($14,000 to $18,000); 50 state and 4 foreign division winners ($1,500 each), and 6 national semifinalists ($1,500 each)

Criteria: Excellence in addressing topic on U.S. constitution; contest open to all high school students

Deadline: State deadlines January 1

Contact: Local American Legion post (www.legion.org) or high school guidance counselor

The National Society of the Sons of the American Revolution Joseph S. Rumbaugh Oration Contest

Awards: One $3,000 (first place), one $2,000 (second place), and one $1,000 (third place) prize

Criteria: Five- to six-minute oration about an event, document, or personality showing the influence of the Revolutionary War on America today. Will be judged on composition, delivery, logic, significance, general excellence, and time limit. Not all of the states participate.

Deadline: Contest held in June. Preliminary state competitions held March/April

Contact: National Society of the Sons of the American Revolution, Joseph S. Rumbaugh Oration Contest, 1000 S. 4th St., Louisville, KY 40203 (502-589-1776; www.sar.org)

SCIENCE AND ENGINEERING

American Physical Society Corporate-Sponsored Scholarship for Minority Undergraduate Students Who Major in Physics

Awards: Twenty-five $2,000 awards, renewable after first year

Criteria: High school seniors, college freshmen or sophomores. Must be a U.S. citizen (or permanent resident) of African-American, Hispanic, or Native American descent, majoring in physics.

Deadline: Early February

Contact: Arlene Modeste-Knowles, Program Coordinator, American Physical Society, 1 Physics Ellipse, College Park, MD 20740-3844 (301-209-3232; www.aps.org/educ)

General Electric Corp./Society of Women Engineers

Awards: $1,000 to $5,000 scholarships available for freshman women entering engineering

Criteria: High school record (minimum 3.5 GPA), teacher recommendation, character reference, essay on why applicant would like to be an engineer. Must be a U.S. citizen.

Deadline: May 15

Contact: Society of Women Engineers, 230 E. Ohio St., Suite 400, Chicago, IL 60611-3265 (312-596-5223; www.swe.org)

Intel Science Talent Search

Awards: Ten awards of $20,000 to $100,000, 30 awards of $5,000

Number of applicants: 1,600

SCHOLARSHIPS OF BROAD INTEREST *continued*

Criteria: Research report, teacher recommendations, high school records, SAT scores
Deadline: Mid-November (call for date)
Contact: Science Service Inc., 1719 N St., N.W., Washington, DC 20036 (202-785-2255; www.sciserv.org)

TEACHING
Horace Mann Scholarships
Awards: One $15,000 scholarship, one $10,000 scholarship, and ten $2,500 scholarships for high school seniors who are dependents of public school employees
Criteria: Academics, written essay, activities, letters of recommendation, test scores
Deadline: March
Contact: P.O. Box 20490, Springfield, IL 62708 (800-999-1030; www.horacemann.com)

Phi Delta Kappa Scholarship Grants for Prospective Educators
Awards: One $5,000 grant, one $4,000 grant, one $2,000 grant, and 30 $1,000 grants, for high school seniors planning to pursue careers as teachers
Criteria: Open to high school seniors, academic record, recommendations, essay, school and community activities
Deadline: January 15
Contact: Phi Delta Kappa local chapters or send SASE to Phi Delta Kappa International, 408 N. Union St., P.O. Box 789, Bloomington, IN 47402-0789 (www.pdkintl.org)

WRITING/JOURNALISM
Edward J. Nell Memorial Scholarship Program
Awards: One $1,000 award, eight or nine $500 awards for intended majors in journalism
Criteria: Students first compete in national writing/photography or yearbook excellence contests. Top entrants qualify to compete for Nell scholarships. Judged on academic achievement, potential for journalism career, leadership qualities, communication skills
Deadline: November 1 for Yearbook Excellence Contest. February 5 for National Writing/Photography Contest
Contact: Quill and Scroll Society, School of Journalism and Mass Communication, University of Iowa, 312 W. Seashore, Iowa City, IA 52242 (www.uiowa.edu/~quill-sc)

Ayn Rand Institute Fountainhead Essay Competition
Awards: One $10,000 first prize, three $2,000 awards, five $1,000 awards
Criteria: For high school juniors and seniors. Essay on the philosophical and psychological meaning of Ayn Rand's novel *The Fountainhead*
Deadline: April 15
Contact: High school English teacher or counselor. Also, www.aynrand.org

Guideposts Youth Writing Contest
Awards: Top ten entrants are awarded scholarships of $1,000 to $10,000
Criteria: Entrants write a first-person story about an inspirational experience, preferably spiritual in nature.

Deadline: November (call for date)
Contact: Young Writer's Contest, *Guideposts* magazine, 16 E. 34th St., 21st Fl., New York, NY 10016 (212-251-8107; www.guideposts.com)

Scholastic Writing Awards

Awards: Five $10,000 awards. Four for general writing and one for nonfiction
Criteria: Outstanding creative-writing ability based on portfolio of student's work
Deadline: Varies
Contact: Send a postcard to The Scholastic Writing Awards, 557 Broadway, New York, NY 10012 (212-343-6493; www.artandwriting.org)

Veterans of Foreign Wars of the United States Annual Voice of Democracy Contest

Awards: More than 50 awards totaling more than $100,000
Criteria: Contestants write and tape-record essays on a patriotic theme. Essays are judged in local, state, and national competitions.
Deadline: November 1
Contact: High school principals or teachers can get official entry forms from local VFW posts (www.vfw.org).

UNION AFFILIATION

National Alliance of Postal and Federal Employees Ashby B. Carter Memorial Scholarship Fund

Awards: Three awards for dependents of NAPFE union members. First place $5,000, second place $3,000, and third place $2,000
Criteria: For Founders Award, community involvement and leadership ability. Must take SAT before March 1.
Deadline: April 1
Contact: Ms. Melissa Jeffries, NAPFE, 1628 11th St., N.W., Washington, DC 20001 (202-939-6325)

A SCHOLARSHIP FOR BEING AVERAGE

Here's a scholarship that turns tradition on its head. At Broward Community College, in Florida, about 250 students a year benefit from scholarships that have been designated for students with C averages. The late Edward W. Seese, a Fort Lauderdale businessman, left the college $4.8 million in 1995, stipulating that the money be used to fund scholarships for C students. He stated in his will that students who earn average grades would be "capable of greater accomplishments" if they did not have to work to finance their education.

Start Your Search Early

Junior year isn't too early to begin hitting the guide-books. Some competition deadlines fall early in the senior year, which doesn't leave much time to send away for applications, prepare essays or science projects, and get recommendations from teachers. A top-notch paper or project that stands a chance in competitive contests isn't one that's slapped together the night before the deadline.

Thinking ahead—say, by sophomore year—also gives your child time to join organizations that offer scholarships, like a 4-H Club or scouting group.

Carefully Read Instructions and Eligibility Criteria

Scholarship sponsors complain that they get many inquiries and applications from students who don't meet the eligibility criteria that's plainly set out in their literature. Encourage your child to read every word to avoid wasting time on applications that are trashed on receipt by the sponsor or disqualified for a small error, such as exceeding a word count for an essay or omitting a required transcript or recommendation.

Ask for Samples of Winning Entries

Most scholarship sponsors will tell you in broad terms what criteria are used to select winners, but reading a winning essay, article, speech, history paper, or science-project proposal can give you real insight into what judges are looking for. Often, they're available for the asking. *How to Go to College Almost for Free: The Secrets of Winning Scholarship Money* (Waggle Dancer Books; $15.40) includes sample winning essays and applications, along with many helpful tips.

After High School

For those who are inclined, scholarship seeking isn't just for high schoolers. There are just as many awards for college sophomores, juniors, and seniors, even though we've excluded them here. The same search tactics—and caveats—apply:

- **Spend some library time** with the guidebooks.
- **Try a computerized search** if it's free or very low cost.
- **Touch base with clubs and organizations,** faculty, and your financial-aid officer on campus.
- **Think creatively about outside groups** that might have a philanthropic interest in a kid like yours.
- **And don't let the scholarship hunt** for relatively few dollars eclipse the more-important task of applying intelligently for financial aid.

Scholarship seeking isn't just for high schoolers. There are just as many awards for college sophomores, juniors, and seniors.

Borrowing Power

Chapter 9

No one wants to borrow their way through the college years. But the reality is that most families can't cover the full expense from cash flow, savings, and financial aid. Even when a college meets 100% of your demonstrated financial need, a portion of the aid package will probably be loans rather than grants. In addition, many families wind up taking out loans to cover a portion of their expected family contribution, because they can't come up with the prescribed amount from cash flow and assets.

Low-rate loans to help foot the bills are plentiful, and most families have no difficulty finding educational loans to fill the gap, or even qualifying for them. The challenge, then, is deciding whether you're willing to take on as much debt as necessary to send your child to whatever school he or she chooses, or whether the level of debt you must assume will play a role in which college you choose. The worksheet on page 233 will help you either way.

Although you probably won't apply for loans until after your child graduates from high school, you should give them some thought as you're making the final choice of a school, in the spring of your child's senior year. By then, you will have received financial-aid offers from the schools and will be able to determine how much you would have to borrow at each one. This chapter will help you evaluate how much debt you can carry comfortably—and how much debt your child may be able to manage after graduation. Once

Good news. College debt is cheaper than it was several years ago, thanks to tax relief and reductions in interest rates on student loans.

you've selected a school and are ready to begin applying for loans, this chapter will help you understand the terms of the various student loans, select a lender, and decide over how much time you want to stretch out the payments.

College Debt Gets Cheaper

But, first, some welcome good news for tuition-paying families: For several reasons, education debt is cheaper than it was several years ago. First, as part of the Taxpayer Relief Act of 1997, students and their parents gained the right to claim a tax deduction for the interest paid on student loans. Then, midyear in 1998, Congress revised the interest-rate formula for student loans, which has reduced the rates on Stafford loans. And the interest rate on student loans is variable; it cannot exceed 8.25%. Rates are adjusted each year on July 1. For the July 1, 2004 through June 30, 2005 period, the rate for loans in repayment was 3.39%.

Student-Loan Interest Deduction

You can now deduct the interest you pay on college loans, even if you don't itemize deductions. The loans must have been used to pay the costs of attendance—including tuition, fees, room, board, books, and personal expenses—for a student enrolled at least half-time in a program leading to a degree, certificate, or other recognized credential. But either the student or the parent can have taken out the loan, and just about any kind of loan qualifies (except a home-equity loan, because the interest is already tax-deductible).

You can deduct up to $2,500 per year—if your adjusted gross income is less than $130,000 for joint filers and $65,000 for individuals. (Those income limits will rise with inflation.) That covers roughly a year's worth of interest on as much as $40,000 in student-loan debt. If you have that much debt, you could save as much as $375 a year if you're in the 15% tax bracket and up to $625 a year in the 25% tax bracket. Who qualifies? To take the deduction, a borrower must be legally liable for repaying the loan and cannot be claimed as a dependent on someone else's tax return. That means there's no deduction if Mom and Dad are repaying a loan for which their child is responsible. So if you want to help with the debt, give your son or daughter the cash to make the loan payment. That way the child gets the deduction, assuming you're not claiming him or her as a dependent. Parents, of course, can take the deduction for loans they've taken out to cover a child's college expenses.

Can the family double-dip if parents are repaying a PLUS (parent) loan and their child is paying back a Stafford student loan? Absolutely. Assuming you meet the other requirements, you can each write off up to $2,500 in interest. Interest is deductible for the full term of the loan.

The Interest-Rate Formula

For Stafford loans taken out since July 1998, the rate on loans in repayment is set annually at the rate of the 91-day T-bill plus 2.3 percentage points, with an 8.25% cap (currently 3.37%). An even lower rate applies while the student is in school and for six months afterward—that rate is set at that of the 91-day T-bill plus 1.7 percentage points, with an 8.25% cap (currently 2.77%). Before Congress changed the formulas in 1998, the rates were set at 3.1 points and 2.5 points, respectively, over T-bill rates, and those formulas still apply to earlier loans.

How Much Debt Is Too Much for Your Child?

If your child is a dependent, the amount of money he or she can borrow under the federal government's Stafford student loan program will be limited to $17,125 over four years ($2,625 in the freshman year, $3,500 in the sophomore year, and $5,500 in the junior

Who qualifies? To take the deduction, a borrower must be legally liable for repaying the loan and cannot be claimed as a dependent on someone else's tax return.

Generally speaking, payments of much more than 10% of gross monthly pay will be a strain for a new grad.

and senior year). That's probably a reasonable borrowing limit for the typical undergraduate. Assuming a 6% interest rate, a student would be expected to make payments of about $189 a month over ten years after graduation to retire that debt. That's about 7.5% of the gross monthly pay of a new grad earning $30,000 a year, and it should become a smaller percentage of pay as income rises over time. Generally speaking, payments of much more than 10% of gross monthly pay will be a strain. Even $240 or so a month on a $30,000 annual salary—or about $1,980 a month in take-home pay—will pinch. If payments are truly unmanageable, a student can stretch repayment out over a longer period of time to reduce the monthly payments. But, as discussed below, that option increases your child's interest costs significantly and should be avoided if possible.

How Much Debt Is Too Much for Yourself?

To get a good ballpark estimate of what your total debt might be at the end of four years, simply multiply the amount you figure you need to borrow for freshman year by four. Your aid package can change from year to year, and your child will probably be expected to borrow more after the freshman year. But it's hard to predict whether that bigger loan will replace some of your debt or cut into other financial aid, such as a grant from the school. Once you've estimated your total debt, use the table on page 232 to estimate what your payments will be.

Say, for instance, you need to borrow $4,000 to attend School X and $8,000 to attend School Y. Over four years, your debt at the first school is likely to be around $16,000, while debt at the second school could approach $32,000.

■ **Assuming you borrow at 7% over ten years,** you'd have to be able to swing $186 (16 × 11.61) a month in loan payments over ten years to pay for School X, and $372 a month (32 × 11.61) for ten years to pay for School Y.

■ **If you want to repay the debt in five years,** your payments would be $317 a month (16 × 19.80) at School X and $634 a month (32 × 19.80) at School Y.

This is a simplified example, and it doesn't take into account the fact that you won't borrow the entire amount at once, and that you may have the option to defer paying principal, or principal and interest, until after your child graduates, which would ease the burden while you're using your income to pay college bills but increase your expenses over the long term. Still, the exercise helps you get a handle on whether the debt you plan to incur will be manageable when it comes time to repay.

You probably will have a gut feeling for how much is too much. But most private lenders will cut you off when the monthly payments on your debts, including a mortgage, exceed 35% to 40% of your gross monthly income. If you're borrowing directly from the federal government, there may be no such income test, but you should probably limit your borrowing to those levels anyway. Committing any more of your income

---

WHY SO MUCH DEBT?

Parents are borrowing far more than they ever did to cover the cost of college. Why? Rapidly rising college costs are an obvious culprit. But in addition, in the early 1990s Congress raised the borrowing limits on federal loans to students and removed borrowing caps entirely from federal PLUS loans, so that parents can now borrow as much as they need to cover college costs, sometimes regardless of their ability to repay.

The rules also made Stafford loans available to students regardless of need—although only needy students qualify to have their interest subsidized while they're in school.

At the same time, Congress altered the federal financial-aid formulas so that they don't count a family's home equity as an asset available to cover college bills. Excluding that resource, which is often a family's largest asset, has made many more families eligible for subsidized student loans.

Subsidized Stafford loans are a very good deal for students, since Uncle Sam pays the interest while your child is in school.

to debt can leave you strapped to pay for food, clothing, transportation, and other essentials. And if you still have a younger child to put through school, you'll probably want to commit yourself to even less debt now, to leave a cushion for a second round of college expenses later.

When You're Ready to Apply: The Loans

If your financial-aid package includes a loan from the school itself, you'll probably receive that money automatically—or will simply see the amount of the loan deducted from your tuition bill. But for most other loans, you'll need to find a lender (except for certain federal loans where Uncle Sam is the lender), complete an application, and wait for approval.

In most cases, choosing a loan is fairly cut-and-dried. You could choose to decline a federal loan offered in a financial-aid package in favor of, say, a private loan such as those described in the next section, but in most cases you wouldn't want to. Subsidized Stafford loans are a very good deal for students, since Uncle Sam pays the interest while your child is in school. And it's tough to do any better than a

LOAN PAYMENTS PER $1,000 OF DEBT

Find where the loan's repayment term and interest rate intersect. Multiply the result there by the number of thousands you're borrowing, such as 10 for a $10,000 loan. The result is your monthly loan payment. To figure out the total cost of the loan, multiply the monthly payment by the number of months in the loan term; for example, 120 months for a ten-year loan.

Loan term	5%	6%	7%	8%	9%	10%	11%
5 years	18.87	19.34	19.80	20.28	20.75	21.25	21.74
10 years	10.61	11.11	11.61	12.13	12.67	13.22	13.78
15 years	7.91	8.44	8.99	9.56	10.14	10.75	11.37
20 years	6.60	7.17	7.75	8.36	9.00	9.65	10.32

DECISION TIME: HOW MUCH SHOULD YOU BORROW?

Even if you're determined to borrow "whatever it takes" to send your child to his or her first-choice college, the worksheet that follows will help you size up just how much "whatever it takes" will be. The table provided on the preceding page will help you determine how much it will cost, over time, to repay the debt. If your choice of a school depends on whether you can manage the resulting debt, these exercises will help you pinpoint how much borrowing you can comfortably afford.

YOUR COSTS
Estimate what you will actually spend, which may be different from the allowances for books, transportation, and personal expenses in your financial-aid package.

Tuition	$ _____
Room and board	_____
Books	_____
Transportation	_____
Personal expenses	_____
Other	_____
Total costs	$ _____

YOUR RESOURCES
Estimate what you can actually contribute, whether it's more or less than your expected family contribution.

The amount you can contribute from:

Monthly income _____ × 12	$ _____
Savings and investments	_____

Your student's contribution from:

Income (including a work-study job and summer earnings)	_____
Savings	_____
Scholarships and grants	_____
Other resources (such as gifts)	_____

Total resources	$ _____
Minus student loans provided in the aid package	_____
Minus parent loans provided in the aid package	_____

ADDITIONAL BORROWING NEEDED	$ _____

Parents will probably remember these low-interest Stafford student loans from their college days as Guaranteed Student Loans.

Perkins loan (a federally funded loan that's administered by schools and has a 5% interest rate). Even unsubsidized Stafford loans are a pretty good deal, given the low rate (3.37% in 2004–2005) and flexible repayment terms.

On other loans, you'll want to select the lowest-cost alternative, based on the loan's interest rate, fees, and repayment terms.

The following sections describe your options among federal and private loans.

Stafford Student Loans

Parents will probably remember these low-interest loans from their college days as Guaranteed Student Loans. These loans, made directly to students as part of their financial-aid package, have been renamed and split into two mirror-image loan programs.

- **If the loan is a Federal Family Education Loan** (FFEL), your child borrows from a bank, savings and loan, or credit union, but the government acts as guarantor—meaning that the government winds up reimbursing the bank if your son or daughter defaults.
- **If the loan is a Federal Direct Student Loan** (FDSL), your child borrows directly from the federal government (through the Department of Education).

You don't get to choose which loan program to borrow from—if your child's school is one of the several hundred participating in the Federal Direct Student Loan program, you get a government loan; if it's not, you get a government-guaranteed loan from a lender of your choice. You are not permitted to borrow through both loan programs in any one semester, but you could wind up with both kinds of loans if your child switches schools, or if the school enters or leaves the direct-loan program during your child's college years.

THE TERMS. In any event, the loan terms, interest rates, and fees for FFEL and direct loans are identical.

The interest rate. The interest rate you pay on these variable-rate loans is adjusted every July 1. The rate calculation for loans disbursed after June 30, 2004, equals the rate on the 91-day Treasury bill plus 2.3 percentage points, with a cap of 8.25%. Through June 30, 2005, the rate was 3.37%.

Most Stafford loans disbursed prior to July 1, 1998, are calculated at the rate of the 91-day Treasury bill plus 3.1 percentage points (currently 4.17%). The rate on all Stafford loans cannot currently exceed 8.25%, regardless of when the loan was made.

Loan fees. In addition to interest, you pay up-front fees that total 4% of the amount of your loan. A 3% origination fee goes to the lender, and a 1% insurance fee goes into the guaranty fund that reimburses lenders for loans in default. Normally these fees are deducted from your loan balance, so from a $2,625 student loan, you really get a check for $2,520, leaving a small difference that has to come from some other resource.

BORROWING LIMITS FOR DEPENDENT STUDENTS. Most undergraduates are considered dependent students (see page 114) and can take out Stafford loans up to the following maximum limits:
- **Freshmen:** $2,625
- **Sophomores:** $3,500
- **Juniors and seniors:** $5,500

However, you can never borrow more than your school's cost of attendance minus any other financial aid you receive, so you may be eligible for less than the maximum. Over all of his or her undergraduate years, a dependent student can borrow no more than a total of $23,000 (which includes a fifth year or more, if necessary).

BORROWING LIMITS FOR INDEPENDENT STUDENTS. The maximum amounts an independent student can borrow in Stafford loans each year (including subsidized and unsubsidized loans, which are explained below) are:

- **Freshmen:** $6,625
- **Sophomores:** $7,500
- **Juniors and seniors:** $10,500

An independent student can borrow up to $46,000 during all his or her undergraduate years. Graduate students can borrow up to $18,500 a year, up to a maximum of $138,500, including their undergraduate Stafford loans.

SUBSIDIZED OR UNSUBSIDIZED? FFEL and Federal Direct student loans may be subsidized, meaning that

---

STUDENT LOANS AT A GLANCE

Loan rates (in parentheses) are as of 2004–2005. They are effective on loans disbursed after July 1, 1998.

TYPE	BORROWER	INTEREST RATE	FEES	TERM
Federal loans				
Stafford	student	91-day T-bill + 2.3 points (3.37%)	4%	10–30 years*
Perkins Loan	student	5%	none	10 years
PLUS Loan	parent	91-day T-bill + 3.1 points (4.17%)	4%	10–30 years*
Private loans				
Nellie Mae EXCEL	parent	prime plus 2.25 points (7.5%)	7%	4–20 years
Sallie Mae Signature Loan	student	prime plus 0 to 3 points (5.25% to 8.25%)	0% to 6%	up to 20 years
TERI Alternative Loan	parent or student	prime rate plus 1.5 points (6.75%)	0% to 6.5%	up to 20 years

*The 10 to 30-year repayment term reflects the extended payment options discussed in this chapter, but 10 years is the standard term.

the federal government pays the interest while the student is in school, during the six months after graduation, and during any period during which the student can defer payments (such as during graduate school). Four years of interest-free borrowing is the best deal going in student loans, so if you qualify for a Stafford loan based on financial need, don't pass it up. The aid packages you receive from the schools will tell you whether you qualify for a subsidized loan.

If not, you'll be offered an unsubsidized Stafford loan, which means that the interest clock begins ticking as soon as your child takes out the loan, even though he or she can defer making payments until after graduation. (For more on the pros and cons of deferment, see page 246.) Unsubsidized loans are available to students regardless of need.

If you have financial need that's less than the annual loan limit, you might be offered a small subsidized loan and an unsubsidized loan. A college junior with just $2,000 of need, for instance, might be offered a $2,000 subsidized Stafford loan as well as a $3,500 unsubsidized Stafford to help cover the family's expected contribution to college costs. (The overall Stafford-loan borrowing limit for college juniors who are dependent students is $5,500.)

Unless you've had a sudden windfall that's going to cover the bills (now wouldn't that be nice?), you should always accept the subsidized loan. Before you accept an unsubsidized Stafford loan, however, compare the costs against other sources of borrowing that may be available. If you can borrow at something less than 6%, using a home-equity loan, for instance, you might want to pass up the unsubsidized Stafford. Bear in mind, though, that usually the student takes out and repays a Stafford loan, while a home-equity loan would be your responsibility—even if you worked

---

FEDERAL AID INFORMATION

Have a question about federal student loans, including rates and repayment? Call the Federal Student Aid Information Center at 800-433-3243 between 8 AM and 8 PM eastern time, Monday through Friday. Operators at the information center can also answer questions about completing the FAFSA financial-aid form.

out an arrangement for your child to reimburse you later.

Incidentally, if you would prefer that the debt be yours rather than your kid's, you still shouldn't pass up a subsidized Stafford student loan. Let Uncle Sam subsidize the interest for four years; then help your child with the payments if you want to relieve him or her of the debt burden.

HOW TO CHOOSE A STAFFORD-LOAN LENDER. Your child should apply for a Stafford loan in the late spring or early summer before heading off to college because processing the loan can take four to six weeks. When the school participates in the Federal Direct Student Loan Program, you don't have to scout around for a lender—the school's financial-aid office will tell you how to apply.

If you have an FFEL Stafford loan, you can choose your own lender. The interest rate and the loan terms will be the same just about anywhere you go, although it's possible to find a lender offering slightly lower fees to attract more student-loan business. The differences aren't huge, so it doesn't pay to spend a lot of time shopping for a lender, but checking with a few might save you a little money down the road.

PAYMENTS ON VARIABLE LOANS

Q. I'm thinking about taking out a variable-rate student loan on which the rate changes monthly. Does that mean my payment would be different every month?

A. No, the payment doesn't fluctuate (unless you're making interest-only payments). Your payments are based on the rate in effect when you take out the loan. Changes in the rate are reflected in the length of the repayment term: If rates fall you'll make fewer monthly payments, and if they rise it will take a bit longer to retire the loan. (On Stafford and PLUS loans, however, the payment can change each year when the interest rate is adjusted in the summer.)

Variable-rate loans are pretty common, and they may be the only choice available from private lenders. They're a good choice if you think rates will fall, but a less desirable one if you think interest rates are heading up.

HOW LONG A DEFERRAL?

Q. My daughter plans to go on to graduate school. How long can she defer payments on her Stafford loan?

A. Your daughter can defer loan payments as long as she's a graduate student at least half-time. In addition, she may be able to get a deferment if she can't find full-time employment or can otherwise show economic hardship. If her Stafford loans are subsidized, the government will pay the interest on her loan while it's in deferment. If they're unsubsidized, the interest will be added to her loan balance. Your daughter can apply to her student-loan lender (the federal government's Direct Loan Servicing Center, if it's a federal direct loan) for deferment (see page 246 for a discussion of the pros and cons of deferment).

With whom does your lender work? If you want to trim your child's costs in repayment, look for a lender that sells its student loans to Sallie Mae. The Student Loan Marketing Association, aka Sallie Mae, is the largest buyer of student loans on the secondary market (where banks sell their loans to raise additional money to lend). Sallie Mae owns or manages student loans for more than seven million borrowers. In order to make its packages of student loans most appealing to investors, Sallie Mae offers the incentive of a one-fourth-percentage point break to student borrowers who repay on time by setting up automatic loan payments from a bank account.

The total savings on a $17,125 balance (the most a graduate who finishes in four years can borrow) over the standard ten-year term could be more than $1,700. To find a bank in your state that sells its loans to Sallie Mae, visit Sallie Mae's Web site at www.salliemae.com.

How often is loan interest capitalized? If you're really ambitious about keeping interest to a minimum, and you're taking out an unsubsidized Stafford loan on which you're deferring both interest and principal pay-

Lots of banks, savings and loans, and credit unions make student loans, so if you like the service where you bank, that's a good place to start.

ments, ask the loan officer how often the bank "capitalizes" the interest on the loan—in other words, how often the interest you're deferring is added to the principal balance. The best possible answer is "once, when the loan goes into repayment." If instead the lender capitalizes the interest, say, monthly, the interest is added to your loan balance each month—and you wind up paying interest on interest.

USE A BANK YOU LIKE. Lots of banks, savings and loans, and credit unions make student loans, so if you like the service where you bank, that's a good place to start. You can also ask a financial-aid officer to steer you to a lender—he or she is likely to know who has a good reputation for processing loans promptly and avoiding errors or delays.

Another alternative is for you to contact your state's guaranty agency for a list of convenient lenders. (Many of the state education agencies listed on pages 132–134 also serve as their state's guaranty agency. Others will be able to direct you.)

STAY WITH IT. Whatever lender your child chooses, it's best to stick with that institution for loans throughout the four years of college, if possible. Keeping your loans all in one place will make repayment infinitely simpler: Your child won't have multiple loan payments to make and won't have to notify multiple lenders each time he or she moves, which recent graduates tend to do frequently.

Perkins Loans

Students with high financial need may qualify for a federal Perkins loan, with a superlow interest rate of 5%. The financial-aid offers you receive from schools will tell you if you're eligible. The schools themselves make Perkins loans, but each institution's loan pool is funded with federal money—and with repayments from graduates. The maximum annual loan for undergraduates at many schools is $4,000.

REPAYMENT. No payments are due on a Perkins loan until nine months after your child graduates or drops below half-time as a student. Typically, the repayment term is ten years or less. On $5,000 of Perkins-loan debt, the monthly payment is $53 over ten years.

A BREAK FOR SOME PROFESSIONS. Unlike Stafford and PLUS loans, Perkins loans can be discharged (canceled) in full or in part when you are employed at certain kinds of work, including these jobs:

- **Full-time teacher,** when your school serves a low-income area, you teach special-education students, or you teach math, science, or other subjects with a shortage of teachers;
- **Full-time nurse or medical technician;**
- **Full-time law enforcement or corrections officer;**
- **Full-time employee of a child- or family-service agency** in a low-income community; or
- **Full-time Peace Corps volunteer.**

PLUS Loans (for Parents)

Unlike Stafford loans, federal PLUS loans are made to parents and aren't part of the family's financial-aid package. (PLUS stands for Parent Loans for Undergraduate Students.) Under this federal program, parents can borrow up to the full cost of attendance at a college, minus any other financial aid the family is eligible for. A family that qualifies for $5,000 in aid at a $20,000 college, for instance, could use a PLUS loan to finance all or part of its $15,000 expected family contribution. Parents are eligible based on their creditworthiness, not financial need, however, and you need not have applied for aid to get a PLUS loan.

As with Stafford loans, there are two parallel PLUS-loan programs. Depending on the school your child attends, you may be borrowing from the federal government under the Federal Direct PLUS-loan program or from a private lender under the Family Federal Education Loan program. Either way, the interest rate is equal to the 91-day Treasury-bill rate plus 3.1 percentage points, but can be no more than 9%. The

Federal PLUS loans are made to parents and aren't part of the family's financial-aid package.

If your school doesn't participate in the Federal Direct program, you can apply for your loan directly with a bank or other lender.

rate is adjusted every July 1. The rate (through June 30, 2005) is 4.17% In addition, there's an up-front fee of up to 4% to cover origination and insurance.

LENDERS. If your school participates in the Federal Direct Student Loan Program, you can get a PLUS loan from the federal government by filling out a Direct PLUS Loan Application and Promissory Note, available from the school's financial-aid office. If you are approved (you must have a clean credit history or have a cosigner), the U.S. Department of Education will send the money directly to your school.

If the loan amount exceeds what you owe the school directly for tuition, room and board, and other fees, you'll get a check for the balance, to be used toward books, transportation, and other out-of-pocket educational expenses.

If your school doesn't participate in the Federal Direct program, you can apply for your loan directly with a bank or other lender. As with Stafford loans, you can use your favorite local bank or credit union, or ask the financial-aid office or your state's higher education agency (see pages 132–134) to direct you to lenders that make PLUS loans. In addition to checking your credit, most private lenders will assess your ability to repay, and can turn you down if you already have significant debt (see pages 245–246). Once you're approved for a loan, the money is usually disbursed directly to the school.

REPAYMENT. You begin repaying a PLUS loan 60 days after the lender pays the school, and you can choose to make full payments from the start or interest-only payments during the college years. The loan term depends on how much you borrow, but ten years is typical. You may be able to extend the loan term to as long as 30 years under the Extended Repayment Plan or Graduated Repayment Plan discussed beginning on page 260. But as we'll show later in this chapter, those options will cost you a bundle in additional interest.

Private Loans

The federal loan programs, particularly the PLUS-loan program, will probably provide you with all the borrowing power you need. But if you're looking for additional funds—or would prefer a private lender to the federal government—several not-for-profit organizations make education loans to students and parents at rates that in most cases are slightly higher than those on PLUS and Stafford loans. Loans for undergraduate education are described below. All three organizations also have loan programs for graduate students.

NELLIE MAE. Besides making Stafford and PLUS loans, Nellie Mae (Braintree, Mass.; 800-367-8848; www.nelliemae.com) offers parents EXCEL education loans at variable rates that are calculated monthly or annually. The annual rate is prime plus 2.25%, calculated August 1, and the monthly rate is prime plus 1%, adjusted if necessary at the beginning of each month. (The prime rate at press time was 5.25%.) You can borrow up to the full cost of college annually, minus any financial aid you receive.

If you're creditworthy, you qualify—regardless of your financial need. You must have a clean credit history (with no major delinquencies) for at least two years, and your debt payments, including a mortgage and the EXCEL loan, cannot exceed 45% of your gross monthly income.

You pay an up-front guarantee fee of 7% (2% with a coborrower), which goes into an insurance fund that covers loan defaults.

SALLIE MAE. In addition to buying Stafford student loans (as described above), Sallie Mae makes its own supplemental student loans, called Signature Loans, for up to the full cost of college, less other financial aid. The interest rate is variable. (It equals the prime rate plus zero to 3%, depending on the creditworthiness of the borrower and whether or not there is a coborrower.) At press time it was 5.25% to 8.25%. A fee

If you're creditworthy, you qualify for a Nellie Mae loan—regardless of your financial need.

of 0% to 6% (depending on the same variables) is sub-tracted from the loan proceeds.

One nice thing about these loans is that your child can take them out at the same time as a Stafford loan at lenders that participate in the Signature Loan pro-gram. That means that all of his or her loans will be serviced as one account. And borrowers are eligible for the on-time repayment discounts described on page 239.

THE EDUCATION RESOURCES INSTITUTE (TERI). TERI (800-255-374; www.teri.org) makes its Alternative Loans for up to the annual cost of college, minus finan-cial aid, to parents or to students, although most stu-dents need a parent as a coborrower. Loan approval is based on creditworthiness, with criteria similar to those for Nellie Mae's EXCEL loans.

TERI offers the loans through several lenders who can serve Alternative Loan borrowers nationwide. They include Bank of America, Charter One Bank, Citizens Bank, and Penn Security Bank. The rate is prime plus 1.5% (6.75% at press time). TERI charges a 0% to 6.5% origination fee, which is determined by the repayment schedule. The fee can be added to your loan balance.

Are You Creditworthy?

Students who take out Stafford loans generally don't have to pass any credit tests. After all, points out an executive with the National Council of Higher Education Resources Programs, student-loan programs were created to make funds available to people who otherwise wouldn't be able to borrow. But for parents, it's a different matter. At the very least— for Federal Direct PLUS loans, for instance—you must have a clean credit history. And if you borrow from a private lender, you'll probably also have to meet certain financial tests. The Education Resources Institute (TERI), for instance, requires borrowers:

- **to have a satisfactory credit history,** and residence and employment history of at least two years;
- **to have sufficient income** to make the required payments;
- **if self-employed,** to have been in business for at least two years; and
- **to be a U.S. citizen,** or permanent resident and have resided in the U.S. for at least the previous two years.

Double-Check Your Credit Report

What if you're creditworthy but your credit report says otherwise? The worst time to find out you've got a damaging error on your credit report is after you've applied for a loan. Instead of taking that risk, do a preemptive checkup by ordering a copy of your report from each of the three major credit bureaus:

- **Equifax:** 800-685-1111
- **Experian:** 866-200-6020
- **Trans Union:** 800-680-7289

As of September 1, 2005, free annual consumer-credit reports are available nationwide. It's best to check your credit a couple of months before you expect to begin applying for loans, so you'll have time to correct errors if necessary.

If you find inaccuracies in your credit file, such as entries for late payment or nonpayment, or inclusion of accounts that don't belong to you, complete the dispute form that accompanies the report. Don't worry about minor mistakes, such as an out-of-date reference for your employer or a current balance that's off by a bit—those things won't affect your ability to get credit.

In response to a dispute, the credit bureau "investigates" by asking the creditor whether the information you're challenging is true. Often this takes care of the error. But an affirmative response from the creditor fulfills the credit bureau's obligation. You'll know the outcome because you'll receive a response to your dispute within 60 days. If the original notation stands, you've got to work on the creditor to fix what it's reporting

The worst time to find out you've got a damaging error on your credit report is after you've applied for a loan.

Resist the temptation to put off making payments against principal. The long-term costs are dramatically higher.

to the credit bureau. Make your case in writing, with copies of any documentation, and ask that a correction be sent to all the credit bureaus to whom the creditor reports.

If the creditor won't concede an error, you can add a 100-word statement to your credit file indicating that you dispute the entry. If you must resort to this, be prepared to explain the dispute when you apply for your parent loan.

The High Cost of Stretching Out Your Payments

When you have a subsidized Stafford loan, Uncle Sam pays the interest while your child is a full-time student, and repayment of principal doesn't start until after graduation. But on unsubsidized Stafford loans, PLUS loans, and some private loans, you must choose whether to:

- **Make full payments of principal and interest** while your child is in college;
- **Make interest-only payments** during that time, deferring the repayment of principal for four years; or even
- **Defer payments of principal and interest** entirely for up to three years.

When the student is the borrower, deferring payments is often the only choice, given his or her lack of income. And sometimes the same is true for parents, given that you're using your income to pay the college bills. But whenever possible, parent-borrowers should resist the temptation to put off making payments against principal. The long-term costs are dramatically higher, and interest-only payments don't do much to help boost your cash flow, anyway.

On a $20,000 TERI loan at an initial rate of 4.75%, for example, making interest-only payments while your child is in school adds four years to the 20-year repayment term—and more than $5,000 to the total cost of the loan. And the "big" break on your payment is only $48 a month. The full monthly payment is $136.05, while the interest-only payment is $88.33. How can that be? As with any loan, payments in the early years cover mostly interest and just a little principal while payments toward the end of the loan cover more principal than interest. Most parents who check the "interest-only" box on their loan application forget that, and are unpleasantly surprised at the higher-than-expected installment that results.

Also contributing to high total loan costs are the superlong loan terms that student lenders offer. These may make the monthly payment affordable, but at what a cost in the long run! You'd never take ten or 20 years to pay off a $20,000 car loan, but education-loan lenders routinely write loans over one to two decades or more. On the 4.75%, $20,000 TERI loan above, the total cost of the 20-year loan with interest-only payments for the first four years is $36,652. With full payments from the start, the total cost is still a whopping $32,652. But cut the loan term in half, to ten years (which increases the monthly payment from $136 to $221), and the total cost to repay the loan is $26,488— about $6,164 less.

There are two ways to go about shortening the term of your loan. One is to ask the lender for a shorter repayment term up front. But if the lender says no (perhaps because it doesn't offer a lesser term or because you don't qualify for a higher payment based on your level of income), or if you'd rather not lock yourself into a higher schedule of payments, you can also accept the longer term and then make prepayments to shorten the loan term on your own. You could, for instance, boost your payment a bit each year as your income increases, or you could make a big extra payment on the loan from a bonus or tax refund. In the example above, adding $85 to the $136 loan payment each month would achieve the same effect as having the loan written up with a ten-year repayment term. Lenders of student loans, whether federal or private, are prohibited by law from

There are two ways to shorten the term of a loan: Ask for a shorter repayment term up front, or make prepayments to shorten the loan term on your own.

YOUR MONTHLY PAYMENT

Your monthly payment on a 5-year education loan

Loan amount	5%	6%	7%	8%	9%	10%	11%
$2,500	$50.00*	$ 50.00*	$ 50.00*	$ 50.69	$ 51.90	$ 53.12	$ 54.36
5,000	94.36	96.66	99.01	101.38	103.79	106.24	108.71
7,500	141.53	145.00	148.51	152.07	155.69	159.35	163.07
10,000	188.71	193.33	198.01	202.76	207.58	212.47	217.42
12,500	235.89	241.66	247.51	253.45	259.48	265.59	271.78
15,000	283.07	289.99	297.02	304.15	311.38	318.71	326.14
17,500	330.25	338.32	346.52	354.84	363.27	371.82	380.49
20,000	377.42	386.66	396.02	405.53	415.17	424.94	434.85

*The minimum payment on Stafford loans is $50 a month.

On a 10-year education loan

Loan amount	5%	6%	7%	8%	9%	10%	11%
$10,000	$106.07	$111.02	$116.11	$121.33	$126.68	$132.15	$137.75
12,500	132.58	138.78	145.14	151.66	158.34	165.19	172.19
15,000	159.10	166.53	174.16	182.00	190.01	198.23	206.63
17,500	185.61	194.29	203.19	212.32	221.68	231.26	241.06
20,000	212.13	222.04	232.22	242.66	253.35	264.30	275.50
25,000	265.16	277.55	290.27	303.32	316.69	330.38	344.38
30,000	318.20	333.06	348.33	363.98	380.03	396.45	413.25

On a 15-year education loan

Loan amount	5%	6%	7%	8%	9%	10%	11%
$15,000	$118.62	$126.58	$134.82	$143.35	$152.14	$161.19	$170.49
20,000	158.16	168.77	179.77	191.13	202.85	214.92	227.32
25,000	197.70	210.96	224.71	238.91	253.57	268.65	284.15
30,000	237.24	253.16	269.65	286.70	304.28	322.38	340.98
35,000	276.78	295.35	314.59	334.48	355.00	376.11	397.81
40,000	316.32	337.54	359.53	382.26	405.71	429.84	454.64

On a 20-year education loan

Loan amount	5%	6%	7%	8%	9%	10%	11%
$25,000	$164.99	$179.11	$193.82	$209.11	$224.93	$241.26	$258.05
30,000	197.99	214.93	232.59	250.93	269.92	289.51	309.66
35,000	230.98	250.75	271.35	292.75	314.90	337.76	361.27
40,000	263.98	286.57	310.12	334.58	359.89	386.01	412.88
45,000	296.98	322.39	348.88	376.40	404.88	434.26	464.48
50,000	329.98	358.22	387.65	418.22	449.86	482.51	516.09

charging prepayment penalties. (See also the discussion of student repayment options beginning on page 259.)

Borrowing from Yourself

Stafford loans, PLUS loans, and even some of the private education loans are the cheapest and most flexible unsecured loans (loans requiring no collateral) you'll find. But you may be able to do better by "borrowing from yourself," which really means borrowing from or against your own assets. In some cases, these secured loans cost even less than a government-subsidized student loan.

Home-Equity Loans

If you've been a homeowner long enough, the equity in your home is another cheap borrowing resource. Not only are interest rates low—typically just above the prime rate (5.25% at press time)—but the interest you pay will probably be tax-deductible, which makes the loan or line of credit that much cheaper after taxes. Homeowners can deduct interest on up to $100,000 in home-equity debt, except when using the money to buy tax-exempt bonds or single-premium life insurance (or, in some cases, when a taxpayer is subject to the alternative minimum tax, which generally affects only high-income taxpayers with many tax deductions).

If you're in the 25% tax bracket, paying 7% on a home-equity loan with tax-deductible interest is the equivalent of paying about 5.25% on an ordinary loan. (To arrive at this equivalent rate, subtract your tax bracket from 1 and multiply the loan rate by that result. In this example, 7% × 0.75—that is, 1 – 0.25—equals 5.25%.) The interest is also usually deductible at the state level, so the equivalent rate can be even a bit lower after taking state taxes into account. An even lower "teaser" rate of interest (typically 4% to 7%) during the first six months or year often makes the

You may be able to do better by "borrowing from yourself," which really means borrowing from or against your own assets.

The interest on a home-equity loan is tax-deductible only if you itemize deductions on your income-tax return.

loan even less costly. Loans don't get much cheaper—unless maybe you're borrowing from the Bank of Mom & Pop.

IT'S DEDUCTIBLE ONLY IF YOU ITEMIZE. There's one caveat that's not often mentioned when bankers and others tout the low after-tax cost of a home-equity loan: The interest is tax-deductible only if you itemize deductions on your income-tax return. If you instead take the standard deduction, because your total deductions are less than $5,000 on a single return or $10,000 on a joint return (for 2005), you don't get to take advantage of the tax benefit of a home-equity loan. Granted, most homeowners do itemize deductions because their mortgage interest, along with other deductions, adds up to more than the standard deduction. But if you're not among the itemizers—perhaps because you've paid off your mortgage or because your mortgage-interest payments are relatively low—you should compare the full home-equity-loan interest rate, not the after-tax rate, against other borrowing options.

LOAN OR LINE OF CREDIT? There are two ways that you can borrow against your home equity:
- **a home-equity loan,** which is essentially a second mortgage for a fixed amount, with a fixed interest rate, or
- **a home-equity line of credit,** which usually has a variable interest rate.

A home-equity credit line is ordinarily the better choice for college borrowers because of its flexibility—as with a credit card, you can tap the credit line (using a checkbook or sometimes even a credit card) to borrow the amount you need when you need it—say, $5,000 each semester for tuition, plus a few hundred here or there when you come up short for books or that plane ticket home for spring break. By contrast, with a home-equity loan, you'd have to estimate your total four-year borrowing needs in advance and pay interest on the entire loan balance from the day you take out the loan.

HOW MUCH CAN YOU BORROW? Traditionally, banks have allowed lines of credit of up to 80% of the equity in your home. But competition, along with the low default record on home-equity loans, has encouraged lenders to approve loans that bring the owner's over-all debt to 90% or even 120% of home equity. If you own a home that's worth $120,000 and the balance on your mortgage is $80,000, the equity in your home is $40,000. Banks that let you borrow up to 80% of your equity (known in banking lingo as an 80% loan-to-value ratio) would approve a line of credit of up to $32,000 (80% of your $40,000 in equity). To get a credit line with a 90% or 120% loan-to-value ratio, you'd probably have to accept an interest rate that's a bit higher than the going rate. The higher charge reflects the risk to the bank that if the value of the home drops, its collateral will be less than the value of the loan.

Even if you have plenty of home equity, resist the temptation to open a credit line for far more than you think you'll need just because there's no additional cost. A giant home-equity credit line can limit your ability to borrow elsewhere to meet other needs be-cause other lenders often consider the full amount of the credit line as existing debt when evaluating your ability to repay, even if you haven't borrowed anything close to the limit.

FINDING THE BEST RATES. A couple of hours on the phone shopping for a low-cost home-equity credit line will save you hundreds, and possibly thousands, of dollars in interest costs over the years you repay the debt. The difference a couple of points can make? On a $15,000, ten-year loan, for instance, you'll repay a total of $21,839 if the interest rate is 8%, versus $19,984 if the interest rate is 6%. That's a difference of $1,855.

You can also check the advertisements in your local newspaper's business section, but be aware that the

Resist the temptation to open a credit line for far more than you think you'll need. A giant home-equity credit line can limit your ability to borrow elsewhere.

The rate you really want to compare is the "fully indexed" rate that goes into effect after the teaser rate expires.

rates banks advertise are usually their "teaser" rates, very low rates that apply only during the first three months to a year that you have the credit line.

Assuming you'll be borrowing and repaying over at least four years, and possibly many more, the rate you really want to compare is the "fully indexed" rate that goes into effect after the teaser rate expires. Let's say Friendly Bank & Trust advertises a 4% line of credit that adjusts to prime plus two points (7.25%) after the first year. Across the street, Good Neighbor S&L offers a credit line at 6% the first year and the prime rate (5.25%) after that. If you're going to take any longer than about two years to repay, you're better off with the less-attractive teaser rate and the lower full rate.

You might take the opposite approach if you're the type of borrower who would take the trouble to "surf" teaser rates—jumping from one lender to another periodically to take advantage of a below-market introductory rate. If the new bank is willing to pay all the closing costs and fees (you may try to negotiate this), that could trim your interest expense by hundreds of dollars in the first year, even if the new loan's fully indexed rate is the same as the one on the old loan. The problem with this strategy is that most home-equity loans involve a blizzard of paperwork, not unlike what you endure when you get your first mortgage. Not everyone is willing to go through that every year or two to save a few bucks.

CONSIDER THE ANNUAL FEES AND CLOSING COSTS. As you shop around, also ask about annual fees and closing costs—typically for an appraisal of your home and for document handling. Many markets are so competitive that banks waive most or all of those closing costs, which otherwise run $400 to $1,000. In that case, however, watch the fine print. Sometimes you're obligated to pay those costs if you close the line of credit within a year without selling your home.

Also bear in mind that if you face a trade-off between a higher interest rate with no closing costs and a lower rate with closing costs, you're probably better off paying the extra cash up front and taking the lower rate, assuming you plan to use the line heavily to cover college bills. The opposite is true if you're setting up a credit line just in case you may need to use it later.

REPAYMENT. Home-equity credit lines offer credit card–like convenience, but also the credit card–like danger that you'll pile up huge interest charges by dragging out payments over years and years. Most credit lines permit interest-only payments during, say, a ten-year borrowing period. After that you must stop borrowing and repay the balance over the next 15 years or so. But if you do stretch payments out that long, you'll repay a small fortune in interest. Borrow $20,000 against your home at 7% and stretch payments (of $180) over 15 years and you'll repay the bank $32,358, of which $12,358 is interest. Repay in five years (at $396 a month) and the total cost is $23,761, or $3,761 in interest.

You'll save if you set up a repayment schedule for yourself, as though you were taking out a car loan, to repay within four or five years of your child's graduation. Use the loan-repayment table on page 232 to get a rough idea what the payments would be on a five-year loan. For a more precise calculation, use a financial (or loan) calculator, such as you'll find on Kiplinger.com; in financial software, such as *Quicken;* or on the Web sites listed on page 196 in Chapter 7. Such a program will allow you to estimate the payment required to retire the loan over varying periods of time so you can settle on a payment that's manageable for you—and stick to it as best you can.

A FINAL CAUTION. The final word on home-equity loans: Even if you could borrow 100% of the equity in your home, never, never borrow more of it than you're confident you can repay. Your home is the collateral, and should you fail to repay the loan, the bank can and will foreclose on your house. At the bare minimum,

> You'll save if you set up a repayment schedule for yourself, as though you were taking out a car loan, to repay within four or five years of your child's graduation.

In retirement plans that permit borrowing, federal limits define how much of your account you can tap.

you should comfortably be able to manage the payment that would be needed to repay the loan in the 15 years required. Five years is far better.

Your Retirement Plan

Many employees have built up considerable sums in company retirement plans, including 401(k) plans, 403(b) plans, and company profit-sharing plans. Should you tap that retirement kitty to pay for your kids' college education?

Maybe. But even if your plan has an attractive-sounding interest rate, and even though the interest you pay winds up in your own account, a home-equity loan is almost certain to be cheaper, if you can get one. And depending on what the investments in your retirement plan are earning, a PLUS loan or one of the education loans on pages 243–244 may also be a less-costly choice. The discussion in the next section will show why. But first, bear in mind that not all retirement plans permit loans:

- **Defined-benefit plans**—those that guarantee set payments based on your salary and years of service— almost never allow loans.
- **But most of the defined-contribution variety,** including 401(k), 403(b), and company profit-sharing plans, allow participants to borrow from them.

The law doesn't allow you to borrow from your IRA, or from SEP-IRAs or Keogh accounts, which are retirement plans for the self-employed.

In plans that do permit borrowing, there are federal limits (under the Employee Retirement Income Security Act) on how much of your account you can tap. You can borrow only up to 50% of your vested balance (which is the amount that's yours to roll over if you quit your job), but no more than $50,000.

MORE EXPENSIVE THAN MEETS THE EYE. A typical interest rate is the prime rate plus one percentage point—and, yes, you pay yourself the interest. But that doesn't make it the free loan it may sound like. In most cases, when you borrow from your retirement plan you in effect realign the investments inside your account. Rather than having the amount of the loan—say, $15,000—in your 401(k)'s stock mutual fund, for example, you have it invested in a college loan. If the interest rate on the loan is 8%, that's what that portion of your retirement money earns while the loan is outstanding. When investments inside the plan are growing at a higher rate than interest charged on the loan, the "bargain loan" rate is deceptive.

Here's why: Say that your 401(k) investments are growing at 11% a year. Borrowing from the plan at 8% means not only paying the 8% out of your pocket but also forfeiting the 3% difference between that rate and the 11% the money would otherwise earn. So 11%, not 8%, is the rate to compare with the cost of borrowing elsewhere.

A retirement-plan loan is a good choice if your 401(k) money is earning less than the going rate on plan loans. In that case, you get a convenient, below-market-cost loan, plus you boost the return on your retirement investments. If you've got your money in a guaranteed investment contract (GIC) that's paying 4%, for example, and you pay off your loan at 8%, taking the loan actually improves what you're earning on your money. (Unless you're very close to retirement, you shouldn't have your retirement money in GICs, but that's another book.) If your retirement stash is spread among various investments, such as GICs, bonds, and stocks, see if you can borrow first from the portion earning the lowest return. That keeps the cost of the loan as low as possible.

IT'S EASY. If a plan loan makes sense for you, it can be wonderfully convenient. Many employers will arrange the loans with a single phone call; there's no credit check (you're borrowing from yourself, after all) and payments are typically deducted from your paycheck. Another plus is that when the money is used for anything other than buying a home, you must repay the loan within five years. You can't even be tempted into

If a plan loan makes sense, it can be convenient. Many employers will arrange loans with a phone call; there's no credit check, and payments are typically deducted from your paycheck.

Now for the big downer on retirement-plan loans: If you're fired or you quit your job, the loan will be due immediately.

stretching the payments over a decade or more and accruing mountains of interest.

BUT THERE ARE STRINGS. Now for the big downer on retirement-plan loans: If you're fired or you quit your job, the loan will be due immediately. If you can't repay it, Uncle Sam considers the loan balance to be a distribution to you. You'll pay income tax on the money and, if you're under age 55, you'll owe a 10% penalty on it, too. Don't borrow from your retirement plan if you fear your job isn't secure or if you think you might change employers soon.

Your Life Insurance Policy

If you have cash-value life insurance (whole life, universal life, or variable universal life), undoubtedly one of the selling points that sounded attractive when you bought it was the ability to borrow against the cash value. You can usually borrow nearly all the cash value in your policy, but unless you started off with a large one-time premium payment, there's typically not much cash accumulated in the first several years of a policy's life. Once you do have some value you can borrow against, the trick—as with retirement-plan borrowing—is to figure out the true cost of taking a loan.

THE TRUE COST. Current rates are around 6% to 8%. (You may have a choice between a fixed rate and a variable rate. As mentioned previously, you'd want to go for the fixed rate if you thought interest rates were going to rise and the variable rate if you thought interest rates were going to fall.) But your real cost may be higher. On a universal-life policy, for instance, many companies pay a lower interest rate on the portion of the cash value you've borrowed. So, as with retirement accounts, you have to add the lost return to the interest rate on the loan to get the true borrowing cost.

Don't buy the insurance agent's classic argument that if you're borrowing at 7% and getting 5% on your money, the net cost of the loan is a bargain 2%. That's hogwash. If the interest rate your cash value earns is ordinarily 8%, the 5% you're getting on the portion you've borrowed against is a three-percentage-point reduction in your investment return. You must add that to the interest you're paying (and you're paying it, even if it's being painlessly subtracted from your premium or from the cash value each month) to get the true cost of the loan. In this case, the true cost is 10%—the 7% interest rate plus the 3-point drop in your rate of return.

The same principle applies to whole-life policies (on which your dividend may be reduced) and for variable universal-life policies (on which the cash value you borrow against may be switched from a stock or bond fund to a money-market fund paying a lower fixed interest rate). So in order to compare the cost of a policy loan with other choices, you have to ask about not only the interest rate but also the impact of the loan on the dividend, interest, or investment return on your cash value.

There are some policy-loan bargains. Many whole-life policies purchased in the mid-1970s offer loan rates of 5% to 6% with no reduction in the dividend. If you have been holding on to one of those old policies, you've got yourself a truly cheap borrowing source.

DO LOANS AFFECT FINANCIAL AID?

Q. How does borrowing against my assets affect financial-aid formulas?

A. Because parents' assets are such a small percentage of the family contribution, you're better off choosing a loan based on its cost, not its financial-aid impact. But since you asked:

- **Investment debt** (such as a margin loan, discussed on page 258) is the most favorable from a financial-aid standpoint—it directly reduces your assets under the federal aid formulas.

- **Because the federal formulas** don't count home equity, a home-equity loan won't improve your official expected family contribution. But it may reduce your assets in the formulas that private schools use to award their institutional grants.

- **Very few schools** look at retirement accounts or cash-value life insurance, so borrowing against those assets is unlikely to have any impact.

While your loan is outstanding, your life insurance policy's death benefit is reduced by the amount of the loan. That could leave you underinsured.

REPAYMENT. If you think the repayment terms on a home-equity loan or credit card are lenient, life insurers are even more easygoing: You can repay the loan however and whenever you like—or never pay it back at all. The trouble is that interest continues accruing as long as the loan is outstanding, and if you don't keep paying enough into the policy to cover at least the interest, you can eventually chew through the remaining cash value and cause the policy to lapse. If that happened, you'd owe taxes on a portion of the amount you borrowed. In effect, you would have cashed out the policy, and while you wouldn't be taxed on the portion that represents your investment in the policy, you would be taxed on the earnings. You might also be leaving your family without insurance protection it needs. You can avoid that by not borrowing the maximum amount allowed or by asking your agent to help you set up a repayment schedule that ensures your policy won't waste away.

Another point to remember is that while your loan is outstanding, your policy's death benefit—the amount your family would receive if you died—is reduced by the amount of the loan. That could leave you underinsured.

Margin Loans

Borrowing "on margin," or against the value of a stock or bond portfolio, may sound like risky stuff for high-finance types. That can be true when the loan is used to buy speculative investments, the value of which can rise or fall suddenly. But borrowing from your broker to pay college bills isn't necessarily risky, and it can even be a pretty good deal.

Rates, which are pegged to the "broker call rate" (what brokerages pay to borrow) are sometimes lower than home-equity loan rates. Rates in 2005 were around 8%. But if you're using the money to pay college bills, the interest isn't tax-deductible, so the after-tax rate is higher.

At most brokerages, you can borrow up to 50% of the value of the stocks or stock mutual funds in your account, and a higher percentage—often up to 85%—of the value of lower-risk investments, like Treasury bonds or municipal bonds. But it's best not to borrow up to the limit, so you can avoid the one big risk in borrowing on margin—the dreaded margin call. If the market value of your stock falls, so does the value of the collateral backing up your loan. If the value dips below a certain point, the brokerage can demand that you pay back part of the loan or deposit extra cash or securities as collateral. If you don't have the cash, you could be forced to sell your stocks, bonds, or mutual funds just after they've plummeted in value. But if you limit your borrowing to 20% or 25% of your account value, the risk of facing a margin call is virtually nil. That's because the value of your securities would have to drop to almost nothing before you'd face a margin call.

Why not just cash in a bond or sell some of the stocks in your portfolio to cover tuition bills? For a couple of reasons:

- **It might make sense to hang on to a good investment** rather than sell right away to cover the bills.
- **You might want to put off paying taxes** on a capital gain, which, by boosting your taxable income in a given year, could also cost you financial aid (see page 152).

There's also the chance that you'll be more disciplined about paying back a margin loan than about saving to replace your investments. But as with other "borrowing from yourself" choices, it's up to you to set up, and stick to, your own repayment schedule (see the box on page 248).

Student Loan "Relief"

It's probably hard right now to imagine you and your child on the other side of four years of college, but here's some food for future thought: Most students face their first student-loan payments six months after graduation. For those whose entry-level salaries won't cover the payments on big debts, the federal govern-

> **Borrowing from your broker to pay college bills isn't necessarily risky, and it can even be a pretty good deal.**

While recent grads will welcome payment relief in the short run, they should pay attention to the long-term cost of a more lenient repayment schedule.

ment's direct-loan program can bring relief—but that relief can be very costly in the long run.

Under the program, graduates choose either the standard ten-year repayment schedule or one of these flexible repayment options:

- **Extended repayment** lets the borrower stretch his or her payments over a longer term, ranging from 12 years to 30 years.
- **Graduated repayment** allows extension of the loan up to 30 years, with lower payments in the early years of the loan and higher payments later when, presumably, your child will be better able to afford it.
- **Income-contingent repayment** allows payments to fluctuate each year based on the borrower's income and level of debt. A graduate with $31,000 in student-loan debt and a $25,000 income would initially owe $264 per month. That compares with $380 under the standard 10-year repayment plan and $264 under a 20-year extended repayment schedule. (These calculations used the maximum interest rate of 8.25%.)

These repayment plans are automatically available to students with direct federal loans, and many private lenders offer similar options, including an "income-sensitive" repayment schedule. (Extended and graduated payment are also available to parent borrowers.)

While recent grads will welcome payment relief in the short run, they should pay attention to the long-term cost of a more lenient repayment schedule. In the example above, the borrower who stretches payments over 20 years pays back nearly $13,743 more in interest than the borrower who manages the 10-year repayment schedule. The total expense may be even greater for graduates in the income-contingent plan because those loans allow what's called "negative amortization." That means that when payments don't cover all the interest due, the unpaid interest is added to the principal balance, on which additional interest compounds. Even though you're making payments, your loan balance is growing, not shrinking.

Graduates can prepay their debt or switch back to a standard plan any time—and they'd be wise to raise payments as soon as they can afford to. Lenders tell students they're making their loans more affordable, which they are in the short run. But by spreading the cost over a longer period of time, they're making the debt more costly in the long run—and increasing the risk that they'll still be paying off student loans when their own kids are ready for college.

Other Ways
and Means

Financial aid, loans, savings, and sometimes scholarships are at the core of most parents' pay-for-college plan. But when those don't stretch quite far enough, a student job, an accelerated-degree program, or installment payment plan can help close the gap. In this chapter you'll find a grab bag of ideas for supplementing your financial resources—or making them go further.

Cost-Conscious Ways to Get a Degree

There's a lot to be said for the traditional four-year path to a college degree that allows a student a healthy mix of social and academic development. But at a time when college costs are soaring, saving a semester's or even a year's expenses by accelerating the usual 15-credits-a-semester pace has become an increasingly popular alternative for students who can handle the load. The fast track certainly isn't for everyone, but it can save a family thousands of dollars. If you have this route in mind, you need to plan ahead, because the courses your child takes in high school and the college he or she chooses can make a difference between being able to graduate early or not.

Another "alternative" route—going to community college for two years before pursuing a bachelor's degree elsewhere—doesn't take advance planning while your child is in high school. It does require some attention to course selection during those community-college years, so that the maximum number of credits will transfer to a four-year school. Careful course selection in order to meet major or program requirements is also important to students who follow the traditional path and want to avoid the expense of an unanticipated extra semester or extra year.

Advanced Placement

One way for your child to get through in fewer than four years is to start taking college-level courses in high school. More than 61% of the nation's high schools offer Advanced Placement (AP) courses. The schools may administer Advanced Placement exams to juniors and seniors, usually after they've completed an AP class in, say, English literature, U.S. history, calculus, or biology. Students who are homeschooled or whose schools do not offer AP courses may participate through independent study or an online course. Exams may also be taken. (For a list of the exams, see the box below.) If the student scores a 3 or better on the exam—on a

---

ADVANCED PLACEMENT EXAMS

Art History and Studio Art
Biology
Calculus (AB and BC)
Chemistry
Comparative Government and Politics
Computer Science (A and AB)
Economics (Macroeconomics and
  Microeconomics)
English Language
English Literature
Environmental Science
European History
French Language
French Literature
German Language
Human Geography
Latin (Vergil and Literature)

Music Theory
Physics (B and C)
Psychology
Spanish Language
Spanish Literature
Statistics
U.S. Government and Politics
U.S. History
World History

The following subjects will be tested for
the first time:
Italian Language and Culture: May 2006
Chinese Language and Culture: May 2007
Japanese Language and Culture: May 2007

Source: The College Board

scale of 1 to 5—he or she usually earns AP credit, although some colleges or universities will require a 4 or even a 5. Each exam, prepared and scored by the College Board, costs $82.

The majority of colleges let students use advanced placement credits to reduce the number of courses needed to complete a degree. A student who passed three AP exams, for instance, might have to take—and pay for—three fewer courses during his or her college career. Some extremely ambitious students exempt themselves from an entire year's worth of classes.

But not all schools are so generous. Instead of giving college credit, some simply let students who've passed AP exams take more-advanced courses as freshmen, but still expect them to take four years' worth of classes. In that case, students get the benefit of skipping introductory courses, but there's no savings on tuition. Other schools limit the number of credits they give for AP exams. Selective schools may not give college credit for AP courses at all but may view them as a plus in the admissions process. If your child is pursuing AP classes, be sure to ask prospective colleges about their policies. Someone with an eye on graduating early will want to give extra weight to a school that will offer full credit for AP work.

Choose Community College

There may still be people who think of community college as a backwater refuge for students who aren't quite, well, smart enough for a "real" college. But you'd better not suggest that to astronaut Robert "Hoot" Gibson, Black & Decker CEO Nolan Archibald, former EPA administrator Carol Browner, former Maryland governor Parris Glendening, or former Seattle mayor Norman Rice—community-college alumni all. With an average annual tuition of around $2,000, community college is an affordable stepping-stone to a four-year degree. In fact, with the help of the Hope Scholarship tax credit (discussed in Chapter 1), many students can complete their first two years of study

With an average annual tuition of around $2,000, community college is an affordable stepping-stone to a four-year degree.

Many community colleges also have guaranteed-transfer arrangements with a number of area colleges, public and private.

with 75% of the cost covered. By earning good grades at a community college, your child can transfer to a "brand name" college or university and earn the same sheepskin as students who paid nearly twice as much.

THE WELCOME MAT. When a community-college student is ready to transfer, will the school of her choice be ready for her? Increasingly, the answer is yes. Many four-year schools go out of their way to encourage community-college transfers and smooth the transition.

In a program called Exploring Transfer, Vassar College, in Poughkeepsie, New York, selects about 40 community-college students each year to spend five weeks taking summer courses, with their tuition funded by a grant.

Smith College, in Northampton, Massachusetts, maintains "articulation agreements" with Miami-Dade (Florida) and Santa Monica (California) community colleges, which means that Smith regularly reviews the schools' course offerings and spells out which of their courses will be accepted for how much credit. More commonly, four-year schools have articulation agreements with a handful of nearby community colleges.

Many community colleges also have guaranteed-transfer arrangements with a number of area colleges, public and private. Students who earn a minimum grade point average at De Anza Community College, in Cupertino, California, for example, can automatically transfer as juniors to one of 11 public and private schools.

Even in the absence of a formal agreement, four-year colleges will readily help students select community-college courses for which they'll receive transfer credit. Many also set aside scholarship money for community-college students.

GOING PUBLIC. Public universities, because of their lower tuition costs, tend to be the most popular choice for community-college students. The University of Virginia and the University of North Carolina at Chapel Hill, for instance, accept a large percentage of their transfer students from community colleges.

In Pennsylvania, all public universities must give first preference to students applying for transfer from Pennsylvania community colleges. Florida and Arizona have similar programs. More than half of the states guarantee admission to selected colleges and universities, both public and private, for in-state community-college students who have an associate's degree, provided they meet state standards such as a minimum GPA.

MAKING THE GRADE. At both public and private schools, admissions officers say that grades are far more important than the reputation of the school from which the applicant is transferring.

Success at a community college can even offer a second chance at a school that turned you down. At Cornell University, a small number of strong applicants who miss the cut straight out of high school receive a consolation offer: Study for a year or two at any accredited college, including two-year colleges, and take courses that will transfer to Cornell. If you complete specified coursework and maintain a certain GPA, you're guaranteed admission.

Four colleges at the University of California–Berkeley make similar offers. The College of Letters and Science, for instance, guarantees junior-year admission to students turned down as high school seniors who subsequently complete required courses and earn a specified GPA at one of about three dozen California community colleges.

FINISHING THE DEGREE. Besides hard work, the other key to admission to a four-year school (and to finishing in four years) is to choose your lower-division courses carefully. A student with a particular school in mind—or better still, a specific program—will encounter the fewest obstacles. He or she will know which accounting, math, and computer-science courses are required to get into the business school at U. Va., for instance, or that a speech class won't transfer to Smith because no equivalent is offered there.

> Success at a community college can even offer a second chance at a school that turned you down.

Earning a bachelor's degree in three years is no walk in the park, even for motivated, ambitious students.

Do community-college students show up at four-year colleges prepared for more-demanding course-work? It's typical for community-college transfers to struggle through an "adjustment semester," admissions officers say, but by graduation most rank on a par with, or even a bit better than, four-year students. There are people who believe that four years in one place is very important, but given the high cost of college, the excellent preparation at many community colleges is a bargain.

Three-Year Degree Programs

Earning a bachelor's degree in three years instead of four can shave thousands off the cost of a diploma. But even for motivated, ambitious students, it's no walk in the park. Getting through in three years usually means taking a heavier-than-normal course load during the academic year and taking classes in the summer, when everyone else gets a break. It doesn't leave a lot of time for much of a social life. Nor does it leave much time for extracurricular activities. But a growing number of students are choosing the accelerated route, anyway, to reduce their costs and get out into the "real" world—or on to graduate school—as soon as possible.

Here are a couple of examples of schools with formal three-year degree programs:

- **At Southern New Hampshire University,** in Manchester, New Hampshire, you can earn a degree in business administration in three years, with a standard course load and no summer sessions required. You'd save a full year's costs—about $26,000.
- **At Upper Iowa University,** in Fayette, Iowa, students who follow a focused program and carry a heavy course load can graduate in three years and still have summers off. They save the cost of the fourth year, currently about $23,500, including tuition, room and board, fees, and books.

If you're receiving financial aid, your savings is the amount you would be expected to contribute toward costs in the fourth year minus the cost of summer classes, not the full cost of tuition. Your savings could be reduced by extra room-and-board expenses, assuming your child stays on campus during a summer term instead of living at home.

Even at schools without a formal path to a three-year degree, students can often create a schedule that enables them to finish a semester or a year early.

Two Degrees in Five Years

Is your child contemplating graduate school, too? That ordinarily adds two years to a student's college career, unless you seek out a college that offers a five-year, joint-degree program in your child's intended major. Such programs allow students to earn a bachelor's degree and a master's degree in five years, which saves you or your child a year of graduate-school tuition and living expenses. Typically, a student has to decide to enroll in the program by his or her junior year—and then begins working graduate-level courses into his or her schedule in place of electives.

At least two colleges throw in the icing on the cake—at Clark University, in Worcester, Massachusetts, and Lehigh University, in Bethlehem, Pennsylvania, the fifth year is tuition-free. Clark, which grants master of arts (MA), master of business administration (MBA), and master of science in professional communications (MS) degrees in five years, boasts that its program saves students close to $63,000. That's $34,890 in tuition and room and board for the sixth year they won't need, plus $28,000 in tuition that the university waives the fifth year. Of course, your savings is less when some of that cost would have been covered by financial aid. At Clark, the most popular combination is an undergraduate degree in economics or psychology and an MBA, and at Lehigh, it's liberal arts and an MBA or engineering and an MS in materials.

Graduation Guarantees

Figuring out how to pay for four years of college is daunting enough without having to foot an extra year or more because your child can't get into the courses

A five-year, joint-degree program in your child's intended major saves you or your child a year of graduate-school tuition and living expenses.

needed to graduate on time. To erase that worry, a small but growing number of schools are offering graduation guarantees.

If a student is unable to complete classes in four years because of something the university does, the school will waive tuition fees for the needed classes at DePauw University, in Indiana. Other schools that have similar guarantees:

- **the Milwaukee School of Engineering**
- **University of the Pacific,** in Stockton, California
- **Augustana College,** in Rock Island, Illinois
- **Regis University,** in Denver

Students still have to get passing grades, so that they don't need to repeat any required classes, and refrain from changing majors late in their college careers, when it could be harder to cram in a new slate of required classes. But if a school overenrolls or fails to offer a needed class, students get to take the course for free. Books and room and board are not covered by the guarantee. Of course, schools don't want to be forced to give classes away, so expect to see stepped-up student counseling. Students at Indiana University, for instance, take part in "mapping" sessions with academic advisors, designed to blueprint which classes to take and when.

THE ULTIMATE GUARANTEE

Some schools go so far as to guarantee students a job after graduation. For example, at Manchester College in North Manchester, Indiana, students who don't land a job that requires a college degree within six months of graduation can take additional undergraduate courses for one year at no cost. The extra coursework gives the student an opportunity to develop practical skills.

Students must participate in extra-curricular activities and an internship or on-campus job, and must take advantage of career counseling. The idea: Students who take those steps, with the school's encouragement, will be so well qualified that they probably won't need to collect on the guarantee.

Even at colleges without a guarantee, advise your child to seek out such counseling, to avoid a senior-year surprise that will prevent him or her from graduating on time. It might also help to remind your child gently that the earlier he or she settles on a major, the easier it will be to complete all the required courses in four years.

Innovative Ways to Pay the Bill for College

When it comes time to actually begin sending checks to the bursar's office, there are ways to trim your costs—or at least ease the burden of a big tuition bill.

Pay Tuition in Installments

Recognizing that it's tough for most parents to cover a $10,000 tuition bill all at once, most colleges let parents enroll in an interest-free installment plan that stretches the cost over 10 or 12 months. These plans are usually administered by a third-party company, such as Academic Management Services (www.amsweb.com) and Key Education Resources (www.key.com/educate). The application on the Web site includes a payment calculator, once you select the payment plan type you wish to use. You will have to specifically ask a financial-aid officer whether such a program is available through the school and what types of payment plans are available, since many schools offer more than one.

While you pay no interest, there's typically an enrollment fee of about $40 to $50, and you must begin making payments in June, July, or August instead of September. (If you don't enroll until September, you may have to make up back payments all at once.) Still, the plans are a good deal, especially for parents who are paying all or part of the college bills from current income and would otherwise have to borrow—or borrow more—to pay the bill on time.

Most colleges let parents enroll in an interest-free installment plan that stretches the cost over 10 or 12 months.

Say, for instance, that you could squeeze $500 a month out of the family budget to cover the college bills, but you face a $10,000 bill all at once on September 1. Instead of taking out a $10,000 loan at the beginning of the academic year, you could take out a $5,000 loan (or open a home-equity credit line) and pay in ten $1,000 installments—$500 from cash flow each month and $500 from the proceeds of the loan or from the credit line. The installment plan eases the sticker shock—and saves you some interest. (In the example above, what you save is equal to the interest on a 10-month, $5,000 loan, which would be about $300, assuming a 7% interest rate.)

Prepay to Lock In or Reduce Costs

At the other end of the spectrum are parents who can afford to pay the bill up front, perhaps from savings. Those parents may be tempted to consider locking in today's costs by paying four years' worth of bills up front. But if tuition increases are slowing, on average, prepayment may not save you much money, if any.

You'll come out ahead only if tuition and other costs rise faster than the 5% or so you otherwise could earn by holding the money in a lower-risk investment such as an intermediate government bond fund until you were ready to pay each year's cost. If the school your child attends has tied its tuition increases to the consumer price index (the measure of inflation that has hovered around 3% in recent years), prepayment will probably cost you money. There's no way to be certain of how much tuition will go up in future years, but an admissions- or financial-aid officer might be able to tell you what's anticipated for the next year or two. You can also ask what the rate of increase has been in recent years and use that figure as a guide.

Student Jobs

Most students can wait until they arrive on campus to begin looking for a job to help pay the college bills. But to land some cooperative education and military opportunities, students must take steps even as they're selecting a college.

A paycheck is a paycheck, and if they're willing to work for $6 to $7 an hour, most students don't have much difficulty finding jobs waiting tables, ringing up retail-store purchases, or pushing paper in a corporate office. But the plum jobs are those that allow a student to marry an academic or career interest with a job that helps cover tuition or living expenses. Most campuses have a career center or job-placement office that can help students find the kind of job they want—whether the top priority is a chance to help a faculty member with research, freedom to study during slow periods (possible for, say, a library checkout clerk)—or the highest possible pay. Sometimes each academic department keeps its own listing of research jobs and other positions related to its area of study.

To land some cooperative education and military opportunities, students must take steps even as they're selecting a college.

An Extracurricular Activity That Pays

At many colleges, residence-hall advisors not only get something nice to put on a résumé, they often also get free room and board and in some cases remission of tuition. Usually, these positions are for upperclassmen. But if your child is interested, he or she should pave the way early on in the freshman or sophomore year by learning how resident advisors are selected. Other student leaders, such as student-body president and newspaper editors, sometimes get some compensation, too.

Cooperative Education

One way students can make a hefty contribution to their own college costs and get a leg up on a good job after graduation is to enroll in a cooperative education program, available at hundreds of U.S. schools. Co-op students get a paying job related to their academic major and either work half-time or alternate semesters of work and study. The only catch is that, in some programs, it can take five years to graduate. The extra time may be worth it depending on what the co-op pays and to what extent the co-op improves the student's chances of getting a job after graduation.

GREAT CO-OP JOBS

What kinds of jobs do co-op students get? Here are a couple of examples.

At American University
- finance assistant, Merrill Lynch
- press assistant, White House press office
- promotions intern, C-Span
- public-affairs assistant, the Smithsonian Institution

At Northeastern University
- production manager, Boston Red Sox
- production intern, MTV Europe
- brand marketing specialist, Atari

THE COST AND BENEFITS. At Northeastern University, in Boston, where 90% of the students participate in the co-op program, the average earnings for roughly six months of work, with alternate quarters of work and study, are about $11,700 which can go a long way toward the annual tuition of $26,990. Earnings are typically much higher than that for students in engineering, computer science, business, and health occupations, but can be significantly lower for students in the social sciences and humanities. Students in the liberal arts who wind up in lower-paying positions may not always come out ahead financially after the cost of the fifth year is taken into account. But even for those students, the work experience and the contacts they make in their professional field offer an advantage when they look for a job after graduation.

Many co-op students at Northeastern University are offered positions with former co-op employers. Employers include the university itself, the U.S. government, the state of Massachusetts, many Boston-area hospitals, the *Boston Globe* newspaper, and corporations including Fidelity Investments, General Electric, Gillette, John Hancock Insurance, Polaroid, Price Waterhouse Coopers, Raytheon, State Street Bank, Sun Microsystems, and Walgreens. In all, about 1,500 companies have former Northeastern co-op students on their payrolls.

THE OTHER PLAYERS. Among the more than 400 other colleges with large co-op programs are:

- **American University, in Washington, D.C.**
- **Drexel University, in Philadelphia**
- **Georgia Institute of Technology, in Atlanta**
- **Rochester Institute of Technology (N.Y.)**
- **University of Michigan–Dearborn**

At many of the schools, including American, students get academic credit for their co-op jobs, which enables them to finish in four years instead of five. But they spend less time on the job, and earn correspondingly less pay than at other schools.

THE JOB THAT MAKES IT WORTHWHILE. What's an ideal co-op job? A former executive director of American University's career center likes to answer the question with the story of a student who mentioned to her that he had enjoyed participating in his high school's thespian society but was majoring in computer science because "Dad says that's where the jobs are." She found him a position at the Folger Shakespeare Theater, where he designed a computerized reservations system—and also assisted with lights and sound during productions.

TIPS FOR FINDING THE RIGHT PROGRAM. If your child already knows what he or she wants to study and is interested in a cooperative-education program that will alternate work and study, take time to explore co-op programs—and the kinds of co-op jobs they offer—while selecting a school. (A few schools even require co-op participation for students in certain departments, such as the engineering and architecture departments at the University of Cincinnati.) An early commitment is necessary at such schools, because students

If you're trying to fill a gap in college financing, you'll have to decide whether the long-term benefits of an unpaid internship outweigh the short-term lack of income.

must begin participating in a co-op by the end of their freshman year.

At schools such as American University where co-ops are integrated into a student's academic schedule (think of it as a class for which the student gets credit and pay), students can sign up in their sophomore year or later.

Either way, a stop at the cooperative-education office during a campus visit can give you an opportunity to look at current job listings and to talk with a counselor about what kind of earnings your child can expect in his or her chosen field. You can learn more about co-op programs at the Web site of the National Commission for Cooperative Education (www.co-op.edu).

Internships

What's the difference between a co-op and an internship? At schools like Northeastern, cooperative education is a formal program you stick with over the entire college career, while an internship is usually a job that lasts just a semester or a summer or that requires a smaller commitment of time per week. At schools like American University, there's less difference in duration between the two opportunities, but students automatically earn course credit for co-op jobs, while they must make special arrangements with faculty to get credit for an internship. And almost all co-ops pay, while some internships pay well, some meagerly, and some not at all. Even when there's no paycheck, internships can be a valuable source of job experience—and sometimes lead to a job after graduation. But if you're trying to fill a gap in college financing, you'll have to decide whether the long-term benefits of an unpaid internship outweigh the short-term lack of income.

As with ordinary jobs, the best place to look for an internship is at your college's career center or job-placement office. Also check with faculty in individual academic departments for information about internships that are listed directly with the department or contacts the faculty may have elsewhere.

Military Service

There are numerous routes to financing a college education with a stint in the military. Here are four:

APPLY TO A MILITARY ACADEMY. At the U.S. Military, Naval, Air Force, Merchant Marine, and Coast Guard academies, students earn a bachelor of science degree on Uncle Sam, who pays for tuition, room and board, and medical care, and provides a stipend for uniforms, books, and incidental expenses. Graduates repay the government with five years of active-duty military service.

Admission to the academies is competitive. Applicants should have good grades and SAT scores, have participated in athletics and extracurricular activities, and be in excellent health. Candidates for the U.S. Military, Naval, and Air Force academies must also have a nomination, most commonly from the student's congressional representative or senator. Students should apply for a nomination in the spring of their junior year. For more information, visit the academies' Web sites (listed in the box on the following page).

GO FOR AN ROTC SCHOLARSHIP. The Army, Navy, and Air Force award Reserve Officer Training Corps scholarships that cover up to full tuition for four years, and pay a small monthly allowance. Students who earn the scholarships, based on grades, SAT scores, and extracurricular activities, must attend one of the more than 1,000 public or private colleges with an ROTC program (or with a cross-enrollment agreement with a school that has one) and spend two to five hours a week, plus time during the summer, in military training. After graduation, there's up to an eight-year service commitment, which will vary depending on the branch of service and the career field. For Army ROTC scholarship winners, the commitment can be fulfilled with four years of active duty or eight years of service in the Reserves or National Guard.

MORE ABOUT THE MILITARY

U.S. Air Force Academy: www.usafa.af.mil
U.S. Coast Guard Academy: www.cga.edu
U.S. Merchant Marine Academy: www.usmma.edu
U.S. Military Academy: www.usma.edu
U.S. Naval Academy: www.nadn.navy.mil
Army ROTC: www.armyrotc.com
Navy Recruiting Command:
www.cnet.navy.mil/nrotc/nrotc.htm
Air Force ROTC: www.afoats.af.mil/rotc.htm

Students hoping for four-year scholarships should apply no later than the fall of their senior year in high school. For information, visit a recruiting office or the Web sites listed in the box above.

TAKE ADVANTAGE OF MILITARY EDUCATIONAL BENEFITS. Aside from scholarship programs, any member of the military can qualify for educational benefits. Active-duty members of the Army, Navy, and Air Force, for instance, can take off-duty classes toward a bachelor's (or graduate) degree, with the service paying 100% of the cost, up to a total of $3,500 per year.

Soldiers can also participate in the Montgomery GI Bill. Those who serve on active duty for three years or more and agree to have their military pay reduced by $100 a month during the first 12 months of service can receive $900 a month toward educational expenses for 36 months after leaving the service.

Combining the two programs, a student could spend three years on active duty, taking as many off-duty classes as possible, then complete his or her degree with the help of up to $32,400 in GI Bill funds. (Additional GI Bill money—up to an additional $50,000—can be earned by enrolling in certain specialties.) Contact a military recruiting office for further details.

JOIN THE RESERVES. Members of the military reserves, as well as members of the National Guard, can also receive GI Bill benefits. With a six-year commitment (typically involving one weekend a month and two weeks each summer), reservists can receive up to $22,000 toward educational expenses (more if you enlist in certain specialties), plus $35,000 in pay. Members of the Army Reserves and National Guard can also qualify to have up to $10,000 in student loans forgiven, which doubles to $20,000 for those who enlist in certain military specialties.

Collegiate Cash Flow

On top of Introductory Economics or History 101, every freshman, like it or not, takes a real-life course in managing money. You will probably be all too aware of the tuition bills, but the hidden costs of college—like pizzas, textbooks, and travel—can easily add up to $3,000 per year per student—or more. And in most cases, it's up to your kid to keep those costs under control, with you as ad hoc and often long-distance financial advisor. You can consider this chapter your instructor's manual for Freshman Finances 101. On the syllabus: guidance on banking, credit cards, and smart cards; how to keep phone bills in check; whether to send your child to school with a car or computer; help with the dorm-versus-apartment and meal-plan versus student-cooking decision; and some tried-and-true money-management tips.

Find a Student-Friendly Bank

College students have special banking needs. They're likely to keep a low or steadily declining balance, have few if any monthly bills to pay by check, and rely mostly on automated teller machines to get cash. So a conventional checking account that charges $5 to $10 a month for unlimited transactions or that requires a substantial minimum balance to avoid fees usually isn't the best way to meet those needs. Enter the "basic banking" account, a no-frills, low-cost account that's ideal for students with uncomplicated financial lives. In a typical basic-banking account, there's no monthly fee, no minimum balance, and no fees for using the bank's own ATM machines. The catch to such accounts is that you get a limited number of free transactions each month—when you make more than six or eight or ten transactions in a month, there's typically a fee. So, before signing up, students should be fairly confident that they won't exceed the limits. Also, some basic accounts are geared to ATM and electronic access only, and charge fees for transactions with live tellers.

Fees for using an ATM that doesn't belong to the bank can also be steep—$1.50 to $3 per transaction. Your first choice should be a bank that has its own ATMs—not just those in the same network, such as PLUS or Cirrus—on or near campus. A bank with a branch or ATM on campus may cater to students by offering low-cost accounts.

If you're providing the spending money, how should you fund the account? You might be able to direct-deposit part of your payroll check or make an automatic transfer at little cost through a bank's direct-payment program. If you send regular checks, though, it gives the student experience with making deposits, as well as withdrawals, and reinforces the point that *you're* providing the money, not the electronic tooth fairy.

Then, of course, there's the matter of making sure your kid knows better than the "I can't be overdrawn, the ATM gave me cash" routine. Has your child ever

WHAT MINIMUM PAYMENTS COST

Here's what it costs to pay off a credit card balance one minimum payment at a time, assuming the interest rate is 18% and the minimum payment is 2.5%, but no less than $10—which is a typical formula.

Item	Cost	Time to repay	Interest	Total cost
Clothes	$ 100	11 months	$ 9.16	$ 109.16
Books	500	7 years	365.42	865.42
Computer	1,500	16+ years	1,865.40	3,365.40
Miscellany	2,500	20+ years	3,365.51	5,865.51

reconciled a bank-account statement? Have you been pitching in as your kids' bookkeeper? Now's the time to give them the tools to do it themselves. If your child hasn't had a bank account, then it's time to open a small one close to home. Either way, balancing the checkbook should be old hat by the time freshman year rolls around.

Once your child turns 18, he or she will be able to get a debit card attached to a checking account. That offers the convenience of using plastic instead of cash, but it will also limit how much trouble he or she can get into. If your child overdraws the account, he or she will be hit with a bounced-check fee. That's an immediate signal to get his or her finances in order, and it beats running up a credit card balance he or she can't pay off.

If your child overdraws on a debit card, he or she will be hit with a bounced-check fee, an immediate signal to get his or her finances in order.

Go Easy on Credit

College students enjoy privileged status as credit card customers—they can qualify for a $500 or $1,000 unsecured credit line without any employment, income, or credit history, even as a freshman. Young adults will never again find it as easy to get credit as they will during their college years. Underwriting is lenient mainly because college students tend to be loyal customers—three in four keep their first credit card for 15 years or more.

But it's a Jekyll-and-Hyde opportunity. Ideally, students save the card for emergencies, pay their bills on time, and graduate with a jump on building a good credit history. But it's easy for the ideal scenario to turn nightmarish: There's so much competition among credit cards to be the first one in a young adult's wallet that it's not unusual for students to get several cards. And after six months to a year, card issuers may increase the borrowing limit. The result: big debts at high rates of interest—and the inevitable phone call home from a son or daughter pleading for a bailout because he or she can't meet the minimum payment—or perhaps has missed payments and is hearing from collectors. If parents can't or won't come to the rescue, graduates start their careers with excessive debt and a blemished credit history.

The best way to avoid either unhappy outcome is to send your student to school with some counsel on how to handle credit. Students are often ill-informed about interest rates, grace periods (an opportunity to pay the bill in full before any interest is charged), and, in particular, the minimum-payment trap: If you make just the minimum payment (say, 2.5% of the outstanding balance) each month, it takes seven years and costs $865 to pay off a $500 purchase at 18%. Make sure your child also knows that credit costs the least when you pay in full by the due date, and that failing to pay at least the minimum payment will wreak havoc with his or her ability to get credit in the future.

Pick the Best Card

Students aren't likely to qualify for a low interest rate, but you can find no-annual-fee cards marketed to students online at www.cardtrack.com or www.cardratings.org. Rates don't vary much, so compare other factors that can add to the cost: late-payment and over-the-limit fees (which banks have become more aggressive about charging), lack of a grace period, and two-cycle billing, which requires at least two back-to-back, no-balance months to avoid interest charges. Also be aware of "teaser," or introductory, rates. These don't last long, so it's better to compare cards at their full rate.

Build a Good Credit Record

A strong credit history can mean lower rates on loans and brownie points with employers, landlords, and insurance companies. The best way to build good credit is to use the card, ideally making several small transactions each month and then paying the bill on time or even early. A good rule of thumb you can give your kids to help them stay on track: Use cash if the purchase will be used up by the time they get the bill or if they're not sure they can pay the bill in full right away.

Should You Cosign?

Sometimes parents cosign their children's credit applications, assuming they'll be able to spot problems before they get out of hand. Not necessarily. One Ohio father cosigned a bank credit card application for his daughter while she was a high school senior. Several months later, maxed out at the $500 limit, she was unable to manage even the minimum payment. Eight months passed, and $272 in late and over-the-limit fees had piled on to the balance before the bank called her father to request payment. "They could send you a postcard to let you know the payments aren't being made," he protested.

But card issuers and other creditors have no obligation to notify cosigners when the primary borrower isn't making payments. "We would hope that a parent who is cosigning would be actively interested in how the student is managing the loan," says a spokeswoman for the bank. That's nice in theory, but if your child is away at school, you may have nothing except his or her word that the card is under control.

Another warning to parents: Creditors usually record an account's payment history on the primary borrower's and the cosigner's credit reports, so your credit history could be tarnished if your child doesn't pay on time. Plus, the open credit line counts as part of your overall credit burden when you apply for a loan yourself. If you think co-owning the credit card is a good idea, you might as well be the primary borrower and let the child be the cosigner or coborrower, advises consumer advocate Gerri Detweiler (see box above). "You'll get the bills, so you'll know whether they're getting paid or not," she says.

Another possibility is to simply give your child a card on your account. It won't help him or her build

---

IF THEY DON'T BELIEVE YOU

Want someone else to deliver the perils-of-credit lecture? "Smart Credit Strategies for College Students," an audiotape recorded by Gerri Detweiler, a consumer advocate and former director of Bankcard Holders of America, is aimed at teens and teaches all the essentials (Good Advice Press, $16.90; 800-255-0899; www.goodadvicepress.com).

a credit history immediately, but it will provide a chance to learn to use credit wisely before the consequences are long-term.

Get Used to "Smart" Cards

College students have been among the guinea pigs used in the banking industry's effort to replace loose change with plastic. Smart cards are basically debit cards with special features. Rather than piling up bills on a credit card whose statement comes once a month, smart cards offer a pay-as-you-go alternative. At more than 430 colleges and universities, students (or their parents) can load money onto a smart card that can be used at pizza joints and other fast-food restaurants on campus, the campus bookstore and other retail venues, and for getting a soda at a vending machine, doing a load of laundry, or making photocopies at the library. Meal-plan credits may also be loaded onto the card, which may also serve as a library card, dorm security key, or electronic ID. Students load their cards with cash at "cash chip machines" or kiosks on campus. They can feed dollars into the machine or transfer money from a bank account using an ATM card. At the point of sale, students run the card through a reader to see the cost of the transaction and the balance left on the card.

What wisdom can students and faculty from schools where smart cards are used pass along to future smart-card users?

Guard the Card Like Cash

On some campuses, smart cards require a personal identification number (PIN) for certain transactions, and the card can be deactivated if it's lost or stolen. But at others, students whose cards go missing may as well have thrown the money away, because the cards lack a PIN to keep others from using them and can't be deactivated, because they're not linked to a central account. The card itself stores information about recent transactions.

Count the "Change"

What if the card is debited $5 instead of 50 cents for a soda out of a machine? The card-bearer will find out when the card comes up short in a reader. On some campuses, students can take their case to an on-campus service center, which can look up recent transactions on a card and correct errors. Elsewhere, vending machines are often programmed so that they can debit only as much as the most expensive item in the machine.

Stick with Credit for Big Purchases

In a dispute with a merchant, smart-card users have no more leverage than if they had paid with cash. If you use a credit card, you can withhold payment and dispute a charge when a product or service isn't delivered as agreed.

Don't Rush Technology

Students warn that ripping a card out of a card reader or cash machine too quickly can cause the entire balance to disappear—which means a trip to the service center to reinstate the value.

A Computer's a Must

You may have felt fortunate to take a typewriter to school, but for today's students a computer is an essential, whether it's brought along from home or purchased—or supplied by—the school.

Every student at Wake Forest University, for example, is equipped with an IBM ThinkPad and color printer—and gets an upgraded machine after two years. The university includes the expense in its tuition. Requiring all the students to have the same equipment and software makes it easier for everyone on campus—students, faculty, and administrators—to communicate via e-mail, says a spokeswoman for the university, and enables professors to make assignments using current software, such as requiring everyone in a statistics class to manipulate data using a certain spreadsheet program.

Requiring all the students to have the same equipment and software makes it easier for everyone on campus— students, faculty, and administrators —to communicate via e-mail.

It's probably best to wait until you've chosen a college to decide on a computer to ensure compatibility with the school's preferred system.

Dartmouth College takes a different approach. It requires a computer and recommends which machines and features will meet most students needs and sets minimum standards. Liberal-arts students can probably get by with the minimum, but computer-science students usually want to have all the bells and whistles. Although Dartmouth leaves it up to you what to buy, the college sells computers to students at discounted prices. It recommends that you buy your computer from them because most of the software you'll need is already installed and they provide on-site service and support for the products they sell.

It's probably best to wait until you've chosen a college to decide on a computer because at some schools IBM-compatible machines are predominant and at others Macintoshes are the computers of choice. Your child will have a much easier time using the campus network—for sending e-mail to professors, for instance—if he or she has a computer that's compatible with everyone else's.

Once you know what your child needs, a family hand-me-down or a secondhand machine, perhaps purchased from a graduating senior, might turn out to be sufficient. Most schools buy computers in large quantities and therefore can offer them to students at substantial discounts, through either a computer center or the campus store. It always pays to comparison-shop, but often the discounted price for students at the campus store is less than a comparable computer would cost at a local discount computer store.

One bright note: You may not need to buy your child a printer. Most colleges have a "printer center" or publicly accessible printers in dormitories and libraries that students can use to print out term papers.

Outfitting the Dorm Room

The first semester of college brings with it the extra expense of equipping the dorm room with sheets, towels, and basic furnishings, such as a clock radio, lamp, or CD player. First, find out what the school provides; some may, for example, provide weekly linen service as part of the room-and-board package. Also, ask what, if anything, it may prohibit from dorm rooms because of fire codes or the like. A little coordination with your child's new roommate can also help trim those costs. When a student at the University of Kentucky got his roommate assignment as a freshman, his mom advised him to call the roommate ahead of time to find out what he was bringing, so that neither would buy anything unnecessary. "My son thought that was odd, but he did it and it worked out well," says his mom. Her son brought a used minirefrigerator and microwave, and his roommate brought a TV and DVD player.

Send the Car?

At many schools, undergraduate students aren't allowed to have cars on campus. But even if they are allowed, can your child get by without one? Many a student will do just as well or better without the expense of gas, parking, and maintenance for a car. But more significant, keeping the car in your own driveway will probably save you a bundle on insurance premiums.

As most parents already know, just listing your teen driver as an "occasional user" of a family car can add hundreds of dollars to the family's auto-insurance premium. Coverage can cost even more when a teen is considered the primary driver—especially if he or she is driving an expensive car. But here's one good piece of news about the cost of college: If you send your child to a college more than 150 miles from home and persuade him or her to leave the car behind, your insurance premium will fall—perhaps back to the comparatively painless premium you enjoyed before your child got a driver's license.

Anticipating wails of protest? Your son or daughter may have a case if the car is headed for a sleepy college town. One Cornell student, for instance, found that it was far cheaper to drive her car in Ithaca, New York,

If you send your child to a college more than 150 miles from home and persuade him or her to leave the car behind, your insurance premium will fall.

Most companies consider students living off-campus to be independent and therefore ineligible for property coverage under their parents' insurance.

than back home in Long Island. The cost of insuring her Chevy Corsica was 45% less than the cost when the car was based at her parents' home.

But stick to your guns if your child is headed for a big-city campus. Insurance can cost as much as 300% more in urban areas than in suburban or rural locales. Plus, if your child is rated as an occasional driver on your current policy, taking the car to school for nine months automatically pushes the student into the higher-priced category of principal driver.

Don't Overlook Property Insurance

Students sometimes learn the hard way that valuables can walk off from dormitories, fraternity and sorority houses, and multiroommate apartments or group houses. Their parents' homeowners insurance often covers the damage, but that's not always the case. A few companies cover students' possessions up to the parents' full personal-property limit. Most cap coverage of a student's property stored away from home at 10% of the parents' personal-property coverage. If, for instance, your house is insured for $100,000 and your personal property for $50,000, your child gets $5,000 worth of protection. Parents' property insurance usually also covers the value of a child's property in transit between home and school.

Students step into a gray area when they move from a dormitory into an off-campus apartment. According to the Insurance Information Institute, in New York City, most companies consider students living off-campus to be independent and therefore ineligible for coverage under their parents' insurance. But some may still cover a student who lives off-campus during the school year but lives at home during the summer. A call to your agent should nail down what your own homeowners policy covers.

A student without coverage should get a renter's insurance policy, which for about $150 a year will cover up to $10,000 to $15,000 of furniture and other possessions.

Bargain Airfares for Students

If college is too far away to make the trip by car, your best bet for finding a cheap airfare is to check the Internet. Web-only fares are a source of bargain fares available only through the Internet. Check sites of online travel agencies such as Expedia, Orbitz, or Travelocity. Also look at low-fare airlines or keep an eye out for fare wars on the major airlines—and book tickets at least 21 days in advance.

Student Universe (www.studentuniverse.com), an online site that partners with Orbitz, enables college students and faculty to travel at discounted rates. Students or faculty register with an ".edu" e-mail address, which must be verified before they qualify to receive travel discounts. Choices of airline or departure time may be limited, but the savings can be worth it. The student or faculty member can make a reservation only for himself or herself through this service.

If you're traveling with a companion, you will need to check other online travel agencies for companion fares—specials for parties of two or more traveling together. To get these fares, you and your companion must always be on the same flight. If one person changes flight plans, that could mean higher fares for each traveler.

Calling Home

How communicating home has changed in such a short time! Not too long ago, students called collect from pay phones in the hall or, more recently, phones in their dorm rooms or apartments. Then the answer was either a calling card tied to the phone bill or prepaid phone cards. While all of these options are still available, today the trend is to use the cell phone or computer e-mail, which reduces the expense to nothing.

Consider a prepaid service plan for your college student's cell phone. There's no long-term contract, and you pay only for the minutes you use.

A collect call is almost always the most expensive, and an ordinary calling card on your long-distance service at home may not be much better, unless you sign up for a special calling-card plan or use one of the many small long-distance carriers.

Or you or your child can buy prepaid phone cards, which come preloaded with a limited amount of calling time, say, 60 or 120 minutes, which keeps students on a budget.

If your child still has an individual hardwired phone line, look into low-cost long-distance plans that charge 5 cents or 7 cents a minute anytime.

But you son or daughter will most probably set off to college with his or her own cell phone. There are a couple of ways to keep costs in check here. Look for an inexpensive national cell-phone family plan that allows you to share a pool of minutes. This can be a good value and offers a simple single bill. Some of the major cell-phone companies offer multiple-line national plans as low as $50 a month and allow unlimited calling among plan members.

Or consider a prepaid service plan for your college student. There's no long-term contract, and you pay only for the minutes you use—with no taxes or fees added to your bill. One University of Pennsylvania student signed up for a prepaid plan because he wasn't sure how often he'd use the cell phone. "I went with a prepaid plan because I could cancel it at any time," he explained. He paid $30 up front for 30 days of service, or until his balance dipped below $5, whichever came first. Nights and weekend calls were free. He nearly always managed to squeeze out 30 days of talk time—he estimated he used about 400 minutes each month, including free time—without having to ante up more cash.

Rates for prepaid-wireless airtime are high compared to traditional cell-phone plans and are not a good deal if you make a lot of calls. But, while you'll have to buy the phone, there's no long-term contract and canceling is usually easy.

The E-Mail Alternative

And here's the ultimate cost-saver: Take advantage of the fact that in most circumstances e-mail is free. Most of the time, students pay nothing to have a university e-mail address or to use the Internet. E-mail is especially economical for students who spend a semester abroad and want to avoid expensive international calls. And look out for what may be the next big advance in long-distance voice communication: Voice over Internet Protocol, or VoIP, the service that taps cable or DSL broadband Internet connections to make and receive calls.

"Help, I'm Broke!"

A desperate "Send money!" phone call from your student halfway through the first semester may be inevitable. But you can try to start your youngster out on the right foot with some sound advice on managing money. And consider offering this assistance *before* he or she sets off to college.

Broach the B Word

Have your child draw up a budget during senior year in high school. A good start is to have him or her keep a record of every expense incurred—down to splitting the cost of a pizza with friends, gas for the car, etc. An expense log is a great way to see where the money goes so adjustments, if necessary, can be made. As freshman year draws near, ask him or her to draw up a budget for the school year. It shouldn't be too difficult to figure out how much textbooks or travel home will cost, but a budget for social activities may be harder to estimate accurately.

Use the Expense Log

Once your child gets to college, suggest he or she again track expenses for a month or two to see where the money is going and arrive at a better target number. Estimating costs by the month rather than by the semester will help. Don't forget incidentals; shampoo,

Ask your child to draw up a budget for the school year. Social activities may be harder to estimate than expenses for textbooks or travel home.

One financial planner suggests sending money monthly or biweekly, "the way they'll get money the rest of their lives."

toothpaste, and other toiletries, for instance, can add up. A review of the log at the end of the semester can pinpoint whether your child is broke because of too many late-night pizzas or because a bigger book budget is in order.

Set the Ground Rules

Let your child know ahead of time exactly what you're paying for and what expenses are his or her responsibility. If you're providing spending money, make clear how much will be provided and when. That improves the chances that your child will reserve some part-time-job earnings to pay the phone bill, instead of spending it all on a Saturday-night date.

Send Money in Small Doses— at Least at First

Some parents think college-age kids should be able to handle a lump sum for the semester or the full college year. But one financial planner suggests sending money monthly or biweekly, "the way they'll get money the rest of their lives." Or you might load your child's smart card with meal-plan credits and money for books at the beginning of each semester, then add some spending money to the card each month.

Questions for Sophomores & Up

Living arrangements are usually pretty straightforward in the freshman year, as most freshmen choose or are required to live on campus. By the sophomore year, your student may be free to consider other options:

Dorm or Apartment?

Can your child save money by sharing an apartment with roommates rather than living in the dorms? A lot of students go this route after freshman year (when many schools require students to live on campus). Depending on the rental market near campus, one-quarter of the rent on a two-bedroom apartment may well be cheaper than the amount you're paying each month for dorm housing. But before you send your child packing, be sure to weigh the extra costs and responsibilities of apartment living.

You may have to cosign your child's rental agreement, and your child and his or her roommates will have to decide whether they want a month-to-month or yearlong lease, in which case they may want a provision that allows them to sublet the property during the summer. You'll probably have to put up an amount equal to a month's rent as a security deposit, and depending on how your child and his or her roommates live, that amount may or may not be refunded.

- **There's furniture to buy,** such as a bed, desk, kitchen table and chairs.
- **The little stuff adds up,** too, like trash cans, cleaning supplies, dishes, utensils, and so forth.
- **And monthly phone bills and utility bills** are other added expenses.

Of course, many an apartment-dwelling student stores books in milk crates, sets up the TV on a board supported by cinder blocks, and lounges on the 15-year-old sofa that formerly resided in the family basement. Even so, be sure to leave some room for surprise costs when you make the dorm-versus-apartment decision.

Meal Plan or Chef Boyardee?

Is three square meals for $13 a day a good deal? That's about what you spend for a full college meal plan, where students can usually choose to eat in the dining hall or get carryout food from, say, a deli or fast-food restaurant. After freshman year, many students decide they can eat better on the same amount of money—or eat for less than $90 a week. Residence halls often have communal kitchens that make it possible for students to cook their own meals.

Of course, a lot depends on how convenient the grocery store is—and whether the student likes to cook. If your child's answer to the meal plan is the

> **Be sure to leave some room for surprise costs when you make the dorm-versus-apartment decision.**

pizzeria or campus tavern every night, you won't save money and you may be concerned for his or her health. But a pair of roommates with a little ability in the kitchen can probably make even $70 worth of groceries go a long way. If they're pooling resources, that saves them each about $40 a week—or $720 a semester.

Index

A

Academic Management Services, 271

Accelerated programs, 268

ACT scores, 195

Advanced placement exams, 264–65

African-American group scholarships, 213

Aggressive-growth funds, 72–73

Airfares, 291

Air Force Academy, 277

Air Force ROTC scholarship, 277

Alabama Prepaid Affordable College Tuition (PACT) Program, 87

Alaskan student scholarships, 213

Albertus Magnus College, 144

Alexander Graham Bell Association for the Deaf and Hard of Hearing, 214

Alternative financial resources, 263–79
  advanced placement exams, 264–65
  community college, 263–64, 265–68
  cooperative education, 273–76
  graduation guarantees, 269–71
  installment tuition payments, 271–72
  military service, 277–79
  student jobs, 272–79
  three-year degree programs, 268–69
  tuition prepayment, 272
  two degrees in five years, 269

Alternative Loans, 244

American Century's Target Maturities Trust, 65

American Institute of CPAs, 96

American Legion
  Auxiliary National President's Scholarship, 220
  National High School Oratorical Contest, 221

American Physical Society Corporate-Sponsored Scholarship for Minority Undergraduates, 221

American Pomological Society, 205

American Postal Workers Union, 212

American University (Washington, DC), 274, 275, 276

America's Best Value Colleges (Owens), 3

Amherst College, 125–26, 129, 131

AMVETS National Scholarships, 220

Annuities, 151–52, 159, 167

Archibald, Nolan, 265

Arizona community colleges, 267

Arizona Family College Savings Program, 87

Arkansas Tax-Deferred Tuition Savings Program (GIFT College Investing Plan), 87

Army ROTC scholarships, 277

Articulation agreements, 266

Ashby B. Carter Memorial Scholarship Fund, 223

Asset protection allowances, 131, 134

Assets
  asset-protection allowance, 177
  available for college, determining, 186, 187
  grandparents of students and, 163–64
  home equity, 130–31
  parents' contribution from, 124
  reducing, 161–65
  shifting, 159–61
  of siblings, 134–35, 179
  of students, 135, 161–63

Assumptions, 23–25

Athletic scholarships, 214–15

ATM machines, 281–83

Augustana College (IL), 270

Automatic transfers to savings, 31, 34

Auto(s)
  insurance, 34, 289–90
  students and, 289–90

Ayn Rand Institute Fountainhead Essay Competition, 222

B

Banks, student-friendly, 281–83

Bates College, 3

Bonds
  borrowing against, 258–59
  corporate bond mutual funds, 67–68
  government bond funds, 61
  U.S. savings, 53–57
  zero-coupon, 62–65

Bonuses, saving, 36

Borrowing. See Loan(s)

Boy Scout scholarships, 215

Brigham Young University, 3

Bright Start College Savings Program (IL), 89

Broward Community College, 224

Browner, Carol, 265

Brown University, 5

Bryn Mawr, 199

Budgeting, 30–31, 293–94
  worksheet, 32–33

Bureau of Indian Affairs, 213

Business equipment, 167

C

California Golden State ScholarShare, 88

Campus visits, 200, 201–3

Capital gains/losses, 153

Career centers, 273

Car insurance, 34

Carleton College, 199

Carnegie Mellon, 145

Car purchases, 35

Cars, students and, 289–90

Carter (Ashby B.) Memorial
Scholarship Fund, 223
Case, Joe Paul, 118–19
Cash flow, parents and, 14–15
Cash flow, students and,
281–96
bargain airfares, 291
calling home, 291–93
car use, 289–90
cash management advice,
293–94
computers and, 287–88
credit cards and, 283–86
dorm room outfitting, 288–89
e-mail, 293
meal plans, 295–96
off-campus housing, 294–96
property insurance, 290–91
"smart" cards, 286–87
student-friendly banks, 281–83
Cell phones, 291–93
Certificates of deposit (CDs),
50–52
Certified Financial Planner
Board of Standards, Inc.,
95
Certified financial planners,
95, 182
Chartered Financial
Consultants, 95
Child support, 175
Choosing a college, financial
considerations, 183–203
employers and, 192
financial aid and, 194–200
financial checkup, 185–88
honors colleges, 190–91
need analysis, 184–85
need-blind admissions,
199–200
public vs. private, 189–90
SAT/ACT scores and class
rank, 195
school financial policies,
197–99
values in specific fields, 191–92
Chronicle Financial Aid Guide,
210
Civic group scholarships, 212
Clark University (MA), 269
Class rank, 195
Clergy living allowances, 175
Clifford, Denis, 38

Closing costs, on loans, 252–53
Coast Guard Academy, 277
Coca-Cola Scholars
Foundation Inc., 216
College Board, 2
AP exams, 265
calculator for college aid, 123
institutional methodology,
112–13, 128, 131
MyRoad database, 211
Web site, 196, 211
*College Board's College
Handbook*, 193
*College Costs & Financial Aid
Handbook*, 17
College Handbook, The, 195
College Illinois, 89
College Match, 193
College planning timeline,
8–9
College Savings Iowa, 89
College Savings Plan of
Nebraska, 91
College Scholarship Service,
103
Collegiate Choice Walking
Tours, 202–3
Colorado Stable Value Plus
College Savings Program,
88
Columbia 300 Inc., 214
Community colleges, 263–64,
265–68
Community scholarships, 212
Computer research, 123
Computers, 167, 287–88
Connecticut Higher Education
Trust (CHET), 88
Consultants, financial aid,
181–82
Cornell University, 267
Costs. *See* Expenses
Council of Better Business
Bureaus, 210
Course selection, 267
Coverdell Education Savings
Account (ESA), 36, 37, 39,
40
restrictions to, 42–43
Cracking the New SAT, 201
Credit bureaus, 245
Credit card debt, 34, 283–86
Credit records, 284

CUNY Brooklyn College, 3
CUNY Queens College, 3
Custodial accounts, 176

D

Dartmouth College, 130, 131,
288
Daughters of the Cincinnati
Scholarship, 220
Day care costs, 36
De Anza Community
College, 266
Debit cards, 286–87
Debt, 164–65
high levels of, 148
long-term, 136
student and, 188
trend of lower cost, 228–29
Defined-benefit retirement
plans, 254
Delaware College
Investment Plan, 88
DePauw University (IN), 270
Detweiler, Gerri, 285
Direct PLUS Loan Application
and Promissory Note, 242
Disabled student
scholarships, 214
Distributive Education Clubs
of America Scholarship
Awards, 218
District of Columbia 529
College Savings Plan, 88
Divorced/separated parents,
117–19, 180, 198–99
*Don't Miss Out: The Ambitious
Student's Guide to
Financial Aid*, 109
Dorm rooms, outfitting,
288–89
Draft registration, 104
Drexel University, 275
Duke, 130, 131

E

Educational Communications
Scholarship Foundation,
216
Education IRAs. *See*
Coverdell Education
Savings Account (ESA)

Education Resources Institute (TERI), 244
Edward J. Nell Memorial Scholarship Program, 222
Electric bills, 34
Elks, 212, 216
Employee Retirement Income Security Act, 254
Employer(s)
  college choice and, 192
  -provided scholarships, 211–12
  -provided tuition benefits, 179
  -sponsored flexible spending accounts, 175
Encyclopedia of Associations, 212
Endowments, 194, 195
Equifax, 245
ESPN Scholastic Sports America Scholarship, 206
Estate taxes, reducing, 44
Ethnic group scholarships, 213
Eureka College, 5
EXCEL education loans, 243
Expected family contribution, 100–101, 107–8, 126
  calculating, 119–23
  student and, 187–88
Expenses, 2
  annual increases in, 4
  average for 2004–2005 academic year, 2–3
  cost of getting into college, 200–203
  cutting, 34–35
  day care, 36
  expected family contribution, 25–26, 27, 100–101, 107–8
  expense log, 293–94
  forecasting total, 6
  inflation and, 4
  sampler, 2004–2005, 17–22
  top ten best value colleges 2004–2005, 3
Experian, 245
Exploring Transfer, 266
Extended loan repayment, 260

F
FAFSA (Free Application for Federal Student Aid), 99, 102–3, 107, 154, 169–78

Family Federal Education Loan program, 241
Farm, family, 124, 178
fastWeb, 211
Federal Direct PLUS-loan program, 241–42
Federal Direct Student Loan (FDSL), 234
Federal Family Education Loan (FFEL), 128, 234
Federal methodology, 102
Federal need-analysis figures, 127
Federal Student Aid Information Center, 237
FinAid, 123
Financial advisors, 95–97
Financial aid, 5–7, 125–49, 151–82
  balancing merit and need, 141–42
  calendar, 106
  child's assets and, 161–63
  deadlines, 103
  debt and, 164–65
  discounts, 140–42
  enhanced packages, 136–38
  expected family contribution, 13, 25–26, 27, 107–8, 126
  extending deadlines for response, 149
  FAFSA forms, 169–78
  federal aid information, 237
  federal methodology, 108–15
  first layer of, 126–27
  "gapping," 138–40
  grandparents and, 163–64
  loans and, 257
  merit-based, 168
  negotiating/appealing, 142–49
  officers, 209–10
  parent as student and, 168–69
  parents' income and, 152–59
  preferential packaging, 136–38
  prepaid tuition plans and, 85–86
  private consultants for, 181–82
  process, 125–27
  PROFILE preparation, 178–80
  reducing assets and, 161–63
  savings and, 165–68
  scholarships and, 127, 207–8
  school adjustment of federal formula, 127–36

shifting assets and, 159–61
  two children in college and, 115–17
  variables, 101–2
  yearly application for, 180–81
Financial Aid for the Disabled and Their Families, 214
Financial Aid Information Page, 196
Financial aid officers, 209–10
Financial calculator, 253
Financial checkup, 188–200
Financial downturns, 148
Financial Planning Association, 96
Financing software, 30
Fiske, Edward, 193
Fiske Guide to Colleges, The, 193, 196
568 Consensus Approach to Needs Analysis, 130
529 plans, 39–42, 87
  see also State-sponsored college savings plans
  grandparent contributions and, 44
Flexible spending accounts, 154–55, 175
  PROFILE and, 179
Florida community colleges, 267
Florida Prepaid College Program, 88
Foreign income, 175
Foreign study, 135, 192–93
401(k) plan, 45, 155, 254–55
Franklin, Benjamin, 34
Free Application for Federal Student Aid (FAFSA), 154, 169–78

G
Gapping, 138
General Electric Corp./ Society of Women Engineers, 221
Georgia Higher Education Savings Plan, 88
Georgia Institute of Technology, 275
GI Bill, 278
Gibson, Robert "Hoot," 265

GIFT College Investing Plan, 87

Gifts
asset shifting with, 163–64
saving, 36

Glendening, Parris, 265
Glenn Miller Scholarship, 217
Graduated loan repayment, 260
Graduate school, 116, 146–47, 269
Graduation guarantees, 269–71
Grandparents, 43–44, 163–64, 187
Guaranteed investment contract (GIC), 255
Guidance counselors, 192, 209
Guidebooks, 192
Guideposts Youth Writing Contest, 222

H

Hanover College, 3
Harness Horse Youth Foundation, 205
Hawaii Tuition EDGE, 89
Hendrix College, 3
High school club scholarships, 211
Hispanic group scholarships, 213
Hobby-related scholarships, 214
Home equity, 187
as asset, 12, 109, 130–31
debt, 164–65, 166, 167, 178, 249–54
Homeowners insurance, 34
Honors colleges, 190–91
HOPE (Helping Outstanding Pupils Educationally), 212–13
Hope Scholarship Credit, 8, 10, 12, 13
community colleges and, 265–66
Horace Mann Scholarship, 206, 222
How to Go to College Almost for Free: The Secrets of Winning Scholarship Money, 225

I

Idaho College Savings Program (IDeal), 89
Illinois college savings programs, 89
Income
accelerating or deferring, 152–59
business, 154
college education and, 7
-contingent loan repayment, 260
extra, as liability, 187
increasing, for college expenses, 15
out-of-the-ordinary boosts in, 158–59
-protection allowances, 123
savings raises, 34–35
of student, 131, 135, 153
Independence, declaring, 114
Index of Majors and Sports, 192
Indiana CollegeChoice 529 Investment Plan, 89
Indiana University, 270
Indian student scholarships, 213
Inflation, 12
Installment payments, 271–72
Institutional aid, 129
Insurance
automobile, 34, 289–90
cutting bills for, 34–35
private mortgage, 35
property (for students), 290–91
term life, 34
Insurance Information Institute, 290
IntelliQuote, 34
Intel Science Talent Search, 206, 221
International funds, 73–74
International study, 135, 192–93
Internet, college resources and, 196
Internships, 276
Investing college money, 47–97
aggressive-growth funds, 72–73
certificates of deposit, 50–52
choosing an advisor, 95–97

conservative stock mutual funds, 70–71
corporate-bond mutual funds, 67–68
international funds, 73–74
long-term, 71–74
money-market mutual funds, 52–53
municipal bond funds, 68–69
mutual fund portfolios, 75–79
savings bonds, 53–57
state-sponsored college-savings plans, 79–95
time and, 48–49
Treasury bills and notes, 57–60
Treasury funds, 60–62
zero-coupon bonds/bond funds, 62–67
Iowa college savings plan, 89
IRAs, 45–46, 155–56
Italian American student scholarships, 213
Ivy League schools, 24–25, 130

J

Job guarantees, 270
Job-placement offices, 273
Jobs, student, 272–79
cooperative education, 273–76
internships, 276
residence-hall advisors, 273
Jordan, Cora, 38
Joseph S. Rumbaugh Oration Contest, 221

K

Kansas Learning Quest 529 Education Savings Program, 89
Kantrowitz, Mark, 196
Kaplan's SAT, 201
Karla Scherer Foundation Scholarship Program, 219
Kentucky Education Savings Plan Trust, 89
Keoghs, 45–46, 155
Key Education Resources, 271
Kiplinger.com, 253
Kramon, Cliff, 203

L

Lebanon Valley College, 144
Lehigh University, 269
Libraries, 35
Life insurance
  borrowing against, 160–61,
    187, 256–58
  term, 34
Lifetime Learning credit,
  10–11
Lindenwood University, 5
Loan(s), 14, 15–16, 227–61
  borrowing from self, 249–59
  cost of, 246–49
  creditworthiness and, 244–46
  deferring payment on, 237, 239
  determining debt load, 229–32,
    233
  financial aid and, 257
  margin loans, 258–59
  payments on variable, 238
  payments per $1,000 of debt,
    232
  Perkins, 240–41
  PLUS loans, 241–42
  private, 243–44
  rates, 236
  shortening term of, 247, 249
  Stafford student loans, 234–40
  student debt and, 188
  student-loan interest
    deduction, 228–29
Louisiana Student Tuition
  Assistance and Revenue
  Trust Program, 90
Lourdes College, 5

M

Maine NextGen College
  Investing Plan, 90
Major, undecided, 192
Manchester College, 270
Mann (Horace) Scholarship,
  206, 222
Mapping sessions, 270
Margin loans, 165, 258–59
Maryland Prepaid College
  Trust, 90
Massachusetts Institute of
  Technology, 6
Massachusetts U. plans, 90
MasterQuote, 34

Meal plans, 286, 295–96
Medical expenses, 136, 146
Merchant Marine Academy,
  277
Merit-based aid, 140, 168,
  190–91
  and need compared, 141–42
Miami-Dade (FL) community
  colleges, 266
Michigan Education Savings
  Program, 90
Michigan Education Trust, 90
Microsoft Money, 30
Military Academy, 277
Military living allowances, 175
Military personnel, children
  of, 214
Military service
  attending a service academy,
    financial aid and, 116
  educational benefits, 278
  military academies, 277
  reserves and National Guard,
    278–79
  ROTC scholarships, 277–78
Miller (Glenn) Scholarship,
  217
Milwaukee School of
  Engineering, 270
Minnesota College Savings
  Plan, 90
Mississippi Affordable
  College Savings, 91
Mississippi Prepaid Affordable
  College Tuition Program
  (MPACT), 91
Missouri Saving for Tuition
  (MOST), 91
Money-market mutual funds,
  52–53
Montana Family Education
  Savings Program, 91
Montgomery GI Bill, 278
Morningstar fund-rating
  service, 41
Municipal bond funds, 68–69
Mutual funds, 52–53, 152–53
  aggressive-growth, 72–73
  conservative stock, 70–71
  corporate-bond, 67–68
  growth-and-income, 70
  international, 73–74
  long-term-growth, 71–72

municipal-bond funds, 68–69
  portfolios of, 75–79
MyRoad database, 193, 211

N

NAACP, 213
National Alliance of Postal
  and Federal Employees
  Ashby B. Carter
  Scholarship, 223
National Association of
  College Admission
  Counselors, 201
National Association of
  Hispanic Nurses, 213
National Association of
  Independent Colleges
  and Universities, 5
National Association of
  Personal Financial
  Advisors, 96
National Commission for
  Cooperative Education,
  276
National Council of Higher
  Education Resources
  Programs, 244
National Federation of the
  Blind, 214
National Federation of Music
  Clubs Competitions and
  Awards, 217
National Foundation for
  Advancement in the Arts
  Recognition and Talent
  Search, 217
National Guard, 278–79
National Hispanic
  Scholarship Fund, 213
National History Day
  Awards, 220
National Honor Society
  Scholarship Program,
  216
National Italian American
  Foundation, 213, 219
National Merit Scholarship
  program, 216
National Society of the
  Daughters of the
  American Revolution
  NSDAR Scholarships, 220

National Society of the Sons of the American Revolution Awards, 221
National Urban League, 213
Native American Scholarship Fund, 213
Naval Academy, 277
Navy ROTC scholarships, 277
NCAA Guide for the College-Bound Student-Athlete, 215
Nebraska college savings program, 91
Need a Lift?, 214
Need analysis, 184–85
Need-blind admissions, 199–200
Need analysis formulas, 100
Nell (Edward J.) Memorial Scholarship Program, 222
Nellie Mae loans, 243
Net worth adjustment, business/family farm, 124
Nevada Prepaid Tuition Program, 91
New College of Florida, 3
New Hampshire UNIQUE College Investing Plan, 91
New Jersey Better Education Savings Trust, 91
New Mexico Education Plan's College Savings Program, 92
New Mexico Institute of Mining and Technology, 3
New York, 529 plans and, 41, 92
North Carolina's National College Savings Program, 92
North Dakota College SAVE, 92
Northeastern University (Boston), 274–75

O

Off-campus housing, 294–96
Official SAT Study Guide for the New SAT, The, 201
Ohio CollegeAdvantage 529 Savings Plan, 92
Oklahoma College Savings Plan, 92

Oppenheimer funds, 41
Oregon, 529 plans and, 41
Oregon College Savings Plan, 92
Owens, Eric, 3

P

Peace Corps, 241
Pell Grant, 126, 128
Pennsylvania community colleges, 267
Pennsylvania Tuition Account Program, 92
Perkins loans, 126, 129, 234, 240–41
Personal Financial Specialist, 95
Personal identification numbers (PINs), 286
Peterson's Four-Year Colleges, 193
Phi Delta Kappa Scholarship Grants for Prospective Educators, 222
Physics majors, 221
Planning timeline, 8–9
Plan Your Estate (Clifford and Jordan), 38
PLUS (Parent Loans for Undergraduate Students), 138, 229, 231, 241–42
Prepaid-tuition plans, 82–95
"contract" type plans, 82–83
financial aid and, 85–86
listed, 87–94
penalties and alternatives, 86, 95
tuition units, 83–84
Prep courses, 200, 201
Princeton University, 130, 135
Private mortgage insurance, 35
Private schools/colleges/universities, 129–30, 146, 189–20
Professional associations, scholarships and, 212
PROFILE Aid form, 103–4, 107, 125, 127, 155, 178–80
Property insurance, 290–91
Public colleges/universities, 25, 27, 190
community college transfers and, 266–67

Q–R

Quicken, 30, 253
Rand (Ayn) Institute Fountainhead Essay Competition, 222
Real estate, 176
Reference Service Press guidebooks, 213
Regis University (CO), 270
Religious group scholarships, 214
Renter's insurance, 290–91
Residence-hall advisors, 273
Resources, alternative. *See* Alternative financial resources
Retirement savings, 44–46, 155, 187
borrowing against, 254–56
Rhode Island CollegeBound Fund, 93
Rice, Norman, 265
Rochester Institute of Technology (NY), 275
Rocky Mountain Coal Mining Institute, 206
ROTC scholarships, 277–78
Roth IRA, 46
Rugg's Recommendations on the Colleges, 192
Rumbaugh (Joseph S.) Oration Contest, 221

S

Salem International University, 5
Sallie Mae
loans, 239, 243–44
Web site, 196
Sam Walton Community Scholarship, 216
Santa Monica (CA) community colleges, 266
SAT
prep course, 200, 201
scores, 195
Savings, 13–14
college vs. retirement, 44–46
custodial accounts, 369
cutting spending, 30–31
determining amount of, 26–30
financial aid and, 165–68

529 plans, 39–42
location of. *See Investing college money*
long range, 28–29
monthly contributions, 29
realistic goals for, 23–25
short range, 27
techniques, 31, 34–36
worksheet, 27
Savings bonds, 53–57, 153–54
Scherer (Karla) Foundation Scholarship Program, 219
Scholarship(s), 205–25
academics and leadership, 216–17
arts, 217–18
athletics, 218
benefits of, 208–9
business, 218–19
categories of, 205–7
directories, 210
effect of, on financial aid, 207–8
ethnicity, 219
financial aid and, 127
government, 219
history, 220
military affiliation, 220
public speaking, 221–22
ROTC, 277–78
search services vs. free databases, 210–11
seeking, after high school, 225
sources, 209–15
teaching, 222
tips for receiving, 215, 224–25
union affiliation, 223
writing/journalism, 222
Scholarship Information for Scouts and Explorers, 215
Scholastic Arts Awards, 217
Scholastic Writing Awards, 223
Seese, Edward W., 224
SelectQuote, 34
Self-employment, 154
equipment purchases and, 157
hiring your children and, 156
tax issues and, 157–58
Semesters abroad, 135, 192–93
SEP-IRAs, 46, 155
Set-aside accounts, 35, 154–55
Sibling assets, 134–35

Signature Loans, 243
"Smart Credit Strategies for College Students," 285
Smith, Joyce, 201
Smith College, 266
Smoking expenses, 35
Social security benefits, 175
Software, tax preparation, 35
South Carolina Tuition Prepayment Program, 93
South Dakota CollegeAccess 529, 93
Southern New Hampshire University, 268
Stafford loans, 126, 128, 180, 228, 231, 234–40
choosing a lender, 238–40
interest-rate formula, 229
subsidized/unsubsidized, 236–37
Stanford, 130, 131
State agency scholarships, 212–13
State grants, 126, 129
State guaranty agencies, 240
State higher education agencies, 132–34
State sampler, of college costs, 17–22
State-sponsored college savings plans, 79–95
prepaid-tuition plans, 82–95
savings-style plans, 81–82
State tax allowances, 122
Stocks, 152–53, 258–59
Strong Capital Management, 41
Student Aid Report (SAR), 102–3, 105, 169
Student Loan Marketing Association (Sallie Mae), 239
Student loans, 14, 15–16
see also Loan(s)
flexible repayment options, 260
"relief," 259–61
Student Universe, 291
Supplemental Educational Opportunity Grants, 129

T

Tax credits, 7–16
examples of, 11–12

Hope Scholarship, 8, 10, 12, 13
Lifetime Learning, 10–11
Tax issues
borrowing against home equity, 250
deductions, 12–13
scholarships/fellowships and, 147
social security tax, 123
state tax allowances, 122
student-loan interest deduction, 228–29
tax preparation, 35
timing taxes and aid forms, 104–5
Treasury strips, 66
zero-coupon bonds and, 63–64
Taxpayer Relief Act of 1997, 228
Telephone expenses, 291–93
Tennessee college savings plans, 93
TERI, 244
Term life insurance, 34
Texas Guaranteed Tuition Plan, 93
Three-year degree programs, 268–69
TIAA-CREF, 41
Timeline, college planning, 8–9
Trans Union, 245
Treasury bills and notes, 57–60
Treasury funds, 60–62
Treasury strips, 65
Tuition
installment payments, 271–72
prepaid-tuition plans, 82–95
prepayment of, to lock in/reduce costs, 272
private school tuitions for younger siblings, 135

U

UGMA (Uniform Gifts to Minors Act), 36–39
Undecided major, 192
Union-awarded scholarships, 212
United Negro College Fund Awards, 219

University of Alaska College Savings Plan, 87
University of California Berkeley, 126, 267
University of California Los Angeles, 3
University of Central Oklahoma, 209–10
University of Cincinnati, 275
University of Massachusetts at Amherst, 209
University of Michigan Dearborn, 275
University of North Carolina at Chapel Hill, 266
University of the Pacific, 270
University of Virginia, 266
Upper Iowa University, 268
U.S. News Ultimate College Guide, 195
U.S. savings bonds, 153–54
Utah Educational Savings Plan Trust, 93
Utility bills, 34
Utility Workers Union of America, 212
UTMA (Uniform Transfers to Minors Act), 36–39, 43

V
Vacation homes, 176
Vanguard funds, 41, 69, 76
Variable loans, 238, 243. See *also* Loan(s)
Vassar College, 266
Vermont Higher Education Savings Plan, 93
Veterans' benefits, 175
Veterans of Foreign Wars of the United States Annual Voice of Democracy Contest, 223
VFW National Auxiliary Young American Creative Patriotic Art Awards, 218
Virginia college savings plans, 94
Voice over Internet Protocol (VoIP), 293

W–Z
Wake Forest University, 126, 287
Wal-Mart Stores Inc., 211
Walton (Sam) Community Scholarship, 216

Washington College (MD), 145
Washington Crossing Foundation National and Regional Awards, 219
Washington Guaranteed Education Tuition, 94
Western Golf Association/ Evans Scholars Foundation Chick Evans Caddy Scholarship, 218
West Virginia SMART 529 Prepaid Tuition Plan, 94
Wilberforce University, 5
William Jewell College, 3
William Randolph Hearst Foundation, 217
Winning Edge: The Student Athlete's Guide to College Sports (Killpatrick), 215
Wisconsin Edvest College Savings Program, 94
Women's Western Golf Foundation, 218
Work-study, 126–27, 129, 174
Wyoming College Achievement Plan, 94
Zero-coupon bonds/funds, 62–67

Share the message!

Bulk discounts
Discounts start at only 10 copies and range from 30% to 55% off
retail price based on quantity.

Custom publishing
Private label a cover with your organization's name and logo.
Or, tailor information to your needs with a custom pamphlet
that highlights specific chapters.

Ancillaries
Workshop outlines, videos, and other products are available on
select titles.

Dynamic speakers
Engaging authors are available to share their expertise and insight
at your event.

Call Dearborn Trade Special Sales at
1-800-621-9621, ext. 4444,
or e-mail trade@dearborn.com

Dearborn™
Trade Publishing
A **Kaplan Professional** Company